HAYEK AND MODEI

HAYEK AND MODERN LIBERALISM

CHANDRAN KUKATHAS

CLARENDON PRESS · OXFORD

1990

Oxford University Press, Walton Street, Oxford OX2 6DP
Oxford New York Toronto
Delhi Bombay Calcutta Madras Karachi
Petaling Jaya Singapore Hong Kong Tokyo
Nairobi Dar es Salaam Cape Town
Melbourne Auckland
and associated companies in
Berlin Ibadan

Oxford is a trade mark of Oxford University Press

Published in the United States
by Oxford Univerity Press, New York

First published 1989
First issued in Clarendon Paperbacks 1990

British Library Cataloguing in Publication Data
Kukathas, Chandran
Hayek and modern liberalism.
1. Political ideologies : Liberalism. Theories of
Hayek, F. A. (Friedrich August), 1899
I. Title
320.5'12'0924
ISBN 0–19–827863–2

Library of Congress Cataloging in Publication Data
Kukathas, Chandran.
Hayek and modern liberalism / Chandran Kukathas.
Based on the author's thesis (doctoral—Oxford University)
1. Hayek, Friedrich A. von (Friedrich August), 1899– —Political
and social views. 2. Liberalism—Great Britain—History—20th
century. 3. Liberty—History—20th century. I. Title.
JC257.H39K85 1989   320'.01'1—dc19   89–3127
ISBN 0–19–827863–2

Typeset by Pentacor PLC, High Wycombe, Bucks
Printed in Great Britain
by Biddles Ltd.,
Guildford & King's Lynn

For Debbie

PREFACE

Hayek scholarship is in a healthy state. Several studies of his economics, of his political ideas, and of his general philosophy have appeared over the last ten years—and more are on the way. An author offering yet another full-length study of Hayek's work is therefore under some obligation to say why.

This study is distinctive in so far as it presents an extended *critical* treatment of Hayek's political philosophy. It makes no attempt to provide a comprehensive survey of Hayek's thought in the way that John Gray's *Hayek on Liberty* does, but focuses more narrowly on the question of the coherence of Hayek's *political* thought. Unlike Eammon Butler's *Hayek*, it tries to go beyond plain exposition to discuss and criticize Hayek's political theory. Norman Barry's *Hayek's Social and Economic Philosophy* does this to some extent but, as the first important study of Hayek's work, was largely devoted to the task of outlining his ideas. The present study, I hope, takes full advantage of the success of these earlier scholars in making Hayek's social philosophy more familiar to pursue the narrower question of the character of Hayek's liberalism.

In this book I advance two theses. The first concerns the coherence of Hayek's defence of a particular conception of liberalism. I argue that, in the end, Hayek fails. While he has many important arguments to offer, his defence of liberalism rests on presuppositions which are philosophically incompatible and which draw him into inconsistency and, on occasion, self-contradiction. The central dilemma of Hayek's political philosophy is, given his view of the limited role reason can play in social life, how is it possible to mount a systematic defence of liberalism without falling victim to the very kinds of rationalism he criticizes? This difficulty stays unresolved in Hayek's political thought because it is informed by two incompatible assumptions about what reason can achieve.

The first assumption is the Humean one that the very idea of philosophical justification of political principles is questionable at best. Hume emphasized the historical nature of society as the product of evolution rather than rational construction, the passionate nature of man as a social creature, and the artificial nature of morality as the undesigned 'invention' which emerged with society to help man cope with his circumstances. His liberal prescriptions are rooted in a suspicion of all abstract rational constructions.

The second assumption is the Kantian one that insists on the importance of rational justification. For Kant, the justification of a liberal conception of justice and the state is thus rooted in a view of man's autonomy, his rationality, and his equal right to freedom.

Modern liberalism has inherited both these lines of argument, although it would be fair to say that the Kantian inheritance is dominant in much of the most recent writing in liberal theory. In Hayek's work we find both these strands of liberal philosophy present. But it is, as I hope to show, an unstable alliance.

I should stress, however, that it is not my concern here to advance any historical theses about the sources of Hayek's thought. This study presents a *philosophical* argument about the problem in Hayek's political thought. It does not try to show that Hayek was *influenced* by Hume and Kant, although it has to be noted that Hayek himself suggests that he has been. I am interested in the presuppositions of Hayek's argument in defence of liberalism, rather than in its origins.

The second thesis advanced in this study concerns the nature of Hayek's contribution to modern liberal theory. I try to show that, despite its difficulties, Hayek's thought does offer a political philosophy which is worth serious consideration by the critics of liberalism and also by its defenders. Hayek's defence of liberalism, unlike many others currently on offer, is grounded in a comprehensive social doctrine. It offers a political philosophy for modern society which actually has something to say about the nature of man and society, and about how this constrains our choice of political principles.

It may interest the reader to know that when I first set out to write about Hayek and modern liberalism I intended to show precisely the opposite of what I now argue: that Hayek's philosophy presents a successful reconciliation of the moral and political philosophies of Hume and Kant. I now think that such an undertaking could never succeed. Others have tried: John Rawls and R. M. Hare spring most readily to mind. The view implicit, but unargued, in the account I advance here is that liberal theorists should turn away from their preoccupation with uncovering Kantian foundations for liberalism, and look again to Hume.

Many people have helped me in the course of writing this book. It is a pleasure to be able to thank them. An earlier version of this study was successfully submitted as a D.Phil. thesis at Oxford University. I would like to thank my friends, and fellow members of the 'Oxford Hayek Society', Hannes H. Gissurarson, Stephen Macedo, Andrew Melnyk, and Emilio Pacheco, for criticizing, and suggesting improvements to, earlier drafts of the thesis. I owe a special debt to John Gray and David Miller for the care with which they read and criticized my work, and also for the kindness they showed me over my four years at Oxford. I am also grateful to my examiners, Raymond Plant and Nevil Johnson, for allowing me to see their written comments to assist with my revisions.

It would have been impossible for me to have completed my studies without the generosity of the British Council, who supported me as an Australian Commonwealth Scholar, and the Institute for Humane Studies, who supported me as a Claude Lambe Fellow at Oxford and, later, as the R. C. Hoiles Post-doctoral Fellow at George Mason University. I am very grateful to both of these institutions. I am particularly grateful to Walter Grinder and Leonard Liggio of the Institute for Humane Studies for the help and encouragement they have given me over these past few years.

My most recent debts are to Brian Beddie, Knud Haakonssen, and Philip Pettit who supplied me with helpful comments on revised portions of the manuscript. My thanks also to the anonymous OUP reader for many helpful suggestions concerning both the structure and content of the book. Responsibility for the final work, however, remains mine alone.

My deepest debt is acknowledged in the dedication.

C. K.

Canberra
May 1988

CONTENTS

ABBREVIATIONS

References to the main works of Hayek, Hume, Kant, and Rawls are indicated in parentheses ( ) in the text using the following abbreviations. (Full citations of these works may be found in the bibliography.)

HAYEK

CL   *The Constitution of Liberty*
CRS   *The Counter-Revolution of Science*
EP   'Epilogue' to *Law, Legislation and Liberty*
IEO   *Individualism and Economic Order*
KES   *Knowledge, Evolution and Society*
MSJ   *The Mirage of Social Justice*
NS   *New Studies in Philosophy, Politics, Economics and the History of Ideas*
POFP   *The Political Order of a Free People*
RO   *Rules and Order*
RS   *The Road to Serfdom*
SO   *The Sensory Order*
S   *The Studies in Philosophy, Politics and Economics*

HUME

D   *Dialogues Concerning Natural Religion*
E   *Essays Moral, Political and Literary*
EM   *Enquiry Concerning the Principles of Morals*
EU   *Enquiry Concerning Human Understanding*
T   *Treatise of Human Nature*

KANT

A/B   *Critique of Pure Reason*
CPR   *Critique of Practical Reason*
CTJ   *Critique of Teleological Judgement*
G   *Groundwork of the Metaphysics of Morals*
MJ   *The Metaphysical Elements of Justice*

RAWLS

TJ   *A Theory of Justice*
KC   'Kantian Constructivism in Moral Theory'

Introduction
Hayek's Enterprise

I. HAYEK'S INTENTIONS

Contemporary political theory has been preoccupied with the place of the state in social affairs. This is not a peculiarly modern concern, since the minds of political philosophers have long been exercised, even if not troubled, by this problem. What bears remarking upon is the coming to prominence of a political outlook hostile to the idea of the extensive state and concerned largely to articulate the case for the reduction of its activities in society. While this outlook has spawned a variety of political philosophies, the arguments displayed may be divided into two major categories.

The first category encompasses those works aimed primarily at exposing the practical inadequacy of the extended state which, it is argued, is unable to achieve its intended goals. Thus political economists such as Samuel Brittan have sought to show that the intrusion of the state into parts of the market-place leads to the exacerbation of economic problems governments seek to avert.[1] Similarly, Milton Friedman has attempted to bring his own economic philosophy to defend the view that government provision of welfare services diminishes the quality, and distorts (in favour of the privileged) the distribution, of those goods.[2]

The second category includes works concerned less to identify the shortcomings of government enterprise than to set out principles specifying the justifiable scope of state action. The most celebrated work in this category is Robert Nozick's *Anarchy, State and Utopia*, which puts the philosophical case for a minimal—and

---

[1] See e.g. his *Participation Without Politics: An Analysis of the Nature and Role of Markets*, 2nd edn. (London, 1979); and also, *The Economic Consequences of Democracy* (London, 1977).

[2] See M. Friedman, *Capitalism and Freedom* (Chicago, 1962); M. Friedman and R. Friedman, *The Tyranny of the Status Quo* (Harmondsworth, 1985).

no more than minimal—state. Taking a quite different philosophical approach, Ayn Rand tried to establish similar conclusions in a series of political novels as well as in theoretical writings outlining more explicitly her 'Objectivist' philosophy.[3]

It would be wrong to suggest that these writers might not fit equally well in either category. Rand, for example, has also produced economic and historical arguments in defence of capitalism.[4] And Murray Rothbard has defended a brand of libertarian anarchism through his writings in economic theory[5] as well as in a treatise in moral philosophy articulating a proprietarian theory of natural law.[6] But, generally, they have insisted on the *separateness* of the two kinds of arguments. For Rothbard, for example, the moral case against the state can be established, and is conclusive, independently of any of the arguments which derive from his economic or social theory. And Rand insists that, ultimately, the defence of capitalism must be presented on 'rational and moral' grounds.[7]

The interesting aspect of the work of F. A. Hayek is its attempt to defend an ideal of a just social order in a *single* philosophy constructed of interrelated arguments from both social and moral theory. Indeed, there is, for Hayek, only a single coherent justification for the classical liberal social order, whose principles do *not* derive from considerations independent of an explanation of the nature of the social world. On the contrary, liberalism—and, so, liberal justice—has its justification in the very nature of social life.

The interest that Hayek's work has for us as readers is not reflected in the greater attention now paid to his social and political writings. In most recent books on political theory Hayek's name is likely to appear—particularly if the work deals with an aspect of liberal theory.[8] Histories of liberalism which reach as far as the present invariably make mention of his writings,[9] and mainstream

---

[3] See in particular her novels *Atlas Shrugged* (New York, 1957) and *The Fountainhead* (New York, 1943). See also R. Nozick, 'On the Randian Argument', in J. Paul and E. Paul (eds.), *Reading Nozick* (Oxford, 1982), 206–31.

[4] See her *Capitalism: The Unknown Ideal* (New York, 1967).

[5] Particularly in *Man, Economy and State* (Princeton, 1962).

[6] *The Ethics of Liberty* (Atlantic Highlands, 1982).

[7] *Capitalism: The Unknown Ideal*, p. 34.

[8] e.g. selections from Hayek appear in M. Sandel (ed.), *Liberalism and Its Critics* (Oxford, 1984).

[9] See e.g. A. Arblaster, *The Rise and Decline of Western Liberalism* (Oxford, 1985); J. N. Gray, *Liberalism* (Milton Keynes, 1986).

journals of political philosophy feature articles dealing with his thought.[10] Yet, despite the publication in recent years of several books on his work,[11] Hayek remains something of a marginal figure in academic debate in political theory. While his work is alluded to, it has not really received the sustained critical attention accorded to John Rawls, Robert Nozick, or Ronald Dworkin, to name three defenders of liberal viewpoints. Part of the reason for this, undoubtedly, is that Hayek's work straddles a number of disciplines. Not only does he draw on the different social sciences, as well as law and economic history, when presenting arguments in political theory, as do other liberal thinkers, but he also has made substantial contributions towards the development of those disciplines, most notably economics. Consequently, a great deal of Hayek's political theorizing appears in works which are not concerned solely with political theory. Indeed, Hayek is, as much as anything else, a social theorist drawing out the implications for political philosophy of the conclusions of his economic, sociological, historical, and to some extent psychological enquiries.

All this points to a more general reason for Hayek's marginal status in academic political theory. In most of his work he has been asking different questions. Since the publication in 1971 of Rawls's *A Theory of Justice*, political theory in the English-speaking world has focused on the question of what kind of state and, more particularly, what kinds of distributive arrangements, are *morally justifiable*. While Hayek does touch upon these issues (and, as I try to show in this book, these issues are unavoidable given his

[10] e.g. most recently, A. Galeotti, 'Individualism, Social Rules, Tradition: The Case of Friedrich A. Hayek', *Political Theory*, 15 (1987), 163–81. See also A. M. MacLeod, 'Justice and the Market', *Canadian Journal of Political Science*, 13 (1983), 551–62; replies by A. W. Cragg, 'Hayek, Justice and the Market', and E. Mack, 'Hayek on Justice and the Market: A Reply to MacLeod', are in the same issue, 563–74; MacLeod's response, 'Hayek on Justice and the Market: A Rejoinder to Cragg and Mack', follows on 575–7.

[11] These include: N. Barry, *Hayek's Social and Economic Philosophy* (London, 1979); J. N. Gray, *Hayek on Liberty*, 2nd edn. (Oxford, 1986); R. Butler, *Hayek: His Contribution to the Political and Economic Thought of Our Time* (London, 1983). Selections from Hayek's various writings form the substance of C. Nishiyama and K. Leube (eds.), *The Essence of Hayek* (Stanford, 1984). Note also the Festschrift celebrating Hayek's 85th birthday: A. Zlabinger and K. Leube (eds.), *The Political Economy of Freedom: Essays in Honour of F. A. Hayek* (Munich, 1984). The most recent work on Hayek, B. L. Crowley, *The Self, the Individual, and the Community: Liberalism in the Political Thought of F. A. Hayek and Sidney and Beatrice Webb* (Oxford, 1987), appeared too late to be considered in preparing this book.

intentions), his primary concern has not been *moral* justification. Political theorists, however, have tended to take interest in his views only in so far as he has offered arguments dealing with this problem. As far as the rest of his work defending a particular view of the good polity goes, it is not unusual to see Hayek bracketed with Milton Friedman, a thinker of very different character, as simply another prominent advocate of free markets or member of the 'new right'.[12] To gain a proper understanding of his contribution to political theory, however, we need to recognize the questions and the concerns that inform his work. In short we need to understand his intentions.

The simplest, if not always the surest, way to uncover a thinker's intentions is to look to his professed aims. Hayek's aims have long been fairly clear: he has wanted to show that socialism in any form is untenable and that the good society must be one governed by liberal institutions upholding the market economy and the rule of law. This aspiration is clearly expressed in the subtitle of his trilogy *Law, Legislation and Liberty*, which reasserts his intention to present 'A new statement of the liberal principles of justice and political economy'. Yet this does not tell us enough: Hayek, after all, is not the first critic of socialism; nor is he the only defender of liberalism. Indeed, the variety of self-proclaimed liberals makes the relationship between liberalism and socialism contentious to say the least.[13] Several other features of Hayek's defence of liberalism need to be noted if we are to uncover his distinctive intentions. First, he devotes considerable effort to showing that the nature of society and human action tells against the possibility of socialist institutions preserving either welfare or liberty. Secondly, he has consistently maintained that the nature of mind and the limited powers of human reason make institutions aimed at organizing society to achieve some desired end, or reconstructing it in accordance with some preferred pattern of distribution, largely

---

[12] See e.g. the mistaken claim of D. Edgar, 'The Free or the Good', in R. Levitas (ed.), *The Ideology of the New Right* (Oxford, 1986), 55–79 at p. 57, that the 'significant characteristic of the political philosophy of both Hayek and Friedman was, and is, not so much their advocacy of laissez-faire economics *per se*, as the belief that the free market is a necessary *and sufficient* condition for the just society'. Not all critics of the 'new right', however, fail to distinguish between the quite different philosophies of Hayek and Friedman. See e.g. N. Bosanquet, *After the New Right* (London, 1983).

[13] On this see J. Waldron, 'Theoretical Foundations of Liberalism', *Philosophical Quarterly*, 37 (1987), 127–50.

unworkable. Thirdly, he has consistently argued, most famously in *The Road to Serfdom*, and more recently in *Rules and Order*, that unless the powers of central government are limited, we are likely to see 'a gradual transformation of the spontaneous order of a free society into a totalitarian system conducted in the service of some coalition of organized interests' (*RO* 2). Finally, he insists that, with these arguments, he is returning our attention to the neglected insights of the early thinkers of classical liberalism, among them Montesquieu, David Hume, Adam Smith, James Madison, Immanuel Kant, and Alexis de Tocqueville.

The last point indicates something more important than Hayek's modesty. It reveals that his work is informed by an awareness that the arguments of classical liberals have, particularly since the nineteenth century, been subjected to the most searching criticism by thinkers who rejected individualism and the attendant liberal vision of a pluralistic social order in which the ineliminable forces of division, competition, and conflict were kept in check by a stable system of laws governing individual conduct. The individualist standpoint was attacked by a series of brilliant writers who, beginning with Rousseau, drew attention to the plight of the individual and the very transformation (for the worse) of human nature in what was then an emerging commercial society. In Rousseau's early discourses we find a clear rejection of the liberal idea of liberty and progress in his attacks on private property, on the market economy characterized by specialization and the division of labour, and on the idea that scientific and technological development invariably contributed to human advancement. This, coupled with a hostility to the notions of political representation and division of powers, saw him develop a doctrine which, in contrast to liberalism, 'linked the constitution of liberty to *egalitarian and communitarian premises*'.[14]

Many of these themes were taken up by Marx, in whose work we find the most sustained attack on the political and economic arrangements of liberal capitalism. As an economic order, despite its great productive power, liberal capitalism was found wanting because it bought productive success at great cost: ultimately, at the cost of demeaning the lives of, and the relations among, human beings. As a political order it was found wanting because, while

[14] S. Seidman, *Liberalism and the Origins of European Social Theory* (Oxford, 1983), 65.

pretending to create the conditions in which the universal interests of all men were respected, it in fact created institutions which merely concealed the divisions among them and enabled particular interests to gain ascendancy.

More importantly, however, Marx went on to describe an alternative society, which would differ from the preceding order in at least two crucial respects. First, as a productive order it would no longer be dominated by the chaotic and irrational competitive processes that characterized capitalism. It would be a more fully planned order, organized by human beings who at last exercised collective control over the economic and social forces which once ruled them. Secondly, men would consequently achieve a freedom possible only in a truly human society in which conflicts among individuals, and between individual and society, had disappeared.[15]

Despite his undoubted importance, Marx is only one among many figures who sought to undermine the presumptions of liberal individualism. Coming from a variety of disparate political and philosophical perspectives, these thinkers shared a hostility to what one writer has described as the 'modern premises' of 'Enlightenment liberalism'.[16] They sought to replace the liberal idea of a pluralistic, secular society with a more communitarian ideal of an organic, spiritually unified social order: 'division, conflict, and competition were supplanted by the ideal of a uniform and common culture which integrates and harmonizes the interests of the individual and the community.'[17]

This political philosophical standpoint provides the target for Hayek's critical attention. Thus some of his earliest work, notably his essay, 'Individualism: True and False' (*IEO* 1–32), and his 1952 study, *The Counter-Revolution of Science*, were concerned mainly to show why the critics of individualism had misdescribed and misunderstood its nature, and why their alternative (socialist) ideals of the good society as orders scientifically organized and directed to achieve the ends of the community were no more than 'beautiful illusions' (*CRS* 247). While he has relatively little to say by way of detailed analysis and criticism of Marx (although his work abounds in critical references to many of Marx's contentions), he devotes

---

[15] For a stimulating critical examination of these themes in Marx, see J. Elster, *Making Sense of Marx* (Cambridge, 1985), 53–107.

[16] Seidman, *Liberalism*, p. 51.

[17] Ibid.

considerable space to criticism of other nineteenth-century fore-runners of socialism, most notably Saint-Simon and Comte.[18] Saint-Simon was a particularly significant target of Hayek's criticism in *The Counter-Revolution of Science*, partly because he regarded that eccentric Frenchman as an especially important influence on Marx and Engels (*CRS* 306–7), but also because he thought that 'insofar as that general socialism which today is common property is concerned, little had to be added to Saint-Simonian thought' (*CRS* 281). Indeed, he attributes to Saint-Simon a prescience he denies to other socialists:

Saint-Simon sees more clearly than most socialists after him that the organization of society for a common purpose, which is fundamental to all socialist systems, is incompatible with individual freedom and requires the existence of a spiritual power which can 'choose the direction to which the national forces are to be applied'. (*CRS* 249)

It is this set of ideas of the good society as one organized and directed by the community pursuing collective goals that Hayek finds most at odds with the ideals of liberalism. The critique of central planning most readily associated with his early work in economics is consistent with his general rejection of those ideas he has found dominant in the nineteenth century and since. Hayek's main concern, in the so-called 'socialist calculation debate', was to show that not only would economic calculation become impossible under socialism (as Ludwig von Mises had argued), but the *knowledge* required for central planning would not be available in the absence of a price system.[19] The arguments Hayek developed in his three essays on socialist calculation published between 1935 and 1940 (*IEO* 119–208) formed the basis of the broader challenge to central planning presented in *The Road to Serfdom* in 1944.

These arguments are also consistent with the concerns of much of Hayek's economic theorizing in the 1930s and 1940s. He then persistently argued that a good deal of economic theory had

---

[18] One might also add Hegel, who forms another prominent target for Hayek in *The Counter-Revolution of Science*. But Hegel's status in this context is problematic inasmuch as many of his views are not as far removed from Hayek's as one might think. See ch. 3 below.

[19] A helpful survey of these arguments appears in A. E. Buchanan, *Ethics, Efficiency, and the Market* (Oxford, 1985), 109–16. A more comprehensive treatment is to be found in D. Lavoie, *Rivalry and Central Planning: The Socialist Calculation Debate Reconsidered* (Cambridge, 1985).

misconceived the nature of the economic problem in assuming that the question for economics was to explain how one might construct a rational economic order if one possessed all the relevant information about preferences and the available means of satisfying them. What really required explanation was how knowledge came to be acquired and correctly utilized and economic activity co-ordinated. Moreover, Hayek continually argued that economic analysis, by 'bringing out the interdependence of the particular phenomena, one upon the other', was able to offer 'an insight into the nature of the economic system as a whole'.[20] This insight consisted in the identification of a co-ordination mechanism which served, in what appeared to be unregulated economic orders, to solve complex co-ordination problems to achieve results that could not be accomplished by deliberate regulation. It was this insight, and its implications, that economists needed to draw out. This would be consistent with the concerns of the great classical economists of the past. He argued this at length in his inaugural lecture at the London School of Economics in 1933. There he stated:

From the time of Hume and Adam Smith, the effect of every attempt to understand economic phenomena—that is to say, of every theoretical analysis—has been to show that, in large part, the co-ordination of individual efforts in society is not the product of deliberate planning, but has been brought about, and in many cases could only have been brought about, by means which nobody wanted or understood, and which in isolation might be regarded as some of the most objectionable features of the system. It showed that changes implied, and made necessary, by changes in our wishes, or in the available means, were brought about without anybody realizing their necessity. In short, it showed that an immensely complicated mechanism existed, worked and solved problems, frequently by means which proved to be the only possible means by which the result could be accomplished, but which could not possibly be the result of deliberate regulation because nobody understood them. Even now, when we begin to understand their working, we discover again and again that necessary functions are discharged by spontaneous institutions. If we tried to run the system by deliberate regulation, we should have to invent such institutions, and yet at first we did not even understand them when we saw them.[21]

[20] F. A. Hayek, 'The Trend of Economic Thinking', *Economica*, 13 (1933), 121–37, at p. 129.
[21] Ibid. 129–30.

So for Hayek, a grasp of the central insights of economics should lead any economist to be sceptical of the idea of social planning and, by implication, of socialism.[22] If economic theory told us anything, it was the need for decentralization rather than central planning and the importance of the very institutions which socialists criticized: money and private property.[23] The need was not for economists to contribute to the task of central planning, but for scholars more generally, with an understanding of the implications of economic analysis, to turn to the question of the proper scope of state activity. The classical writers, he suggested, had neglected this important task of distinguishing the *agenda* from the *non-agenda* of government, and 'thereby allowed the impression to gain ground that *laissez-faire* was their ultimate and only conclusion'.[24] And he added: 'To remedy this deficiency must be one of the main tasks of the future.'[25] The greater part of Hayek's work attempts to take up this task, so to revive the waning fortunes of classical liberalism.

This philosophy, he argued in 1960 in *The Constitution of Liberty*, has been going through 'one of its periods of decline': it

[22] Thus Hayek wrote in 'The Trend of Economic Thinking', p. 135: 'I have discussed planning here rather than its older brother socialism, not because I think that there is any difference between the two (except for the greater consistency of the latter), but because most of the planners do not yet realise that they are socialists and that, therefore, what the economist has to say with regard to socialism applies also to them. In this sense, there are, of course, very few people left to-day who are not socialists.'

[23] '. . . we have definitely to give up the opinion which is still widely prevalent, that, in the words of John Stuart Mill, "there cannot, in short, be intrinsically a more insignificant thing, in the economy of a society, than money".' So wrote Hayek in *Prices and Production* (London, 1932), 110. He does quote Mill more favourably elsewhere when he notes that Mill, 'stated one of our present main problems in unmistakable terms' when he observed in the first edition of his *Principles of Political Economy* that ' "The principle of private property has never yet had a fair trial in any country".' Mill, 'then still a true liberal', had written: ' "The laws of property have never yet conformed to the principles on which the justification of private property rests. They have made property of things which never ought to be property, and absolute property where only a qualified property ought to exist . . . if the tendency of legislators had been to favour the diffusion, instead of the concentration of wealth, to keep them together; the principle of private property would have been found to have no real connexion with the physical and social evils which have made so many minds turn eagerly to any prospect of relief, however desperate" ' (quoted in *IEO* 110).

[24] A conclusion, Hayek observes, which 'would have been invalidated by the demonstration that, in any single case, State action was useful.' See 'The Trend of Economic Thinking', p. 134.

[25] Ibid.

'has made little progress during the last hundred years and is now on the defensive' (*CL* 7). The need was not for a new philosophy so much as for a new statement of the liberal viewpoint which reformulated the insights of classical liberalism in the light of modern experience. 'The experience of the last hundred years', he suggested, 'has taught us much that a Madison or a Mill, a Tocqueville or a Humboldt, could not perceive' (*CL* 8). Again in *Law, Legislation and Liberty* he argued:

In these circumstances it seems important to ask what those founders of liberal constitutionalism would do today if, pursuing the aims they did, they could command all the experience we have gained in the meantime. There is much we ought to have learned from the history of the last two hundred years that those men with all their wisdom could not have known. (*RO* 1–2)

Hayek's intention has been to provide a restatement of the philosophy of classical liberalism which answers the criticisms raised against individualism more generally and, yet, remains true to the aspirations of its founders. Quite clearly, he hopes that this undertaking will offer a political philosophy which is appropriate for the modern world.

In pursuing this course, it is an important part of Hayek's intentions to establish certain substantive theses. The concluding passage of *Law, Legislation and Liberty* offers some indication of what Hayek himself thinks these are:

We ought to have learnt enough to avoid destroying our civilization by smothering the spontaneous process of the interaction of the individuals by placing its direction in the hands of any authority. But to avoid this we must shed the illusion that we can deliberately 'create the future of mankind', as the characteristic hubris of a socialist sociologist has recently expressed it. This is the final conclusion of the forty years which I have now devoted to the study of these problems since I became aware of the process of the Abuse and Decline of Reason which has continued throughout that period. (*POFP* 152)

This summary does indeed identify the most important theme running through Hayek's work. The one line of argument that he has consistently followed is that demands for ' "conscious" control or direction of social processes' (*CRS* 153) can never be met. Attempts to gain control, to direct social development, in his view, can lead only to the loss of liberty and, ultimately, the destruction of civilizations. The implication to be drawn from this is plain: 'as individuals we should bow to forces and obey principles which we cannot hope fully to understand, yet on which the advance and even the preservation of civilization depend' (*CRS* 162).

This standpoint suggests the most striking contrast with the views of Marx, for whom human freedom could not be won until man gained control of those social forces which, as products of his own creation, had worked to dominate and control him. Alienation would be overcome, and human freedom achieved, only when the autonomous life of social objects and forces was destroyed. This would only be achieved under socialism, for not till then would we see the conscious, purposive ordering of production by the producers. As Marx puts it in volume 1 of *Capital*, 'the life process of society, which is based on the process of material production, does not strip off its mystical veil until it is treated as production by freely associated men, and is *consciously regulated by them in accordance with a settled plan*'.[26]

For Hayek this hope is delusive. While Marx suggests that there will come a stage in human history when man will acquire the capacity to control social processes, Hayek concedes no more than that, in the course of history, men may come again and again to *believe* that they can do so. This, he observes pessimistically, 'may well prove a hurdle which man will repeatedly reach, only to be thrown back into barbarism' (*CRS* 163).

Man will not acquire the capacity to control or redesign society, according to Hayek, because of the limited powers of human reason. The 'constitutional limitations of the individual mind' (*CRS* 161) suggest that it will never be able to comprehend the processes of human interaction as a whole, so to 'make use of all knowledge in a systematically integrated form' (*CRS* 161). Moreover, the 'fact that no single mind can know more than a fraction of what is known to all individual minds sets limits to the extent to which conscious direction can improve upon the results of unconscious social processes' (*CRS* 178). Those who do not recognize this, he dubs 'rationalists' or 'constructivist rationalists'. The most important thesis he advances in his criticism of the demand for collective social control is that this form of rationalism is the source of

---

[26] *Capital*, I (New York, 1967), 80, quoted in J. N. Gray, 'Marxian Freedom, Individual Liberty, and the End of Alienation', in E. Paul, F. Miller, J. Paul, and J. Ahrens (eds.), *Marxism and Liberalism* (Oxford, 1986), 160–87, at pp. 172–3.

misunderstanding and folly. In his view, it is the failure to accept the limitations of human reason which lies at the heart, not only of 'modern socialism, planning and totalitarianism' (S 85), but of all those social doctrines which view social institutions as the products of human construction and, so, capable of human redesign. Indeed, he finds the 'errors' of constructivist rationalism manifest also in utilitarianism, contractarianism, and legal positivism. The inclination of the rationalist, in Hayek's view, requires all social arrangements to be evaluated by human reason before they are accorded respect or allegiance. This is an impossible demand, and one which is destructive of the most important of social institutions: morality (CRS 163–4).

It is because he holds to these substantive theses that Hayek seeks to defend the much criticized individualism in a liberal philosophy 'based on an evolutionary interpretation of all phenomena of culture and mind and on an insight into the limits of the powers of the human reason' (S 161). His intention is to provide a defence of liberal principles which is based in an understanding of the 'spontaneous' character of social processes, which recognizes that 'all knowledge and all civilization rest on tradition' (S 161), and which is suspicious of any attempt to reconstruct society or its morals.

It would be a mistake, however, to think that Hayek's writings are concerned exclusively with questions of social theory. While an understanding of the nature of the social world is important, this in itself is not enough to establish firm conclusions about the principles that should govern any social order. Once again, it is worth noting that Hayek has been highly critical of those who wish to move too quickly from the conclusions of economic theory to advocate the extension of 'private property' and 'freedom of contract' in what is misleadingly described as a 'laissez-faire' politics. Thus, at the first meeting of the Mont Pélerin Society in 1947, in his paper ' "Free" Enterprise and Competitive Order', he argued:

As far as the great field of the law of property and contract are concerned, we must, as I have already emphasized, above all beware of the error that the formulas 'private property' and 'freedom of contract' solve our problems. They are not adequate answers because their meaning is ambiguous. Our problems begin when we ask what ought to be the contents of property rights, what contracts should be enforceable, and how contracts should be interpreted or, rather, what standard forms of contract should be read into the informal agreements of everyday transactions. (*IEO* 113)

Accomplishing this task requires nothing less than the elaboration of a normative political philosophy, from which standpoint we might tackle the problem of interpreting or giving content to these legal notions of property and contract. It requires the articulation of 'a philosophy of men's living together' (*CL* 7). Clearly, this is very important for someone whose sympathies lie with the liberal view that a political order should not be dominated by the organized pursuit of particular collective goals. For if social arrangements are not determined by such ends, the question that immediately arises is: what arrangements should there be, and what is their rationale? To deal with this question Hayek produced, in 1960, his first major statement of liberal philosophy, *The Constitution of Liberty*, and twelve years later, *Law, Legislation and Liberty*.

Hayek's answer was that human relations should be governed by arrangements which preserved *liberty*—with liberty understood as 'independence of the arbitrary will of another' (*CL* 12). A large part of Hayek's concern over the past three decades has been to articulate more fully this conception of freedom. In this regard, it has been his intention to defend three theses. The first is that a free society is one governed by the rule of law. The second is that justice is served only if the law operates to delimit the scope of individual freedom. The third is that the idea of 'social justice' is inconsistent with, and even destructive of, justice and the rule of law because it seeks to modify or reconstruct social arrangements in the light of substantive conclusions about the desirable distributive structure of society.

Two main concerns thus inform Hayek's work when it is understood as an attempt to restate the political philosophy of liberalism. The first is to show how the idea of a liberal social order is consistent with a proper understanding of the nature of social forces and of the limits of human capacity to control them. The second is to articulate the normative principles which underlie the liberal ideal of a free society.

2. APPROACHING HAYEK

Having identified Hayek's intentions, it would be as well to ask what makes his thought worthy of extended investigation. A full answer can only come at the end of this enquiry; but something may be said now. There are several reasons why his work merits attention. The first is that he offers what is perhaps the most sustained and comprehensive response since Weber[27] to the social theorists who have criticized liberalism as an inadequate social philosophy resting on an implausible understanding of human nature and human society. Indeed, while liberalism continues to be derided as a doctrine lacking the fuller account of the economic, political, and historical processes governing social interaction, necessary for any philosophy purporting to be a philosophy for human beings,[28] Hayek's writings offer a liberal philosophy not susceptible to that criticism.[29]

Secondly, such an enterprise is of interest because liberalism is still besieged by detractors who continue to draw inspiration from its earliest critics: from Rousseau, Hegel, and Marx. Contemporary political theory is replete with writings criticizing both early and modern liberal writers from a variety of perspectives. This literature also points to any number of alternative views of the good society, extolling the virtues of participatory democracy,[30] or a more communitarian politics,[31] or market socialism,[32] to name but a few

[27] On this see J. Shearmur, 'Hayek and the Wisdom of the Age', in A. Seldon (ed.), *Hayek's 'Serfdom' Revisited* (London, 1984), 67–85.

[28] This criticism has been put by contemporary writers such as R. P. Wolff, *Understanding Rawls: A Reconstruction and Critique of* A Theory of Justice (Princeton, 1977), 194–210. Similar criticisms are made from a 'socialist feminist' perspective by A. Jaggar, *Feminist Politics and Human Nature* (Brighton, 1983), 27–48.

[29] J. Dunn, in his essay, 'Liberalism', in his *Western Political Theory in the Face of the Future* (Cambridge, 1979), 4 n., is perceptive in noting that Hayek and Popper come nearest to presenting 'a comprehensive liberal theory', but mistaken, as I hope to show, when he suggests that neither 'offers a very robust conception' of human beings.

[30] See e.g. C. Pateman, *The Problem of Political Obligation: A Critique of Liberal Theory* (Berkeley, 1985); B. Barber, *Strong Democracy: Participatory Politics for a New Age* (Berkeley, 1984).

[31] See e.g. M. Walzer, 'Philosophy and Democracy', *Political Theory*, 9 (1981), 379–99, and *Spheres of Justice: A Defence of Pluralism and Equality* (Oxford, 1983); M. Sandel, 'The Procedural Republic and the Unencumbered Self', *Political Theory*, 12 (1984), 81–96, and 'Morality and the Liberal Ideal', *New Republic*, 7 May 1984, 15–17.

[32] See e.g. K. Nielsen, *Radical Egalitarianism* (Totowa, 1984).

examples. Hayek's work is worthy of consideration because it tries to defend a version of liberalism which is free of some of the deficiencies commonly attributed to it.

Finally, the very idea of restating liberal philosophy as a coherent whole by returning to the ideas of its founders is an interesting one, since the liberal tradition harbours theorists who offered very different justifications for similar liberal beliefs. Hayek's concern to offer a defence of the liberal ideal which both shows it to be consistent with the conclusions of social theory and elucidates the *normative* principles of a liberal social order suggests that he is bent upon providing a justification of liberalism which not only draws on different kinds of argument, but also presents them in a coherent theory.

The question is whether such a thing is possible. After all, Hayek's critique of socialism, informed as it is by his critique of constructivism, rests on a social theory. His theory of the free society and defence of the rule of law, on the other hand, make much greater use of particular moral conceptions which he is at pains to elaborate in an attempt to offer an account of justice, liberty, and coercion. The danger for Hayek is that such an enterprise may not succeed. Indeed, the idea of restating the philosophy of liberalism through the arguments of the classical liberal thinkers may be untenable because, even if these thinkers share certain fundamental political commitments, they may do so for different reasons. In other words, there may be more than one 'philosophy' of liberalism, and to try to present them in a single construction may create inconsistency.

This danger presents itself most forcefully in the contrasting liberal philosophies of Hume and Kant. While they undoubtedly shared important political commitments inasmuch as they upheld the ideal of liberty and stressed the importance of the rule of law, the maintenance of property distinctions, and distribution according to individual entitlement or rights, their reasons for upholding what amounts to a liberal view of justice could not differ more.

If we take seriously Hayek's claim that he is simply restating the philosophy of liberalism of the Enlightenment, it does, however, look as if his philosophical presuppositions are to be found precisely in the moral and social philosophies of David Hume and Immanuel Kant. We find in Hayek's work a political philosophy with foundations[33] in the liberal social theory of David Hume and the thinkers of the Scottish Enlightenment and in the liberal moral theory whose individualist foundations were explored most thoroughly by Kant. It is not surprising to find him claiming that the philosophies of Hume and Kant, far from being incompatible, are in fact complementary: what Kant had to say about the notion of universal laws, Hayek avers, 'seems to derive directly from Hume' (*S* 117), whose own political theory had its roots 'in his analysis of the circumstances which determined the evolution of the chief legal institutions' (*S* 111). The question, however, remains: are they in fact compatible or complementary, or do they stand in irreconcilable conflict.

Hayek is not alone in thinking that their philosophical standpoints are reconcilable. John Rawls clearly saw his liberal political philosophy as offering 'a viable Kantian conception of justice'[34] detached from its metaphysical surroundings and relocated in a Humean understanding of the 'circumstances of justice', so recasting Kant within the 'canons of a reasonable empiricism'.[35] While Hayek does not explore the philosophical problems involved as comprehensively or as deeply as Rawls does, his enterprise may be understood as a similar, if less self-conscious, restatement of the liberal philosophy in a construction which presents both the social and moral theories, most readily associated with Hume and Kant respectively, in a single consistent and compelling theory.[36]

For many critics, Rawls's conscious philosophical endeavour does not, however, succeed[37] precisely because the philosophical standpoints of Hume and Kant are not reconcilable. This does not augur well for the success of Hayek's enterprise, since he too may

---

[33] The word 'foundations' is used here in a loose sense, since the very question of whether liberalism, or any political theory, can have 'foundations' is open to dispute. On this see D. Herzog, *Without Foundations: Justification in Political Theory* (Ithaca, 1985), who argues against foundationalism (and also sees Hume as a theorist who is anti-foundationalist).

[34] 'The Basic Structure as Subject', *American Philosophical Quarterly*, 14 (1977), 159–65, at p. 165.

[35] Ibid.

[36] Other commentators have proffered similar interpretations. Gray, *Hayek on Liberty*, p. 8, suggests that 'One of the most intriguing features of Hayek's political philosophy is its attempt to work out a *tertium quid* between the views of justice of Hume and Kant.' And N. MacCormick, in *Legal Right and Social Democracy* (Oxford, 1982), 6 n., avers that Hayek's view of the compatibility of Humean and Kantian doctrines is not only plausible but insightful.

[37] See M. Sandel, *Liberalism and the Limits of Justice* (Cambridge, 1982).

be led to defend substantive views which are inconsistent or contradictory.

The success of Hayek's argument is the primary concern of this book. The conclusion it reaches is that he does not succeed because the different arguments he presents to defend 'the principles of a liberal social order'[38] rest on philosophical presuppositions which remain incompatible, namely those of Hume and Kant.

Hayek sees himself drawing on the arguments of a liberal tradition. Yet this tradition contains many philosophies, some openly critical of their 'liberal' predecessors. Liberalism's Humean inheritance emphasizes the historical nature of society, the passionate nature of man, and the artificial nature of morality. The Kantian inheritance, however, emphasizes man's autonomy, his rationality, and his equal right to freedom. One insists that all moral and political issues be approached within the framework of existing practice. The other is explicitly constructivist, maintaining that practice should be judged by the universal values of justice and freedom.

Since the primary concern of this study is to evaluate Hayek's enterprise, and so to assess his contribution to modern political theory, and liberal theory in particular, its focus is on precisely the question of the coherence of the philosophical assumptions which underlie Hayek's attempt to offer a justification of the liberal social order. The conclusion it reaches is that Hayek's attempt fails because the philosophical assumptions which underpin his social theory are inconsistent with those underlying his attempt to justify liberal principles. It tries to show, first, how Hayek's view of the nature of human knowledge and his account of the nature of social order lead him to develop arguments for liberalism grounded in a profoundly anti-rationalist stance; and, secondly, how his desire to secure this defence in a set of normative principles upholding individual freedom lead him to adopt, at the same time, a more rationalist approach to the problem of justifying his liberal theory of justice.

To accomplish this task, we begin with an examination of Hayek's liberal inheritance in the thought of Hume and Kant to suggest why taking Hayek seriously requires some recognition of the distinct kinds of argument advanced in his political theory. We

---

[38] This is the title of one of Hayek's best known essays which offers a succinct statement of his political philosophy (S 160–77).

then turn (in ch. 2) to an examination of Hayek's theory of knowledge which emphasizes that the limitations of human rationality make it impossible to construct rules of justice from some transcendental or Archimedean perspective. The nature of knowledge counsels against attempts to derive any rationalist defence of a particular conception of just distribution and also suggests that practical efforts to enforce distributive patterns cannot succeed. This view leads Hayek to reject the kind of individualist defence of liberal justice offered by Rawls.

Despite his differences with Rawls, however, Hayek clearly wishes to defend what remains an individualist political theory. Unlike Rawls, he grounds his defence in a social theory which purports to show where the critics of individualism have gone astray. Thus his theory of 'spontaneous order' rejects the claim that an individualist moral culture, which upholds the justice of distribution according to entitlement (rather than merit or desert or need, for example), cannot sustain the bonds of community. More than this, he tries to show that order is most likely to be sustained in societies in which individualist conventions accord entitlements or property rights to individual persons or associations.

Indeed, only in such societies will the unintended consequences of individual action generally be benign rather than destructive. Chapter 3, while critical of aspects of the theory of spontaneous order, indicates the force of Hayek's social theory. It must, however, be recognized that, just as Hume's philosophy sought only to caution against rationalist inspired justifications of existing authority or of revolutionary reform, this theory is able, at most, to suggest the limits to which any social order can be moulded or controlled by individuals or governments, whether well- or ill-intentioned. The social theory does not indicate precisely where these limits lie, or how they should be identified, for this would require some account of how individual entitlements or property rights ought to be defined. In short, if Hayek is to claim that the theory of spontaneous order suggests that individual 'liberty' is essential for the maintenance and flourishing of the social order he must also produce an account of liberty which identifies the *scope* of individual freedom and so the proper scope of government.

This is a task whose importance Hayek willingly concedes, for he denies that he is any sort of conservative, insisting that his philosophy has sought to secure the validity of particular liberal *principles*. Here, as we shall see in Chapter 4, Hayek turns to Kant in an attempt to account for justice as that condition in which the freedom of each is compatible with the freedom of all under universal laws. We shall also discover, however, that the conception of liberty Hayek develops in his Kantian defence of the rule of law is unable to secure the normative claims he thinks derive from his social theory. To see whether these claims *can* be given any normative justification we shall have to turn directly to the question of what kind of moral theory could underpin Hayek's defence of liberalism. And Chapter 5 makes clear why the nature of Hayek's social theory, and the anti-rationalism which lies at its heart, makes the elucidation of a coherent moral philosophy justifying his view of liberal justice a very difficult, if not hopeless, undertaking.

Hayek's political philosophy is an ambitious endeavour to articulate the intellectual foundations of a liberal society. Yet his enterprise goes wrong in its very beginnings: in its assumption that it is rationalism, particularly as it is manifested in the attempt to give a deductively sound justification for a morality, that is the source of all that is hostile to the Open Society. It is this assumption that is most at odds with the attempt to establish the principles of a liberal social order. Understanding the character of Hayek's enterprise, and where it breaks down, should afford us a firmer standpoint from which to assess his contribution to liberal theory, and to ask how contemporary political theory more generally might proceed from here.

I

Hayek's Liberal Inheritance

I. HUME

When Hayek commends for their prescience and their insight the early thinkers of the Enlightenment, more often than not he has Hume in mind. In his essay on 'The Legal and Political Philosophy of David Hume' he suggests that the neglect of Hume's political theory is remarkable because it offers 'probably the only comprehensive statement of the legal and political philosophy which later became known as liberalism' (*S* 109), and he speculates that the reason is the 'erroneous belief that Hume himself was a Tory rather than a Whig' (*S* 109). Hayek's view looks like a persuasive one. While Hume advances a political theory with conservative leanings,[1] he retains a secular, individualist philosophy strongly committed to liberty, constitutionalism, and the rule of law. This is underlined by critics of liberal individualism such as Alasdair MacIntyre and John Finnis, who identify Hume as the first (and most formidable) target of their criticisms.[2]

Hume's starting-point is an anti-rationalist theory of morals which claims that moral distinctions are not derived from reason: morality 'consists not in any *matter of fact*, which can be discovered by the understanding' (*T* 468). He thus rejects those arguments which assert that virtue consists in conformity to reason: 'that there are eternal fitnesses and unfitnesses of things, which are the same to every rational being that considers them; that the immutable measures of right and wrong impose an obligation, not only on human creatures, but also on the Deity himself' (*T* 456). Whether

---

[1] See e.g. D. Miller, *Philosophy and Ideology in Hume's Political Thought* (Oxford, 1981), 2 and 187ff. The view of Hume as a conservative has been questioned by J. Robertson, 'The Scottish Enlightenment at the Limits of the Civic Tradition', in I. Hont and M. Ignatieff (eds.), *Wealth and Virtue: The Shaping of Political Economy in the Scottish Enlightenment* (Cambridge, 1983), 137–78, at p. 176 n.

[2] A. MacIntyre, *After Virtue: A Study in Moral Theory* (London, 1981), 45–54; J. Finnis, *Fundamentals of Ethics* (Oxford, 1983), and *Natural Law and Natural Rights* (Oxford, 1980), 343.

or not he found a clear alternative to ethical rationalism,[3] he is certain that reason's primary task is the discovery of the truth or falsehood of matters of fact and the identification of relations of ideas. Reason may influence the direction taken by the passions but cannot create them and is not able to motivate the will directly. Reason is set apart from moral judgements or perceptions which can 'excite passions and produce or prevent actions' (T 457), and it can only influence human conduct indirectly, in its capacity as the 'slave of the passions' (T 15): 'Either when it excites a passion by informing us of the existence of something which is a proper object of it; or when it discovers the connexion of causes and effects, so as to afford us means of exerting any passion' (T 459).

This is not to say that reason is unimportant in moral discourse; 'moral reasoning' is still possible, but it concerns means and ends. We might agree or disagree about the moral quality of actions, but reason cannot identify any objectively praiseworthy or blameworthy quality in an action. Moral evaluation is subjective, but it is neither private, arbitrary, nor without foundation. Hume does not deny the possibility of moral discourse. He only wishes to establish that morality cannot be a rationalist, abstract science. Ethics must be founded not on abstract principles discovered by reason, but on observation and experience.

Hume is not a moral relativist, for he does not deny the possibility of criticism. Following Nicholas Capaldi[4] we might make a distinction between moral relativism and moral relativity. Relativism denies the possibility of criticism; moral relativity allows for it precisely because it recognizes that all explanations are informal, that informal rules do not form a closed logical system, and that this implies that 'even our morality is subject to revisions and reconsideration.'[5] In denying moral absolutism, Hume embraced moral relativity but not moral relativism.

Hume's main intention was to show that reason played a limited and derivative role in the development of morality, and that it was not able to establish absolute or eternal standards for the evaluation of human conduct. All standards had to be established

---

[3] See J. Harrison, *Hume's Moral Epistemology* (Oxford, 1976), 110–25, which suggests five views which might have been Hume's, none of which are *wholly* consistent with his moral thought.

[4] 'Introduction: The Problem of Hume', in D. F. Norton, N. Capaldi, and W. L. Robison (eds.), *McGill Hume Studies* (San Diego, 1979), 3–22, at pp. 19–20.

[5] Ibid. 18.

historically by a consideration of human nature as it has revealed itself in human history. Otherwise, there 'are no manners so innocent or reasonable, but may be rendered odious or ridiculous, if measured by a standard unknown to the persons' (*EM* 330); and it is all too easy to set such improbable standards as might suit only our own rhetorical or philosophical purposes.

This attitude has important implications for Hume's political philosophy which rejects abstract, ahistorical standards for the social and political order. He thus denied the *rationalist* theories of his time, including versions of contract theory and natural law theory,[6] as well as *providentialist* or theistically grounded political theories.[7] One important form of rationalist theory stems from Descartes's injunction that all opinions should be seen as false until they can be made to 'conform to the uniformity of a rational scheme'.[8] A rational scheme would consist in a set of propositions that were intuitively certain or derived from similarly indubitable propositions. In his epistemology Hume rejected this method because the 'Cartesian doubt, . . . were it ever possible to be attained in any human creature (as it plainly is not) would be entirely incurable; and no reasoning could ever bring us to a state of assurance and conviction upon any subject' (*EU* 150). In his politics Hume was equally concerned to reject the Cartesian outlook because it appeared to question all existing authority and social standards by judging the social order atemporally. Cartesianism in politics required that historical society be contrasted with the timeless and rationally ordered society, thus suggesting to many that it be remodelled in accordance with a standard of perfection. Descartes himself, of course, had little to say about politics, and Hume does not attribute to him these political intentions. But there is no doubt about his 'conscious distancing of his science of man from Cartesianism'.[9]

The rejection of rationalism in politics is most evident in Hume's criticism of Whig attempts to justify the existing system of power

---

[6] See D. Forbes, *Hume's Philosophical Politics* (Cambridge, 1978), ch. 1.

[7] See D. Livingston, 'Time and Value in Hume's Social and Political Philosophy', in Norton, Capaldi, and Robison (eds.), *McGill Hume Studies*, pp. 181–201.

[8] *The Philosophical Works of Descartes*, trans. E. Haldane and G. Ross, 2 vols. (New York, 1955), i. 89.

[9] D. Forbes, 'Hume and the Scottish Enlightenment', in S. C. Brown (ed.), *Philosophers of the Enlightenment* (Brighton, 1979), 94–109, at p. 109. See also E. C. Mossner, *The Life of David Hume* (Oxford, 1980), 104, 486, and *passim*.

'by founding government altogether on the consent of the PEOPLE', supposing 'that there is a kind of *original contract*, by which the subjects have tacitly reserved the power of resisting their sovereign, whenever they find themselves aggrieved by that authority with which they have, for certain purposes, voluntarily intrusted him' (*E* 452). While Hume thought the Constitution worthy of support, its justification was not to be found in philosophical abstraction. As a system which favoured liberty it was simply the happy outcome of several accidents in the course of British history. It was not necessarily suitable for every nation, nor could it be judged superior by invoking rationalist principles. 'Let not the establishment at the Revolution [of 1688–9] deceive us, or make us so much in love with a philosophical origin of government, as to imagine all others monstrous and irregular' (*E* 459).

Hume's attack on providentialist justifications of the existing order emerges most clearly in his criticism of the Court party which, 'by tracing up government to the Deity, endeavour[s] to render it so sacred and inviolate, that it must be little less than sacrilege, however tyrannical it may become, to touch or invade it in the smallest article' (*E* 452). He did not deny religion a place in the social order, but rejected this along with all other attempts to judge the world by abstract or external standards of perfection. Religion had its 'proper office', which was 'to regulate the heart of men, humanize their conduct, infuse the spirit of temperance, order and obedience' and so silently enforce 'the motives of morality and justice'.[10] It was dangerous only when it overstepped its bounds: 'When it distinguishes itself, and acts as a separate principle over men, it has departed from its proper sphere and has become only a cover to faction and ambition.'[11]

These arguments are significant because they show Hume's antipathy towards attempts to construct a rational philosophical foundation or justification of existing human practice. His defence of a liberal view of justice is grounded in a 'conservative' acceptance of existing order as the framework for all moral and political thought.

For Hume, the rules of justice, like all moral rules, are not abstract or discoverable by reason, but contingent and variable,

[10] Hume, *Dialogues Concerning Natural Religion*, ed. H. D. Aiken (New York, 1975), 88.
[11] Ibid.

arising historically in different forms. Moreover, justice is an 'artificial virtue',[12] because there is no natural motive to just conduct. Justice only has meaning in society, that is, in an order concerned to secure *property*. Yet, like many other social institutions, it is also to be understood as an institution which emerges because of the nature of man. On his own, man is unable to cope with the 'infirmities' with which nature has burdened him. Society allows him to overcome these difficulties through the division of labour (*T* 485). Conflict would emerge within society, however, because of man's limited benevolence, which renders each individual insecure in the possession of *external goods*: the possessions he has acquired by 'industry and good fortune' (*T* 487).

Indeed problems arise because of two crucial features of human nature. First, man is an 'interested' creature who is *not* indifferent to his surroundings: he is spurred to action by a variety of motives, ranging from ambition, avarice, and self-love, to vanity, friendship, and public spirit (*EU* 83). 'That perfect *disinterestedness* so often pretended to, is never expected in multitudes and parties; seldom in their leaders; and scarcely even in individuals of any rank or station' (*EU* 85, my italics). Secondly, man is also a poor judge who often fails to see his 'real' or 'permanent' interests and is allured by present pleasure and advantage (*EM* 205). These weaknesses are incurable in human nature, so man must palliate what he cannot cure (*E* 36). The palliative is society and the institutions of justice, law, morals, and government, which either serve to make it man's immediate interest to behave disinterestedly or make the outcome of his (selfish) actions disinterested.

Justice emerges because of human *nature* and its *circumstances*. If man were different, or his situation not one of scarcity, justice would not be necessary (*EM* 183–5). Justice is not the result of any explicit contract or agreement but more like a *convention* (T 489–90). Hume's explanation of this convention is similar to Edna Ullman-Margalit's account of the emergence of 'co-ordination norms'.[13] Hume explains the emergence of conventions as solutions

---

[12] On Hume's view of justice as 'artificial' see J. Moore, 'Hume's Theory of Justice and Property', *Political Studies*, 24 (1976), 103–19; P. S. Ardal, *Passion and Value in Hume's Treatise* (Edinburgh, 1966), ch. 9; and J. L. Mackie, *Hume's Moral Theory* (London, 1980), 76–119. More generally, see also D. Miller, 'Justice and Property', *Ratio*, 22 (1980), 1–15.

[13] *The Emergence of Norms* (Oxford, 1977), ch. 3.

to co-ordination problems which do not depend on explicit agreement. Ullman-Margalit has pointed out that co-ordination norms do *not* come about as solutions to problems in achieving *co-operative goals*—in many cases the co-ordination achieved is an end in itself. Often the end is 'the mere achievement of a sort of harmony and accord concurrent with a state of co-ordination equilibrium'.[14] The solutions may become norms because those who found certain potential solutions 'conspicuous' or 'salient' were successful and were imitated, thus establishing a regularity of behaviour.[15] Hume explains the emergence of rules of property in much the same way. 'I observe, that it will be for my interest to leave another in the possession of his goods, *provided* he will act in the same manner with regard to me. He is sensible of a like interest in the regulation of his conduct' (*T* 490). There is no contract or agreement, but there is a certain tacit understanding, which is strengthened through practice.

Once justice is established, however, man's relationship to it changes, and this development is of crucial importance. Once rules of property are established, as the unintended consequence of the actions of individuals acting from self-interest, these rules begin to acquire a moral character. Hume offers different reasons for this in the *Treatise* and in the *Enquiries*, but central to both explanations is the view that justice is not the product of rational design or agreement but an unintended outcome. 'This system, therefore, comprehending the interest of each individual, is of course advantageous to the public; *tho' it be not intended for that purpose by the inventors*' (*T* 529, my italics).

As Knud Haakonssen observes, to see justice as an unintended result of individual action 'must be one of the boldest moves in the history of the philosophy of law'.[16] It avoids an excessive Hobbesian rationalism and thus the dangers of legal positivism, yet it keeps justice out of the metaphysical world of theology without closing the door to a secular theory of natural law. Hume is able to explain the development of a 'sense of justice', the importance of which permits him the prescriptive judgement that laws should be made with a view, not to some abstract principle of right, but to the

---

[14] Ibid. 133.
[15] Ibid. 84.
[16] K. Haakonssen, *The Science of a Legislator: The Natural Jurisprudence of David Hume and Adam Smith* (Cambridge, 1981), 20.

fact that individuals are aware of their interests and have a sense of justice. 'Where a civil law is so perverse as to cross the interests of society, it loses all its authority, and men judge by the ideas of *natural justice*, which are conformable to those interests' (*EM* 197 n.).

Two fundamental values inform Hume's social thought: human survival (or 'safety' or 'security') and liberty. These do not conflict and Hume does not suggest that any trade-off is needed to secure one or the other. On the contrary, liberty cannot be had without security, nor security without liberty. To secure these two values strict justice is necessary, for only strict justice looks to the permanent interests of society and, thus, comprehends the real interests of the individual. A more flexible conception of justice would open the door to all kinds of abuses for it would not just maintain the rules of property but deliver judgements based on abstract conceptions of right or desert or equality or 'public interest'. Money should thus be returned to misers or seditious bigots even if the public's *immediate* interest *might* be better served by its appropriation. Since justice was to preserve the stability of possession, it would be inconsistent to assert that the confiscation of property, for the public benefit, is just. In other words, the individual may not be sacrificed to the public advantage, for 'that policy is violent which aggrandizes the public by the poverty of individuals' (*E* 266).

Hume brings two kinds of arguments to the defence of this theory of justice: arguments about the nature of commerce and of politics. In both cases he seeks to demonstrate the value of stability and public liberty attained through the impartial prosecution of laws of property. First, he argues that, as it provides security, government is the prerequisite of economic improvement because individuals do best when free to pursue their own interests. Security benefits both individual and public: 'as private men receive greater security, in the possession of their trade and riches, from the power of the public, so the public becomes powerful in proportion to the opulence and extensive commerce of private men' (*E* 261). For this reason individuals should, as much as possible, be left free to choose their own pursuits: any attempt to manipulate the individual for particular benefits to the public will founder on the rock of human nature.

Sovereigns must take mankind as they find them, and cannot pretend to introduce any violent change in their principles and ways of thinking. . . . the less natural any set of principles are, which support a particular society, the more difficulty will a legislator meet with in raising and cultivating them. *It is his best policy to comply with the common bent of mankind, and give it all the improvements of which it is susceptible* (E 266, my italics).

Hume also argued that one of the advantages of the commerce that results from public liberty is greater equality.[17] Merchants who make great profits tempt others to imitate them, thus leading to more industry, greater demand for labour, and hence higher wages (*E* 270–1). Not only is such an equality 'most suitable to human nature', but also adds to the happiness of the poor, and to the power of the state, and lessens the burden of taxation on all (*E* 271). Such equality is, however, only of value if it is the product of the wealth created by people secure under the rule of law. Any attempt to enforce equality would impoverish society, 'and instead of preventing want and beggary in a few, render it unavoidable to the whole community' (*EM* 194).[18] Worse, it would require the most severe exercise of tyrannical authority to enforce.

Hume's economic arguments for strict justice are closely allied with the arguments he draws from his 'science of politics'. If liberty and security are to be attained, it must be recognized that in politics virtue has little part to play, and rules of justice should not be formulated in a way that gives great discretionary power to political authority. Politics is dominated by factions and the great task of the science of politics is to explain what kinds of *constitutional* arrangements will curb the activities of factions and control their harmful effects. Hume sees politics as the domain of élites and emphasizes the changes in behaviour of individuals acting as members of political groups.

---

[17] More recently, Friedman has argued that the free market promotes greater equality in the distribution of wealth, as well as greater wealth. See M. and R. Friedman, *Free to Choose: A Personal Statement* (London, 1980), 146–8.

[18] Hayek puts a similar case, arguing that inequality acts as a spur to material progress, from which the poor have most to gain (*CL* 44), and that once the poor start to advance materially, their *relative* position in society will also improve: 'Those forces which at first make inequality self-accentuating thus later tend to diminish it' (*CL* 48).

In politics, Hume observes, the primary actors are generally men of ambition. And while such men may not be vicious or evil, the fire of ambition, 'the most incurable and inflexible of all human passions',[19] is always fuelled by interest and by faction. The political scientist must assume that in politics every man is a 'knave', though it is strange 'that a maxim should be true in *politics* which is false in *fact*' (E 42).

We cannot rely on the benevolence or virtue of political actors if liberty, and security of possession, are to be preserved. To rely on the 'goodwill of our rulers' is to 'have no security at all' (E 41–2). The only solution is to have a sound constitution whose general rules keep interest groups and ambitious individuals in check. It is the rules rather than the individuals who govern that ensure the security and liberty of society. To depart from strict justice, the justice that comes from the impartial prosecution of rules of property, is to submit to the politicization of justice. The only consequence can be to put the liberty and safety of society in the hands of the successful political group.

David Miller has tried to show that Hume's is essentially a conservative philosophy, albeit one with strong liberal elements.[20] For him, Hume's thought reflects the views of the eighteenth-century aristocracy, in its assumptions about human behaviour and its vision of society. This accounts for Hume's emphasis on economic progress, cultural refinement, and learning. While he thought the British Constitution could be made more secure by stripping away the historical myths that encrusted it, he nevertheless had a strong commitment to the political establishment. It is hard to say whether establishment ideology was liberal or conservative, Miller suggests, largely because in eighteenth-century Britain there was no perceived incompatibility between liberal demands for personal freedom and the rule of law, and conservative commitments to institutional continuity, authority, and social hierarchy. The French Revolution forced people to reveal their true commitments and liberals generally supported the Revolution's libertarian ideals, rather than establishment authority. Had Hume been forced to reveal the strengths of his different commitments, Miller argues, his conservatism would have emerged from the

---

[19] Hume, *The History of England from the Invasion of Julius Caesar to the Accession of George III*, 8 vols. (London, 1810), i. 258.
[20] *Philosophy and Ideology in Hume*, 'Conclusion'.

ideological background into the philosophical foreground and he would have defended authority and hierarchy more strongly than liberty. Had he been forced to respond to the Revolution as Burke was, his similarly conservative commitments would have emerged as clearly. We get an inkling of this in Hume's hostility to the Wilkes riots. When violent popular demonstrations broke out in protest at John Wilkes's trial for libel, and at attempts to prevent him entering the Commons, Hume reacted angrily against the radicals and in favour of the political establishment. While Hume's general political attitude seems urbane when contrasted with Burke's more strident conservatism, it is, therefore, largely a matter of time and circumstance. Hume was undoubtedly a conservative of an unusual kind, for he was a sceptic whose epistemology prevented him from defending the old regime or conservatism; but he was an establishment conservative none the less.

I would argue for a different account of the relationship between the liberal and conservative facets of Hume's thought. If he is indeed a conservative it is because of his philosophical commitments, not his ideological assumptions. While his hostility to the Wilkes protests betrays a conservative outlook, this is not because he felt any ideological attachment to the establishment. Hume saw the Wilkes affair as a confrontation 'between the Mob and the Constitution' where 'the Mob', as Donald Livingston notes, was understood to include not only those chanting 'Wilkes and Liberty' but the entire Whig literary and political establishment.[21] To say that Hume was a man of the establishment is wide of the mark because his political writings, far from betraying an affection for established power, assume that politics is the arena in which élites compete for power, and the masses are manipulated. The Whig élite, he argued, took several steps dangerous to liberty while claiming to secure the Constitutional settlement and royal succession according to Whig principles, although the body of the party 'had no passion for that succession, otherwise than as a means of securing liberty'. Whig party members and followers 'were betrayed into these steps by ignorance, or frailty, or the interests of their leaders' (E 141).

Hume is a conservative not because of any ideological attachment to the establishment, but because his anti-rationalist (and anti-providentialist) philosophy set him against anything ideological—

---

[21] D. Livingston, *Hume's Philosophy of Common Life* (Chicago, 1984), 328.

whether that ideology sought to justify established order by appeal to theistic principles or to overthrow that order by appeal to abstract (say, contractarian) principles. He was not a conservative for the reasons that moved Burke who, as a member of the Whig establishment, had been sympathetic to Wilkes. Burke defended the Constitution because he valued order and regarded actions subversive of order as against nature. These views stemmed not from his hostility to the Revolution but from his Christian metaphysics, from his view that God is 'the lawful Author of our being' and 'the Author of our place in the order of existence'.[22] Hume may have shared Burke's liberal views in economics, but he would have rejected completely Burke's attachment to party and his providentialist justification for established order. The only striking thing about Hume's conservatism is that it is grounded, not in any sympathy for the establishment, but in a scepticism that was deeply suspicious of attempts to construct abstract justifications of any particular political order. It is hardly surprising that Dr Johnson dismissed him as a 'Tory by chance'.[23]

These considerations are important for an understanding of Hume's political philosophy which, as MacIntyre has noted,[24] shares with Hobbes the individualist presuppositions which lie at the core of liberalism. While he defended 'liberal' values of property, constitutionalism, the rule of law, individual liberty, and the right of rebellion, his reasons for doing so stemmed from a (mitigated) scepticism about the possibility of securing these values with abstract philosophical justifications. This scepticism inclined him to give conservative reasons in support of liberal values, emphasizing the dangers of attempting to reform or entrench a Constitution (which favoured liberty) in accordance with philosophical ideals. While convinced of the 'violence' of policies which aggrandized the public at the expense of individuals, he shied away from any attempt to elevate this individualist predisposition into philosophical principle. His case for the protection of individual entitlements is thus grounded in a conservative emphasis on the dangers of expanding public authority rather than in any doctrine of individual rights. More generally, the case for rules of justice

---

[22] Quoted in M. Freeman, *Edmund Burke and the Critique of Political Radicalism* (Oxford, 1980), 18.
[23] J. Boswell, *Life of Johnson*, ed. R. W. Chapman (Oxford, 1983), 1214–15.
[24] *After Virtue*, esp. ch. 1, and *passim*.

ensuring the stability of property, its transference by consent, and the performance of promises is that the persistence of society depends on the observance of these 'laws of nature' (*T* 526). There is no doubt in Hume's mind 'that all men have an implicit notion of the foundation of those moral rules concerning natural and civil justice', that they 'arise merely from human conventions, and from the interest which we have in the preservation of peace and order' (*T* 569). Kant, of course, had no doubt that Hume was wrong and presented a very different justification for a similarly liberal political theory.

2. KANT

As political philosophers, Hume and Kant have much in common. Both are individualists who emphasize the importance of private property, distinguish between the public and private domains of social life, and, more generally, separate reason from the passions. They also assume a separation of the right from the good. Here is, however, the source of the most profound conflict: Hume maintains that 'right' is dependent upon human evaluation of what is good, an evaluation which is contingent even if not wholly arbitrary; Kant insists that the right is not a matter of contingency, subject to the vagaries of human nature, but is to be identified independently of the claims of desire—by reason.

Kant's moral theory rests on two basic interrelated claims: first, that the individual is capable of *practical* reason, for reason not only enables us to *judge* but also motivates us to *act*; secondly, the individual is free because reason enables him to grasp the moral law or the unconditional practical law which leads him to awareness of his freedom. Reason shows the individual what he 'ought' to do and what he 'ought' to do he must be *able* to do: so he must be free. 'Freedom and unconditional practical law reciprocally imply each other' (*CPR* 29). Reason, however, does what experience cannot: it reveals to us our freedom by revealing the moral law. Experience can reveal only the 'law of appearances and the mechanism of nature, the direct opposite of freedom' (*CPR* 29). Reason, however, exhibits the moral law 'as a ground of determination which is completely independent of, and not to be outweighed by, any sensuous condition' (*CPR* 29).

Kant denies the empiricist claim that reason is no more than a calculating faculty serving human desires, unable to move individuals to act, and repudiates the contention that morality can be explained by psychology and has no rational or universal foundation. To defend this Kant had to show two things: first, that the idea of freedom was essential to any understanding of morality, indeed to morality itself; and secondly, that freedom could not properly be understood empirically. To take the latter step first, we can see the difficulty involved in conceiving freedom purely empirically if we consider the fact that 'the will of every man has an empirical character', which is 'nothing but a certain causality of his reason' (A 549, B 577). Since this empirical character can only be discovered from the appearances which are its effect (using the rules which govern experience), it follows that all human action in the world of appearance is 'determined in accordance with the order of nature, by their empirical character and by the other causes which cooperate with that character' (A 549, B 577). This leads Kant to conclude that, 'as regards this empirical character there is no freedom' (A 550, B 578). We may study that character as *anthropologists* seeking the motive causes of human behaviour in man's physiology (A 550, B 578); but this will not help us understand human freedom.

But if freedom cannot be understood empirically, how should it be regarded? Kant answers that it must be viewed 'transcendentally' as the capacity of undetermined reason to exercise the power of causality. While *man* himself, as an empirical being, as an 'appearance', is subject to causality because there 'is no condition determining man in accordance with this character which is not contained in the series of natural effects, or which is not subject to their law—the law according to which there can be no empirically unconditioned causality of what happens in time' (A 552, B 580)— *reason* is not an appearance and hence is not subject to the 'conditions of sensibility': 'the dynamical law of nature, which determines succession in time in accordance with rules, is not applicable to it' (A 553, B 581). Reason therefore 'acts freely' because it is not determined in the sense of being conditioned by 'grounds' antecedent in time. In showing that reason lies in this realm of the undetermined, beyond the realm of nature, Kant believes he has shown that freedom and the law of nature can exist independently of each other and 'that causality through freedom is at least *not incompatible* with nature' (A 558, B 586).

Yet Kant also has to show why this freedom is essential to any understanding of morality. Here he argues that, while freedom cannot be demonstrated a priori, it can be shown that a rational agent must act on the presupposition of freedom. Indeed, 'to every rational being possessed of a will we must also lend the Idea of freedom as the only one under which he can act' (G 109). Only when this is true of a rational being can it be seen to be capable of practical reason—i.e. capable of exercising 'causality in regard to its objects' (G 109). Should reason be conceived of as directed from without, the subject's judgements would be determined not by reason but by impulsion. This is impossible if we wish to conceive of a being as rational and as conscious of his causality with regard to action—i.e. as endowed with a *will* (G 109). Rational beings, for Kant, *are* endowed with a will: 'Will is a kind of causality belonging to living beings so far as they are rational' (G 107). While non-rational beings are the subjects of *natural necessity*, rational beings are characterized by the fact that they can operate independently of determination by alien causes. Thus, in possessing a will, a rational being is at least *negatively* free (G 107). A wholly lawless free will, however, is self-contradictory and so free will must be understood positively as something that acts according to laws. Since these laws could not be imposed from without, they must be self-imposed. If this is the case, freedom means *autonomy* and, since autonomy is the principle of morality, 'a free will and a will under moral laws are one and the same' (G 108).

Now, Kant's reasoning appears to be circular. He argues that we must think ourselves free because we are born under moral laws and then claims that we must be under moral laws because we think of ourselves as free. Kant himself notes this in the *Groundwork* (G 111). While he does attempt to answer this objection here, his remarks in the *Critique of Practical Reason* are more illuminating. There he argues that freedom is the necessary condition of the moral law's *existence*, but the moral law is the only condition under which freedom can be *known*. Freedom would exist regardless of our awareness of the moral law; but only because we do know the moral law are we aware of our freedom. Freedom is thus the *ratio essendi* of the moral law, but the moral law is the *ratio cognoscendi* of freedom (CPR 4 n.).

In the *Groundwork* Kant's answer to the question of the circular relationship between freedom and the moral law is, however, more complex. There he seeks to explain not only what these concepts mean but also how the moral law is justified. His answer is based upon a distinction he makes between the *sensible world* and the *intelligible world*. The former is the world of appearances—which are all that we can know, apart from ideas which come to us of our own volition. The sensible world varies considerably according to the sensibilities of the observer, but the intelligible world is always the same (G 111). In so far as man is acquainted with himself empirically, he knows himself as a member of the sensible world. These appearances of himself must, however, have some grounds if the appearances are to be of something. Because of this, and because he knows that he is capable of consciousness and can will ideas, man must acknowledge the existence of a *receiver* of sensations, and this *self* belongs to the intelligible world—of which he knows nothing further (G 112). Now this is not to say that man has two, separate selves. It simply means that man can comprehend himself from two different perspectives: he has 'two points of view from which he can regard himself and from which he can know laws governing the employment of his powers and consequently governing all his actions' (G 113). When we see ourselves as free we see ourselves as members of the intelligible world and recognize the autonomy of the will and its consequence: morality. When we see ourselves as obligated we see ourselves as members of both the sensible world and the intelligible world at the same time (G 113).[25]

The fact of these two standpoints enables Kant to explain what he understands by moral obligation. If there were only one standpoint and man was solely a member of the intelligible world, his actions would *necessarily* accord with the principle of autonomy; if man were solely a member of the sensible world his actions would *necessarily* be subject to the laws of nature. But the fact that man is of both worlds means that he *ought* to allow his will as a member of the intelligible world to prevail, in spite of the fact that he is also a member of the sensible world. His actions *ought* to be in accord with the autonomy of his will. Kant's confusing justification of this claim rests on his assertion that '*the intelligible world*

---

[25] For a more detailed analysis which examines the different 'selves' in Kant's moral philosophy see R. P. Wolff, *The Autonomy of Reason: A Commentary on Kant's* Groundwork of the Metaphysics of Morals (New York, 1973), 201–9; also 9–15.

contains the ground of the sensible world and therefore also of its laws' (G 114).

Whether or not Kant is successful in this attempt to secure the foundations of morality, the point to note is the nature of the Kantian project. Kant wants to show that there can be moral principles that are absolutely binding, that is, binding regardless of the contingencies of nature. To defend morality, as Hume did, by reference to the world of experience, gives the subject not autonomy but heteronomy. Moral imperatives become no more than hypothetical imperatives of prudence and not categorical imperatives.

The most common criticism of Kant that arises out of this deontological interpretation of his moral theory is that his moral law lacks content and so cannot effectively inform moral judgement. The only moral law he has derived from the nature of reason is the formal law of self-consistency, which rules out inconsistent principles but cannot enable us to choose from among consistent principles.[26] To do this he would, as Robert Paul Wolff has noted, have to produce an account of the objective and obligatory ends derived purely from the concept of rational agency.

This view has, however, been challenged by those who see in Kant a stronger teleological commitment which identifies objective and obligatory human ends. To examine this interpretation we must enquire further into his moral philosophy.

'The theory of justice', Kant tells us in the *Metaphysics of Morals*, 'constitutes the first part of the theory of morals' (*MJ* 3). While his theory of justice does have its foundations in his moral theory, one development in his morals must be noted. In the *Groundwork* he made the mistake of equating freedom with following the moral law and so was led to the absurd conclusion that no free act can ever be wrong, since a free act is, by definition, an act guided by the moral law. Kant does not get into this same difficulty in his later ethical writings because he makes an important distinction between two concepts of will: *Wille* and

---

[26] See Wolff, *Autonomy of Reason*, pp. 210–12; R. C. S. Walker, *Kant: The Arguments of the Philosophers* (London, 1978), 159 (who also suggests at pp. 147–50 that closer study shows that beneath Kant's careless statements lies a more plausible, if less developed, theory); B. Aune, *Kant's Theory of Morals* (Princeton, 1979), 121, notes that without appeal to a teleological conception of nature the categorical imperative may become too weak a moral principle.

Willkür.[27] A person has free *Wille* in so far as he has autonomy or acts on the basis of a universal moral law of reason, but has free *Willkür* in so far as he has freedom of choice. Freedom of *Willkür* refers to 'independence from determination by sensible impulses; this is the negative concept of freedom' (*MJ* 13). Freedom of the *Wille*, on the other hand, refers to the 'capacity of pure reason to be of itself practical', through the 'subjection of the maxim of every action to the condition of its fitness to be a universal law'—i.e. it refers to the positive concept of freedom (*MJ* 13). While the *Wille* is the source of moral legislation (and so is the same in everyone), the *Willkür* is the faculty of deciding to act or choose. This distinction is important because in Kant's theory of justice laws are concerned to control *Willkür*.

These laws are 'laws of freedom' or *moral* laws and are of two kinds: juridical and ethical. This is an important distinction for it is no less than a distinction between the *legality* of an action and its *morality*. An action has legality when the law itself makes a particular action a duty. It has the quality of morality, however, when the reason for performing the action is the duty itself, i.e. the duty does not exist because of the law (*MJ* 18–19). This is why Kant says that 'Duties in accordance with juridical legislation can be only external duties because such legislation does not require that the Idea of this duty, which is internal, be of itself the ground determining the will [*Willkür*] of the agent' (*MJ* 19). Thus the duty to obey traffic regulations is a duty to a purely juridical law. Ethical legislation, however, requires that actions be performed simply because they are duties, whether or not they are juridically commanded: in fact, it applies 'generally to everything that is a duty' (*MJ* 19). So truth-telling, for Kant, is a duty to a purely ethical law, for the obligation here stems from nothing other than the morality of the action. Ethical legislation does, however, extend to cover external actions in the sense that one has an ethical duty to perform one's legal duty: 'all duties, simply because they are duties, belong to Ethics' (*MJ* 20). Indeed, while many duties are directly ethical, because of the ethical duty to perform non-ethical duties, all duties are *indirectly* ethical (*MJ* 21). The significance of the difference between the two kinds of duties is indicated by the fact

[27] On this see Walker, *Kant*, pp. 147–8; J. G. Murphy, *Kant: The Philosophy of Right* (London, 1970), 82–6; K. Ward, *The Development of Kant's View of Ethics* (Oxford, 1972), 168–71.

that duties which are not juridical, but purely duties of virtue are not enforceable: while I can be coerced to keep my promise because it is a duty of justice (a juridical duty), I cannot be coerced to give money to the poor. I can be coerced to pay taxes levied (a juridical duty to obey the law) but cannot be coerced to give to charity (a duty of virtue). Justice, Kant notes, generates the authorization to use coercion (*MJ* 35–6). But what is justice?

Justice is not simply what the law of the land commands: to find out what justice is one must abandon empirical principles and search for it in pure reason (*MJ* 34). Justice has three defining characteristics: (*a*) it applies only to the external, practical relationships between persons whose actions can influence each other; (*b*) it applies only to the relationship between persons' wills, and not to a person's wishes or desires or even his needs, which are the concern of acts of benevolence or charity; (*c*) it does not take into account the end a person intends by his actions (*MJ* 34). The only thing that must be considered when applying the concept of justice is the 'form of the relationship between the wills insofar as they are regarded as free, and whether the action of one of them can be conjoined with the freedom of the other in accordance with a universal law' (*MJ* 34). This concept of justice is given a more general expression when Kant writes: 'Justice is therefore the aggregate of those conditions under which the will of one person can be conjoined with the will of another in accordance with a universal law of freedom' (*MJ* 34).

A situation is just if there is *harmony* in the relations among freely acting individuals inasmuch as no one is coerced or impeded in his actions by anything other than the freedom of others, whose freedom is defined by the *same* moral principles. Justice prevails when the freedom of the individual, or individual rights, are in harmony because regulated by the moral laws by which all are bound, and which, indeed, define their freedom or their rights. To act justly is to act in accordance with the laws of freedom and not overstep the bounds of one's freedom by infringing the freedom or violating the rights of others.

The question of distributive justice, then, pertains not to the distribution of goods and bads but to the distribution of *freedom*. Civil society is characterized by distributive justice not because it has a mechanism for distributing goods and bads but because it is a juridical state of affairs in which there exists a public law governing the external relations among individuals (*MJ* 70–1). In the state of nature private law may exist because there may be societies governed by, for example, conjugal or paternal rules of behaviour (*MJ* 70), but it is only when people enter a relationship which involves mutual rights that they enter a juridical state of affairs, and only then does justice exist (*MJ* 70). This is because justice involves the *authorization* to use coercion to secure rights. In the state of nature external relations are characterized by violence rather than legitimate coercion because there exists no means of determining when coercion is legitimate: it is a state of lawless freedom (*MJ* 72).

Kant's view of justice as possible only in a juridical condition in which each person's property is secured, and his insistence that the postulate of public law comes out of private law, commanding men to abandon the state of nature for the state of distributive legal justice, seems to indicate that he does not try to characterize justice independently of *all* ends. In so far as he thinks that justice, like morality, is not to be justified by material and subjective ends, his is a deontological theory. Yet in so far as his legal and moral theory are founded on a theory of objective ends, it appears to be teleological. The objective end Kant presents is that condition in which each individual's freedom is in harmony with the freedom of all others. And the reason he gives for seeing this as an objective end is that the only (ultimate) end of creation or existence is *man*, who is the only being whose causality is teleological or directed to ends, and who is yet unconditioned by nature because he is *free* (*CTJ* 99). Indeed man is distinguished by his freedom to choose his own ends or purposes, and for this reason the condition which offers the greatest scope to human self-legislated ends is the objective end that should be sought. This is the real end of nature: to attain that condition in which human ends can flourish. And this condition is one in which there exists 'a constitution so regulating the mutual relations of men that individuals' striving one against another is opposed by a lawful authority centred in a whole'—and this 'whole' can only be a '*civil community*' (*CTJ* 96). In Kant's understanding of the nature of civil community we see most clearly his conception of the relationship between freedom and justice, for the constitution of a just society is nothing less than the constitution of liberty.

Justice, for Kant, is closely tied to freedom in two ways. First, the foundations of morality lie in the fact of individual freedom. Justice can be commanded only because of the freedom which makes choice and morality possible. Secondly, the end of justice is to secure freedom under law, so that freedom, the source of human flourishing, can be given its greatest expression. 'The highest task which nature has set for mankind must therefore be that of establishing a society in which *freedom under external laws* would be combined to the greatest possible extent with irresistible force, in other words of establishing a perfectly *just civil constitution*.'[28] A just society or constitution must be one in which each individual's freedom is compatible with the freedom of others because any other set of arrangements would, by making the infringement of one individual's freedom the means to another's ends, deny that individual freedom is of fundamental value, rendering it a purely instrumental good rather than an unconditional good.

This consideration of Kant's theory of justice brings us back to the question of whether he presents us with a deontological ethic or one which is teleological. The reason for seeing it as teleological is that he 'does not think that the sphere of morality can be characterized independently of *all* ends, only of all material and subjective ends.[29] The objective end that appears to guide Kant's construction of principles of morality is that condition in which men are free and able to live in harmony. Morality thus becomes teleological because it is directed towards the end of securing the objective end of a harmonious society. The right is thus defined not independently of the good but according to an objective conception of the good. Right action is defined as action that may be performed because its maxim can be a universal law of nature and the universal law of nature refers not to causal laws (for many things are causally possible that are not morally possible) but to teleological laws: laws which have man as the final end of nature.[30] This end or good is objective because it is not the end sought by the parochial desires of an individual pursuing happiness, but the ultimate end of nature, since man himself is the *'ultimate end* of nature' (*CTJ* 92).

Yet Kant's remains a deontological theory rather than a teleological one because of the nature of his account of social harmony as an objective end. While this end is objective inasmuch

---

[28] Kant, 'Idea for a Universal History', in H. Reiss (ed.), *Kant's Political Writings* (Cambridge, 1970), 41–53, at pp. 45–6.

[29] Murphy, *Kant*, p. 76.   [30] Ibid. 92–3.

as it is not defined according to the subjective preferences of its members for happiness, it is *not* objective in the sense of being independent of the moral theory to which it relates. The end of social harmony does not guide our defining of the moral law; it is the moral law itself which gives us this conception of the objective end of morality.

The moral law is the formal rational condition of the employment of our freedom, and, as such, of itself alone lays its obligation upon us, independently of any end as its material condition. But it also defines for us a final end, and does so *a priori*, and makes it obligatory upon us to strive for its attainment. This end is the *summum bonum*, as the highest good *in the world* possible through freedom (*CTJ* 118).

It is our moral faculty alone which makes it possible to conceive of an end (*CTJ* 123). In nature, independent of our projections, there may be many ends, but no final end is discoverable in nature. 'Hence, just as the idea of this final end resides only in reason, so it is only in rational beings that such an end itself can and must be sought as an objective possibility' (*CTJ* 123).

The foundation of Kantian justice is not a teleological justification of morality but a deontological account of the laws of freedom commanded by reason.[31] So it cannot be said that Kant's moral system ultimately relies upon a particular construction of an 'objective' form of the good. Kant's moral theory remains open, however, to Wolff's objection that the only moral law he has derived is the purely formal law of consistency, which offers us no *substantial* test of the rightness of human action.

Kant gets into deeper trouble when he concludes from his original postulate that justice is the aggregate of conditions in which the will of one can be conjoined with the will of another in accordance with a universal law of freedom ('the concept of justice in external relations' (*MJ* 71)) that there exists a postulate of public law which says: 'If you are so situated as to be unavoidably side by side with others, you ought to abandon the state of nature and enter, with all others, a juridical state of affairs, that is, a state of distributive legal justice' (*MJ* 41). With this move he argues that the juridical condition of distributive legal justice, or the civil state,

---

[31] For a teleological reading of Kant see P. Riley, *Kant's Political Philosophy* (Totowa, 1983). This has been criticized in J. Ladd's review in *Political Theory*, 12 (1984), 124–7.

must be *understood as* the product of a social contract among the people in which they 'give up their external freedom in order to take it back as the members of a commonwealth' (*MJ* 80) in which the individual abandons his 'wild, lawless freedom in order to find his whole freedom again undiminished in a lawful dependency, that is, in a juridical state of society' (*MJ* 81). This freedom is abandoned as a matter of moral obligation, for Kant, as it is commanded by justice that men seek to enter a juridical state, and this is why in the civil state man exists in a 'lawful dependency', for his dependency in this state 'comes from his own legislative Will [*Wille*]' (*MJ* 81). But because this membership of the state is the product of my *Wille*, as issuing directly from the moral law (which commands me to enter this, the only condition in which justice can obtain), I cannot, as a member of the state, repudiate its commands or laws, for to do so would be to repudiate the moral law.[32]

We thus find Kant arguing that the people owe the state unconditional obedience and are duty bound 'to endure even the most intolerable abuse of supreme authority' (*MJ* 86). To threaten disobedience or rebellion is to threaten a return to the state of nature. Thus 'juridical status, legitimacy, is possible only through subjection of the general legislative will [*Wille*] of the people' (*MJ* 86). Now once this is accepted, any opposition to law on grounds of its immorality or injustice would be immoral or unjust.

The basic problem of Kant's moral and political philosophy might be labelled the problem of *universalizability*. All his major difficulties stem from his failure to produce 'an a priori valid substantive test of the rightness of wrongness of every possible human policy'.[33] In his moral philosophy, as we have seen, the Categorical Imperative is unable to guide our choices from among competing sets of *consistent* principles of action. The consequence for his political philosophy is that he is unable to give any content to the innate or natural rights he wishes to accord to every

[32] 'If men deliberately and intentionally resolve to be in and to remain in this state of external lawless freedom, then they cannot wrong each other by fighting among themselves; for whatever goes for one of them goes reciprocally for the other as though they had made an agreement to that effect. . . . Nevertheless, in general, *they act in the highest degree wrongly by wanting to be in and to remain in a state that is not juridical*, that is, a state of affairs in which no one is secure in what belongs to him against deeds of violence' (*MJ* 72, my italics). See also C. Taylor, 'Kant's Theory of Freedom', in Z. Pelczynski and J. N. Gray (eds.), *Conceptions of Liberty in Political Philosophy* (London, 1984), 100–22, at pp. 110–13.

[33] Wolff, *Autonomy of Reason*, p. 212.

individual, for the formal principle enjoining the harmony of individual freedoms commands no more than that people not hold contradictory rights without specifying what these rights are. The Kantian ideal republic thus provides little guidance to the framers of constitutions in the real world, for while they are told that 'All forms of State are based on the idea of a constitution which is compatible with the natural rights of man,'[34] they are not told what these natural rights are. Having rejected the Humean, empiricist approach which identifies rights and obligations by investigating society and human nature, Kant is unable to make any plausible claims about the best (ideal) constitution for imperfect, natural man. He posits an ideal constitution for ideal men and then commands that men act according to the moral law which itself commands that they seek to enter such a condition. Ultimately, this amounts not so much to a political theory of the just constitution for imperfect man as a moral theory of the nature of the perfect man.

3. TAKING HAYEK SERIOUSLY

As our brief enquiry into their political thought suggests, the philosophies of Hume and Kant contrast sharply with each other. While both these thinkers of the Enlightenment defended liberal views of justice which stressed the importance of the rule of law, the maintenance of property distinctions, and distribution according to individual entitlement or rights, they offered very different justifications for such similar positions. Hume was concerned to show that the maintenance of such liberal principles could not, finally, be given an abstract or universally binding rational justification: a justification which abstracts from a historically established constitution governing a particular social order. This concern has its roots in Hume's epistemology which works towards the conclusion that we cannot 'defend . . . reason by reason' (T 187): the foundations of human understanding lie not in man's powers of reason, for 'If we reason a priori, anything may appear to produce anything' (EU 164). Rather, the basis of human understanding is experience, 'which teaches us the nature and bounds of cause and effect, and enables us to infer the existence of one object from that of another' (EU 164). Taking the view that 'the foundation of

---

[34] Kant, 'The Contest of Faculties', in H. Reiss (ed.), Kant's Political Writings (Cambridge, 1970), 177–90, at p. 187.

moral reasoning, which forms the greater part of human knowledge, and is the source of all human action and behaviour' (*EU* 164) is also *experience*, Hume recommended a mitigated scepticism which recognized the existing order as the appropriate starting-point for philosophical reflection about tastes, morals, and politics.[35]

Kant sought to uphold precisely what Hume denied: the autonomy of reason. This involved the rejection of Hume's metaphysics which, in denying reason's capacity to establish a necessary connexion between cause and effect, 'inferred that Reason completely deceives herself with this concept, in falsely taking it for her own child, whereas it is nothing but a bastard of the imagination fathered by experience'.[36] It also meant rejecting the idea of securing moral knowledge in an understanding of human nature: 'A metaphysics of morals cannot be founded on anthropology.'[37] Thus when Kant came to defend a liberal view of justice, his defence was founded not in a conservative regard for the authority of the historically given but in the view that the will of man considered as a *rational being* must be regarded as the source of universally binding law.

The question before us now is, why is this contrast significant if we wish to understand Hayek's political philosophy? After all, Hume and Kant not only wrote their major works some two centuries ago, but also were moved to write them by quite different concerns. Inspired by Rousseau, Kant's intentions were to direct the concerns of moral philosophy away from happiness to freedom.[38] His ultimate philosophical objective, in this regard, was 'the reconciliation of nature scientifically understood, with the requirements of moral life'—the reconciliation of human conditionality with human worth.[39] Hume's intention, in his political writings, was to bring to the analysis of politics the temper of a philosopher, and so to undermine the claims of those immoderate men of party

---

[35] A fuller defence of this interpretation of Hume is in Livingston, *Hume's Philosophy of Common Life*, esp. ch. 12 and also pp. 25–33.

[36] Kant, *Prolegomena to any Future Metaphysics That Will Be Able to Present Itself as a Science*, ed. and trans. by P. G. Lucas (Manchester, 1978), 6.

[37] Kant quoted in F. Copleston, *A History of Philosophy*, Vol. 6: *Modern Philosophy*, Part II: *Kant* (New York, 1964), 104.

[38] See S. M. Shell, *The Rights of Reason: A Study of Kant's Philosophy and Politics* (Toronto, 1980), 21–23, 61, and *passim*.

[39] Ibid. 11.

who sought to bolster their political claims with abstract philosophical justifications. Hayek's intentions seem a good deal
removed from the concerns of these eighteenth-century men.

Yet the contrast between Hume and Kant becomes important
precisely if we take seriously Hayek's intentions, and in particular
his claim to be offering a *restatement* of the philosophy of liberalism
presented by earlier thinkers. If their theories do in fact stand in
irreconcilable conflict, as separate defences of the liberal philosophy, Hayek's restatement of liberalism would have either to
embrace one and reject the other, or risk presenting an account of
liberalism which rests on inconsistent premises. It is the latter
course that Hayek chooses, for he sees no fundamental incompatibility between the views of Hume and Kant as far as their social
philosophies are concerned.

Now, this is not to say that Hayek goes to any great lengths to
show that the views of Hume and Kant can be reconciled: *that* is
not part of his concern. He does indicate quite clearly, however,
that he regards their views as complementary, with Kant's legal
philosophy seen as a development of ideas found initially in Hume.
In 'The Confusion of Language in Political Thought', he argues that
the 'end-independent character of rules of just conduct has been
demonstrated by David Hume and most systematically developed
by Immanuel Kant' (*NS* 77). And in his essay on Hume's legal and
political philosophy he suggests that Kant's theory of the categorical imperative, far from being the source of his theory of the
Rechtsstaat, was probably developed by applying to morals the
concept of the rule of law he found in 'Whig or liberal doctrines' of
the government of laws deriving directly from Hume (*S* 117).[40]
Clearly, Hayek himself thinks of Hume and Kant as central figures
in the liberal tradition, and throughout his writings he refers to
their contributions as the basis of modern liberal theory—and
liberal legal theory in particular. Thus, in 'The Principles of a
Liberal Social Order', he suggests that liberalism's 'essential
distinction' between rules of just conduct implicit in the idea of the
rule of law, and the particular commands issued by authority for
the purpose of organization, was 'made explicit in the legal theories
of . . . David Hume and Immanuel Kant', although it 'has not been
adequately restated since' (*S* 166). In the introduction to *Law*,

[40] See also Hayek, *MSJ* 166–7.

Legislation and Liberty he states that, on the issues which are his main concern, 'thought seems to have made little advance since David Hume and Immanuel Kant, and in several respects it will be at the point at which they left off that [Hayek's own] analysis will have to resume' (*RO* 6).

Yet what makes it most clear that Hayek's restatement of the philosophy of liberalism rests on Humean and Kantian presuppositions is not the fact that he occasionally so describes his enterprise. It is the arguments themselves which suggest this most strongly. Hayek's critique of constructivist rationalism, and his account of the evolution of rules of conduct in the theory of spontaneous order, are strikingly Humean in character. His political philosophy is, to a considerable extent, founded in Humean assumptions about the nature of society and the place of justice within it. He sees morality as a social institution composed of rules of conduct which have evolved with the social order and derive their legitimacy, ultimately, from the fact that they facilitate the co-ordination of human activities and enhance society's prospects of survival. He thus follows Hume in regarding justice as an institution which enables man to cope with his circumstances, and in denying that the rules of justice can be discovered by reason. At the same time, however, Hayek appears to reject the idea of such a 'conservative' justification of the liberal order. In attempting to uncover the *principles* of a liberal social order he turns to a Kantian emphasis on the importance of freedom as the master principle of the Great Society. His conception of freedom as 'independence of the arbitrary will of another' is indeed strikingly Kantian, emphasizing as it does that liberty means 'the absence of a particular obstacle—coercion by other men' (*CL* 19).

Taking Hayek seriously requires that we recognize two distinct kinds of argument advanced in his political philosophy. While both kinds of argument are brought to birth by the same concern or intention—to develop an intellectually sustainable defence of liberalism in a restatement of the fundamental tenets of liberal doctrine—they remain separate arguments. Any serious evaluation of Hayek's enterprise must, then, address the question of whether these arguments are compatible and mutually reinforcing, or simply inconsistent claims rooted in conflicting philosophical assumptions.

2

Constructivism and Justice

I. INTRODUCTION

Just as Hume's politics drew attention to the threat posed by the rationalistic (contractarian) doctrines of the establishment Whigs, who failed to appreciate that the Constitution was the fragile product of history, so Hayek has tried to identify the threat to 'our civilization' stemming from a more modern failure to understand how human interaction is governed by rules which have evolved over generations and which cannot be given any rational foundation. This concern is reflected in his 'conviction' that 'the most important political (or "ideological") differences of our time rest ultimately on certain basic philosophical differences between two schools of thought, of which one can be shown to be mistaken' (RO 5). This mistaken philosophical approach is 'rationalism'—or, more precisely, 'constructivist rationalism'—which infects several fields of theoretical enquiry through such doctrines as legal positivism and utilitarianism (RO 6). The 'great tragedy of our time' is the destruction of values occasioned by this constructivist rationalism which, failing to recognize 'the status of values as independent and guiding conditions of all rational construction', in fact dethrones 'the indispensable foundation of all our civilization' (RO 6–7).

We begin our enquiry into Hayek's political philosophy with an examination of his claims about the nature and significance of the limits of human reason. The nature of mind and human knowledge, for him, places serious constraints on our talk about justice, and limits what we can accomplish in its name. The tendency of this philosophy is, like Hume's, basically negative: it seeks not to produce a positive account of the foundations of justice in the good society but to indicate why, ultimately, the free society does not rest on foundations which can be uncovered (or constructed) by reason. As we shall see, this outlook is at odds with Hayek's proclaimed intention to set out the principles of a liberal social order. But first the task of this chapter must be completed. The next four sections will outline Hayek's account of the nature of the mind and knowledge and his critique of 'constructivism', explain the relationship between his attack on constructivism and his theory of justice by comparing his thought with that of Rawls, and, finally, raise some of the problems which emerge from this view of the relation between epistemology and justice.

2. THE NATURE OF MIND AND KNOWLEDGE

Hayek's main concern in philosophy has always been to identify the nature and limits of the power of reason to comprehend the world. He tackles this problem most directly in his work on theoretical psychology, *The Sensory Order*, which defends a view of mind not as a passive receiver of sensations from the external world, but as an active mechanism characterized by the physiological capacity to *classify* the phenomena encountered by the sensory organs. His theory posits three structures, the relations among which account for the nature of knowledge:

1. 'The physical order of the external world, or the physical stimuli, which for the present purpose we must assume to be known, although our knowledge of it is, of course, imperfect.'

2. The neural order of the nervous fibres which transmit impulses 'which, though undoubtedly part of the complete physical order, is yet part of it which is not directly known but can only be reconstructed'.

3. 'The mental or phenomenal order of sensations (and other mental qualities) directly known although our knowledge of it is largely only a "knowing how" and not a "knowing that", and although we may never be able to bring out by analysis all the relations which determine that order' (*SO* 39).

Hayek's central thesis concerns the relations between the second and third structures, for he argues that the mental or phenomenal order is produced by the physiological processes of the brain and nervous system responding to stimuli. The neural order, then, is largely an 'apparatus of classification' which produces sensory (and other mental) qualities by determining the system of connexions or impulses in the nervous system. His basic claim is that 'we do not first have sensations which are then preserved by memory, but it is as a result of physiological memory that the physiological impulses are converted into sensations' (*SO* 53). Thus he explicitly rejects the

'storage' theory of memory which asserts that with every experience some new mental entity representing sensations or images
enters the mind to be retained until recalled (SO 105). He offers an
empiricist account of mental events which rejects the empiricism of
Locke[1] and Hume. Its distinctiveness becomes clear in the
differences between its associationist account of the 'structure of
the mental order' and Hume's associationism. It rejects the
'traditional conception of individual impulses' which sees 'associat-
ive processes as simple chains of impulses where physiological
impulses correspond to mental units' (SO 119). Instead of a purely
associationist account of mental qualities, Hayek offers a physiological theory of associationism:

> The physiological impulse owes its mental quality to its capacity of evoking
> other impulses, and what produces the succession of different mental
> qualities is the same kind of process as that which determines the position
> of the impulses in the order of mental qualities: it possesses such a quality
> only because it can evoke a great variety of associated impulses.
> Associationism, in other words, is not something additional to the
> appearance of mental qualities, nor something which acts upon given
> qualities; it is rather the factor which determines the qualities (SO 119).

In describing the neural order as a system of classification, Hayek
presents a theory of the act of knowing which parallels Kant's
account of the 'pure concepts of the understanding' or 'categories'.
For Kant, 'the act of putting different representations together, and
of grasping what is manifold in them in one (act of) knowledge' (A
77, B 103) is called an act of 'synthesis' rather than an act of
'classification', but the similarity between this account and Hayek's
is striking. For Kant, 'Synthesis in general . . . is the mere result of
the power and imagination, a blind but indispensable function of
the soul, without which we should have no knowledge whatsoever,
but of which we are scarcely ever conscious' (A 78, B 103). Hayek
puts a similar case for seeing the act of knowing as an *unconscious*
act of synthesis even more strongly, arguing that the operations of
the mind are guided by a number of 'supra-conscious' rules of
which we can never acquire an understanding. Not only are our
perceptions and actions governed by 'rules' we are unable to
specify, but our capacity to understand and explain is limited by the

[1] For Hayek's criticisms of Locke see *The Sensory Order: An Inquiry into the
Foundations of Theoretical Psychology* (London, 1952), 18 n., 30, and 32.

fact that we cannot account for those rules which govern that capacity to understand and explain (*S* 60). If the brain is seen as an instrument of classification, we must accept that 'we may understand its *modus operandi* in general terms, or possess an explanation of the principle on which it operates,' but may never 'by means of the same brain, be able to arrive at a detailed explanation of its working in particular circumstances . . .' (*SO* 188–9). There is, he suggests, a general principle which applies to all conscious and rational processes: 'the principle that among their determinants there must always be some rules which cannot be stated or even be conscious' (*S* 62).

Hayek's account of the nature of knowledge does, however, differ from Kant's in a number of important respects. The most obvious difference is that, for Kant, the 'pure concepts of the understanding', which are fixed in number and function, 'apply *a priori* to objects of intuition in general' (*A* 79, *B* 105). Understanding or knowing is explained not physiologically but metaphysically, and the faculty of understanding is held to be non-empirical or undetermined in so far as it is not modified or reshaped by experience. Hayek adopts a different viewpoint inasmuch as he sees the classificatory apparatus, which enables us to experience and to know, as a physiological product itself subject to modification by experience. Indeed it is the still developing product of evolution:

this system of connexions is acquired in the course of the development of the species and the individual by a kind of 'experience' or 'learning'; . . . it reproduces therefore at every stage of its development certain relationships existing in the physical environment between the stimuli evoking the impulses (*SO* 53).

The evolutionary character of Hayek's epistemology takes his theory of knowledge closer to that of Karl Popper. He accepts Popper's argument that knowledge is never acquired inductively: that induction is neither a psychological fact, nor a fact of ordinary life, nor one of scientific procedure.[2] The capacity to generalize comes first, and hypotheses are then tested and corroborated or refuted according to their effectiveness as guides to action (*NS* 43). Thus as an organism 'plays with a great many action patterns of which some are confirmed and retained as conducive to the

[2] See K. Popper, *Conjectures and Refutations: The Growth of Scientific Knowledge* (London, 1976), ch. 1.

preservation of the species, corresponding structures of the nervous system producing appropriate dispositions will first appear experimentally and then either be retained or abandoned' (NS 43).

While this resembles Popper's view of the growth of knowledge as the product of repeated trial and error, it is even closer to Donald Campbell's Popperian account of evolutionary epistemology as 'an epistemology taking cognizance of and compatible with man's status as a product of biological and social evolution'.[3] For Campbell, human evolution has been characterized not only by 'gains in adaptive capacity, in stored templates modelling the useful stabilities of the environment, in memory and innate wisdom', but also by the more dramatic 'gains in mechanisms for knowing, in visual perception, learning, imitation, language and science'.[4] For Hayek, similarly, the impact of the environment on organisms leads them not only to respond by processing data to be stored for later recall, but, more importantly, to adapt their behaviour and purposes, and indeed the structure of the mechanisms of knowing to ensure survival. The continued existence of these organic structures is 'made possible by their capacity of responding to certain external influences by such changes in their structure or activity as are required to maintain or restore the balance necessary for their persistence' (SO 82). Indeed, he suggests that the mind consists of a system of abstract rules governing action, each rule governing a class of actions, and that changes in the environment eliciting new responses not only compel the application of a rule but also engender changes in the rules of action (NS 43). There are no fixed categories of understanding but only constantly adjusting mechanisms of perception; man's *capacity* to know is developing as much as his knowledge is growing.

Hayek differs from Kant in another important way. He does not draw a distinction between 'appearance' and 'reality' or ask if or how we can know 'things in themselves' (SO 4–5). While he is like Kant inasmuch as he argues that we cannot have certain knowledge that is unaffected by the mechanisms which enable us to know, he explains this differently.

---

[3] 'Evolutionary Epistemology', in P. A. Schilpp (ed.), *The Philosophy of Karl Popper*, 2 vols. (La Salle, 1974), i. 413–63, at p. 413. See also Popper's favourable response to Campbell in vol. 2: 'Campbell on the Evolutionary Theory of Knowledge', ii. 1059–64.

[4] Campbell, 'Evolutionary Epistemology', p. 413.

Firstly, Hayek argues that the mental order is ultimately a part of the physical order but a part 'whose *precise* position in that larger order we shall never be able to determine' (*SO* 5). The reason for this is that we can never produce an explanation of the operation of the mind which *at the same time* explains how we are able to present that explanation.[5]

Secondly, Hayek criticizes the distinction between 'reality' and 'appearance' on the grounds that there is no difference between one variety of sense experience and another such that one is truer or more real than another. For example, to accept only the procedures used by the physical sciences as valid tests or criteria of 'reality' would 'force us to regard the various constructs of physics as more "real" than the things we can touch and see, or even to reserve the term "reality" to something which by definition we can never fully know' (*SO* 5). This would pervert the original meaning of the term 'real', and he suggests that it not be used in scientific discussion. Like Popper, he is committed to what we might call conjectural realism (*SO* 173–6).

Thirdly, Hayek's explanation of our inability to obtain knowledge unaffected by the mechanisms we use to test our various perceptions places great emphasis on human ignorance: a limitation that has its origins in the very nature of any 'knowing' organism. The organism seeking to adapt to its surroundings does so using its apparatus of classification to construct models of the environment to simplify the task of adaptation. It does this by selecting some elements from a complex environment as relevant for the prediction of events important for its persistence. While this kind of model-building may be more efficient than any alternative, there are limits to the extent to which such a microcosm can contain an adequate reproduction of the significant factors of the macrocosm (*SO* 131). Fortunately, not all events in the world are fully interdependent, so an organism can make predictions using a selection of the totality of events. Nonetheless, the successful organism of 'knowing' remains largely 'ignorant' of the totality of processes in the environment, and there is an element of uncertainty in its constructions of reality.

One important aspect of his epistemology, however, is particularly Kantian: his account of knowledge as *rule-governed*. In 'The

---

[5] But see R. Nozick on self-subsuming explanation, in his *Philosophical Explanations* (Oxford, 1984), 119–21, 131–40.

Primacy of the Abstract' he describes the mind according to 'the system of abstract rules which govern its operation' (NS 43). Indeed, the primary characteristic of an organism is 'a capacity to govern its actions by rules which determine the properties of its particular movements', so that 'what we call mind is essentially a system of such rules conjointly determining particular actions' (NS 42). This view is at the base of Hayek's account of the act of knowing as rule-guided behaviour:

. . . all the 'knowledge' of the external world which such an organism possesses consists in the action patterns which the stimuli tend to evoke, or, with special reference to the human mind, that what we call knowledge is primarily a system of rules of action assisted and modified by rules indicating equivalences or differences or various combinations of stimuli (NS 41).

While Kant presents a metaphysical, rather than a physiological account of the rule-guided nature of knowledge, his views closely resemble, and illuminate, Hayek's theory. In the first *Critique* Kant characterizes the faculty of understanding as a 'faculty of rules' which is always 'investigating appearances, in order to detect some rule in them' (A 126). More than this, rules are necessary if we are to 'know', for these rules enable us to organize experience: 'without such rules appearances would never yield knowledge of an object corresponding to them' (A 159, B 198). Kant's concept of the 'understanding' is much like Hayek's conception of the mind as a system of abstract rules, applied when an object or 'appearance' is encountered, so that these objects may be 'classified' or 'known'. In Kant, the actual application of the (correct) rule is the work of the faculty of *judgement* ('the faculty of subsuming under rules' (A 132, B 171)). But how exactly judgement is exercised cannot be fully explained because distinguishing whether or not something comes under a rule can only be done 'by means of another rule' (A 133, B 172), and to apply this rule would again require judgement.

This is precisely what Hayek means by the operation of supra-conscious or meta-conscious rules: the exercise of judgement by the application of rules of a higher order.[6] Like Kant, he maintains that

---

[6] The number of meta-rules is potentially limitless, for as soon as a higher stage rule is identified, the rule governing its identification and application must be assumed (but remains unidentified). This view is shared by Michael Polanyi who argues that: 'our rules for establishing true coherences—as against illusory ones—are and must remain indeterminate. Any rules we have must be applied, of course;

these rules cannot be articulated. While Kant likens the ability to apply rules to the possession of a particular talent acquired through practice rather than instruction (*A* 132, *B* 172), Hayek likens it to our ability to make linguistic judgements in the course of learning a language. This linguistic sense or *Sprachgefühl* has its basis in our possession of highly abstract rules governing our actions (*NS* 46).

The unarticulated character of much of our knowledge is of special significance for Hayek, who regards the capacity to act in accordance with abstract rules as older, and more important, than the capacity to articulate those rules through language (*NS* 47). Hayek's thesis is that knowledge is not merely manifested in conscious reflection and communication but embodied in the practices of individuals—and societies. Most of our knowledge is in fact *tacit* knowledge—'knowing how' rather than 'knowing that'.[7] This embodiment of knowledge in action is more clearly expressed in the German language, which distinguishes between *wissen* and *können*, but in English 'know how' may be understood as 'the capacity to act according to rules which we may be able to discover but which we need not be able to state in order to obey' (*S* 44).

That knowledge or knowing is governed by *rules* which guide *action*[8] is important for Hayek for two reasons which bear upon his theory of justice. First, the fact that unarticulated *rules* are 'used' by the mind to solve the epistemological problems which confront it when faced by the world of complex phenomena is analogous to the way in which social rules are 'used' by the individuals of society to solve the epistemological problems posed by social life: problems involving knowing how to act (and so, to co-ordinate and

and to do this, we must have additional rules for their application. But we cannot go on having specific rules for the application of specific rules for the application of specific rules ad infinitum. At some point we must have "rules" of application (if we call them that) which we cannot specify, because we must simply dwell in them in a subsidiary way. They are a part of our deepest commitments. But for this reason they are not specifiable.' See M. Polanyi and H. Prosch, *Meaning* (Chicago, 1975), 61. (What is obscure, however, in Hayek as well as in Polanyi, is why we must have, or be thought to have, ultimate rules.)

[7] A distinction made by Gilbert Ryle, *The Concept of Mind* (Harmondsworth, 1976), 26–60. See also M. Polanyi, *The Tacit Dimension* (London, 1967), esp. p. 20 where he argues that 'the process of formalizing all knowledge to the exclusion of any tacit knowing is self-defeating.'

[8] 'Rule, in this context means simply a propensity or disposition to act or not to act in a certain manner, which will manifest itself in what we call a *practice* or custom' (*RO* 75).

distribute). Our social behaviour is rule-governed just as is our mental activity. The implication of the rule-guided nature of our knowledge is that, just as the mind is limited in its capacity to articulate the rules *upon which its operation depends*, so is the individual limited in his capacity to articulate the rules *upon which the operation of society depends.*[9]

The rules which govern the working of society, and ensure its survival, are, for Hayek as for Hume, rules of justice. In general, we are unaware of how these social rules enable us to overcome the epistemological problems posed by human circumstances. This view of the human predicament as characterized by epistemological problems is a central and distinctive feature of Hayek's political and economic thought. While thinkers like Hume and Adam Smith had seen the problem for man as the scarcity of goods, and the remedy in rules of justice and the division of labour, for Hayek the main problem is to know how to act in a complex environment only a part of which any mind can comprehend. While for Hume there would be no room for justice in a society of abundance (or terrible rather than moderate scarcity), for Hayek there would be no room for justice in a society of omniscient persons (*MSJ* 39). 'Like all abstractions, justice is an adaptation to our ignorance—to our permanent ignorance of particular facts which no scientific advance can wholly remove' (*MSJ* 39). Rules of justice guide man by defining the range of permissible actions, making his environment more predictable.

The second reason why the fact that knowledge is governed by unarticulated rules is important for Hayek is that our capacity to follow yet unformulated rules explains not only our ability to master language, but also our possession of a 'sense of justice' or *Rechtsgefühl* (*S* 46, *NS* 45). This sense of justice is similar to Hume's conception of 'natural justice' to which rules or laws must conform if they are to be accepted by society (*EM* 197 n.). While Hume's point is that laws which contradict the sense of justice are likely to be disobeyed and so cause disruptions, Hayek is more interested in explaining how this 'sense' enables us to change

---

[9] Note the absence of an exact parallel here. The rules which govern the mind's operation might be divided into 'personal' rules, of which we may be conscious, and 'sub-personal' rules, which, as rules governing involuntary actions, may not be accessible. All social rules, however, are, in principle, accessible. This distinction was drawn to my attention by Philip Pettit.

existing rules. When our intuitions lead us to question particular rules, the formally *articulated* rule is seen to be inconsistent with the unarticulated rules guiding our judgement. When we say that a rule we thought to be just is unjust in a particular case, we mean that 'it is a wrong rule which does not adequately define what we regard as just, or that the verbal formulation of the rule does not adequately express the rule which guides our judgement' (*MSJ* 32). As we shall see, this view of our knowledge of justice is the basis of Hayek's arguments against any attempt to specify all (or too many) rules of justice through centralized legislatures. The nature of this knowledge is such that a great deal of it cannot be articulated but must remain embodied in the *procedures* which express it. Implicit in this attitude is a view that what we regard as just is as much subject to change as those unarticulated rules governing our mental operations are altered by experience.

Hayek's theory of knowledge also bears the methodological imprints of his predecessors in the Austrian school of economics. Indeed, the Austrian approach to the social sciences, particularly as evident in the work of Carl Menger and, to a lesser extent, Ludwig von Mises, throws some light on Hayek's explanation of the nature of our knowledge of our social institutions, of each other, and of ourselves. While no Austrian economist exerted a direct influence on Hayek's social thought, it is clear that the dominant concerns of the Austrians—the significance of time for economic actors; the importance of ignorance, uncertainty, and error in human action; the nature of human institutions as the unintended products of individual action; and the subjective nature of our knowledge of society and of our valuations of human goods—are also present in his social theory, and in his epistemology in particular.

The matter of the *ignorance* of human actors was touched on partially by Menger in his *Problems of Economics and Sociology* where he shows an awareness that in some situations ignorance of the unintended results of actions works more 'effectively' towards certain desired ends than would conscious planning.[10] As Schneider observes, it was Hayek who did most to exploit this particular insight,[11] explaining why, in some circumstances, 'ignorance' is

---

[10] See C. Menger, *Problems of Economics and Sociology*, ed. with an introduction by L. Schneider, trans. F. J. Nock (Urbana, 1963), esp. bk iii and app. viii.

[11] See ibid., 'Introduction', 16.

more effective than 'knowledge'. Here again the distinction between articulated or theoretical knowledge and tacit or unarticulated knowledge is crucial. Ignorance has instrumental value in those situations in which knowledge exists embodied in rules of whose value (or existence) individuals are unaware. This knowledge might manifest itself either in the mental rules which guide individual behaviour or in the social rules which regulate his conduct—or both. By allowing themselves to be guided by their instincts, or by the practices of their society, individuals in many circumstances will be led to better outcomes than they could expect from conscious planning or from what Thomas Sowell calls 'articulated rationality'.[12] 'Better outcomes', here, are ones which enhance the individual or group's ability to adapt or survive.

Hayek, as we saw, has two behavioural theses (NS 41): a psychological thesis emphasizing how unarticulated knowledge embodied in instincts or dispositions enables individuals to adapt to their environment despite their 'ignorance'; and a sociological thesis explaining how unarticulated rules embodied in social practices also enable individuals to produce superior outcomes without seeking consciously to do so.

For Hayek, the 'ignorant' individual is not without access to knowledge even if he is unaware of what knowledge he can draw upon. Inasmuch as he acts according to rules he is guided by knowledge embodied in them: in habits, customs, and rules of just conduct. In more complex societies, governed by rules manifested in various institutions (such as money), the individual needs to understand much less of his environment to survive and prosper because he is able to utilize more knowledge he does not possess (RO 15). This view underlies Hayek's understanding of economics and the economic order. Like Hegel,[13] he sees the economy or, as he prefers to call it, the 'catallaxy', not as a separate realm to be understood abstracted from the processes of social life but as intelligible only within the system of rule-governed relationships among individuals in the extended order of society.

In expounding these theses in economics, Hayek was developing the arguments of von Mises, whose efforts had been devoted to showing the impossibility of rational calculation in a socialist

---

[12] *Knowledge and Decisions* (New York, 1980), 102.
[13] See R. Plant, 'Hegel and Political Economy I', *New Left Review*, 103 (1977), 79–92, esp. p. 91.

economy.[14] Mises had criticized that variant of socialism which did not recognize that economic value was subjective: 'Valuation can only take place in terms of units, yet it is impossible that there should ever be a unit of subjective use-value for goods.'[15] Judgements of value did not *measure* but established grades or scales and, in the exchange economy, the 'objective exchange-value' of commodities becomes the unit of economic calculation. In a monetary exchange economy *money* is the good used as the unit in which exchange-values are defined. While the value of money may fluctuate in that its value in relation to other goods constantly changes, money or monetary calculation 'fulfils all the require-ments of economic calculation' in so far as it enables us to judge the relative values of all goods and so to make production plans involving processes stretching over long periods of time.[16]

The heart of Mises' criticism of socialism is that, without a free market, there would be no pricing mechanism and, without that, given the defects of calculation in terms of labour rather than money, there could be no economic calculation.[17] While Hayek generally accepts this Misesian position, his contribution to the critique of socialism was to show that the fundamental problem in economics is not a *calculational* problem but an *epistemological* one. As he explains in 'The Use of Knowledge in Society', the problem we want to solve when we seek to construct a 'rational economic order' is not a logical problem which can be overcome if we possessed all relevant information concerning preferences and the factors of production. This is because the data from which economic calculus begins are never given complete to a single mind who could work out their implications. Rather, the nature of the problem of a rational economic order is 'determined precisely by the fact that the knowledge of the circumstances of which we must make use never exists in concentrated or integrated form but solely as the dispersed bits of incomplete and frequently contradictory knowledge which all the separate individuals possess' (*IEO* 77).

This position itself has its roots in the subjectivist approach to the

[14] See L. von Mises, 'Economic Calculation in the Socialist Commonwealth', in F. A. Hayek (ed.), *Collectivist Economic Planning: Critical Studies in the Possibilities of Socialism* (London, 1935), 87–130; *Socialism: An Economic and Sociological Analysis*, trans. J. Kahane (Indianapolis, 1981), esp. chs. 5 and 6.

[15] Mises, 'Economic Calculation', p. 96.

[16] Ibid. 98–100.

[17] Ibid. 111.

social sciences that characterized the Austrian school. Hayek takes subjectivism a step further by asserting that even the data of the social sciences are subjective phenomena. For the social scientist such things as tools, food, medicine, weapons, words, and acts of production are thus concepts which refer not to some objective property possessed by those things but 'to views which some other person holds about the things' (*IEO* 59). This attitude is consistent with Hayek's view that all our observations are theory-laden: there are no facts that are given to us free of the constructions which enable us to ascertain them. This is as true of historical data as it is of facts we learn through more 'direct' observation: 'what we call historical facts are really theories which, in a methodological sense, are of precisely the same character as the more abstract or general models which the theoretical sciences of society construct' (*IEO* 71).

The extension of the subjectivism of the Austrians is of crucial importance for Hayek's theory of justice, for it transforms the way in which he regards the economic problem of society. The problem is not how to *distribute* goods or resources but how to *co-ordinate* their use so that their employment correctly reflects their relative value.

The economic problem of society is thus not merely a problem of how to allocate 'given' resources—if 'given' is taken to mean given to a single mind which deliberately solves the problem set by these 'data'. It is rather a problem of how to secure the best use of resources known to any of the members of society, for ends whose relative importance only these individuals know (*IEO* 77–8).

On the basis of this view that the distribution of resources is not 'the social problem' Hayek constructs his argument against seeing justice as a problem concerning the allocation of goods. Indeed, rather than seeing justice as posing a question about the right distributive outcomes or distributive procedures, he regards justice as the *answer* to the question 'how do we co-ordinate individuals' actions in society given our limited epistemological powers?' He presents a Humean answer to a modified Humean question. Hume's solution to the social problem created by the moderate scarcity of resources and the limited benevolence of individuals was to institute rules of justice. Hayek offers the same answer, but redefines the social problem: it is not that we are not benevolent, but rather that we cannot know how to co-ordinate our activities without rules (of justice) to guide us.

This raises several questions about justice. First, if justice is the solution to the problem of co-ordination and not a question about the rightness of outcomes or distributive procedures, what kinds of rules of justice should there be? Secondly, can we not answer this question by constructing rules of justice on the basis of our preferred outcomes, and embody these rules in procedures that will secure these outcomes? Justice would still be the solution to the problem of co-ordination, but the standard against which we would assess the rules would be the outcomes they aim at. Thirdly, in the absence of such a test of the rules of justice, is there no way of deciding what is to count as a just or an unjust rule? Hayek has attempted to meet these objections in what has amounted to a critique of 'social justice'. The first part of that critique is an attack on what he has labelled 'constructivism'.

3. THE CRITIQUE OF CONSTRUCTIVISM

Hayek's main charge against constructivists is that they lie under the 'synoptic delusion' that all relevant facts can be known to some one mind 'and that it is possible to construct from this knowledge of the particulars a desirable social order' (RO 14). They do not see that we cannot 'assemble as a surveyable whole all the data which enter into the social order' (RO 15). Nor do they acknowledge either the importance for social theory of the extent of human ignorance, or the limitations of science—which is a tool of limited use as it cannot solve the problem of the utilization of dispersed knowledge. What, then, is constructivism?

'Constructivist rationalism' is a conception of the formation of social institutions which 'assumes that all social institutions are, and ought to be, the product of deliberate design' (RO 5). It is equated with what Popper calls 'naïve rationalism' and contrasted with Hayek's 'evolutionary rationalism' and Popper's 'critical rationalism'. Hayek offers a fuller definition of constructivism in 'Kinds of Rationalism':

Rationalism in this sense is the doctrine which assumes that all institutions which benefit humanity have in the past and ought in the future to be invented in clear awareness of the desirable effects that they produce; that they are to be approved and respected only to the extent that we can show that the particular effects they will produce in any given situation are preferable to the effects another arrangement would produce; that we have it in our power so to shape our institutions that of all possible sets of results that which we prefer to all others will be realized; and that our reason should never resort to automatic or mechanical devices when conscious consideration of all factors would make preferable an outcome different from that of the spontaneous process (*S* 85).

Hayek sees implicit in this variant of rationalism a theory of mind which conflicts with his own, a 'false conception of the human mind as an entity standing outside the cosmos of nature and society, rather than being itself the product of the same process of evolution to which the institutions of society are due' (*RO* 5). Having concluded in *The Sensory Order*, and in his essays on the philosophy of mind, that the individual was incapable of distancing himself from the *cosmos of nature* so as to account fully for its operation, Hayek maintains that it is similarly impossible for man to distance himself sufficiently from the *cosmos of society* to construct a complete account of its structure. Such an account, he argues, would involve an attempt to produce a complete explanation of how society and its institutions have evolved and will evolve, by people who, at the same time, do not know how they themselves are evolving as the members of those institutions, or know how their explanations may affect the development of those institutions.

Hayek traces constructivist rationalism back to Descartes, whose 'radical doubt' led him to refuse to accept as true anything which could not be logically derived from premises that were themselves beyond doubt. The consequence of adopting such a position, Hayek argues, was the rejection of the validity of rules of conduct which could not be justified in this way. It led, indeed, to morals, religion, law, language, money, and the market being thought of as deliberate constructions. And the constructivist account of history was most fully expounded in the conception of the formation of society by a social contract—first in Hobbes and, later, in Rousseau (whom Hayek, following Robert Derathé, sees as a direct follower of Descartes). Of the contractarians Hayek also objects that, 'Even though their theory was not always meant as a historical account of what actually happened, it was always meant to provide a guideline for deciding whether or not existing institutions were to be approved as rational' (*RO* 10).

The crucial feature of constructivism is its refusal to see the limitations of reason. Hayek regards reason not as a capacity that enables man to stand outside nature or society, to explain or to evaluate, but as the product or creation of 'civilization' and human evolution, which enables man to calculate, to compare values, and to identify contradictions in thought and in action (*NS* 20, *CL* 24). Because he sees reason as unable to 'rise above' the civilization that produces it, or identify an Archimedean point from which to view the world, he argues that 'the social process from which reason emerges must remain free from its control' (*CL* 38).

This is, in many respects, an unusual argument. It is more commonly argued that reason is hindered, or even bound, by the social processes that condition human knowledge. Philosophers such as Jürgen Habermas, indeed, seek ways to free our cognitive faculties from the social structures that condition our understanding, so that knowledge can both be acquired and communicated without the distorting effects of human interests, ideology, or traditions. Similarly, Rawls attempts to show how the individual subject may be understood as a being, unencumbered by the interests that otherwise govern his action, who can make rational decisions about principles of justice unconstrained by the influences of wealth, social position, luck, or natural ability (*TJ* sect. 24, *KC* 529). For Hayek, however, no such thing is possible, for our cognitive ability is deeply rooted in the social process. Indeed, any attempt to use reason to control or direct the social process threatens not only to impede the development of our powers of reason but also to bring the growth of knowledge to a halt. Knowledge is the product of freedom and experiment—and cannot be produced by reason.

We might conceive of a civilization coming to a standstill, not because the possibilities of further growth had been exhausted, but because man had succeeded in so completely subjecting all his actions and his immediate surroundings to his existing state of knowledge that there would be no occasion for new knowledge to appear (*CL* 38).

Hayek's view of the limitations of reason thus lead him to argue against those political theories which seek to organize society or to bring it under the control of rational conceptions of the good. His epistemological views lead him to deny the possibility of arriving at such a determinate conception that is not arbitrary, governed by an individual will, and ultimately totalitarian. Thus he rejects the possibility of reaching an ahistorical, extra-social conception of justice. His arguments against constructivism, in this regard, are most explicit in his criticisms of utilitarianism which he sees as a variant of this kind of rationalism. The utilitarianism Hayek criticizes is undoubtedly that of Bentham and J. S. Mill rather than any theory of the functions of rules and institutions in society. He follows Hume inasmuch as he sees justice as a system of rules which serves the general welfare by co-ordinating the actions of individuals so that they may pursue their often separate purposes, yet does not seek to justify any particular rule of justice by appealing to its utility. The distinction Hayek makes is one between 'means-utility' and 'ends-utility' (*MSJ* 18). While Hume defended rules of justice on the ground that justice was a useful 'means' of ensuring that individuals could pursue their interests without their actions coming into conflict, he did not seek to gauge the justice of rules by any determinate 'end' towards which they might tend.[18] Hayek puts two particular, and one more general, criticisms of utilitarianism. He rejects 'act' utilitarianism as incapable of accounting for the existence of rules, for if actions should be judged or taken on the basis of calculations of the likelihood of greater happiness or satisfaction being produced, rules become redundant. If the value of a rule governing conduct is confirmed by calculations of the felicific consequences of an action, then that rule is unnecessary as the felicific calculus has priority. If the rule is discredited by such calculations and overridden, then the rule is pointless. (Unfortunately, Hayek does not pause to consider certain obvious and plausible utilitarian replies.)[19]

The rule utilitarians are criticized as unable to explain the existence of rules without assuming the existence of other rules not accountable for by utilitarian considerations. To judge the utility of

---

[18] Haakonssen uses Hayek's distinction between 'means-' and 'ends-utility' to explain why Hume is not a utilitarian in the way Mill and Bentham were. See *The Science of a Legislator: The Natural Jurisprudence of David Hume and Adam Smith* (Cambridge, 1981), 195. See J. Harrison, *Hume's Theory of Justice* (Oxford, 1981), 87–8, who also argues that Hume was *not* a utilitarian.

[19] See J. J. C. Smart, 'An Outline of a System of Utilitarian Ethics', in J. J. C. Smart and B. Williams, *Utilitarianism: For and Against* (Cambridge, 1980), esp. sect. 7, 'The Place of Rules in Act-Utilitarianism'; P. Pettit amd G. Brennan, 'Restrictive Consequentialism', *Australasian Journal of Philosophy*, 64 (1986), 438–55.

any one rule one would always have to assume that, among the determinants of its utility, there would always be some other rules that were accepted and observed and not subjected to utilitarian calculations (*MSJ* 20). If all rules were followed only on the basis of utilitarian calculations, the uncertainty of utilities (and calculations) of other individuals would make behaviour unpredictable and all calculation exceedingly difficult.

The general criticism of utilitarianism which lies behind Hayek's more particular objections to this variant of constructivism is that it does not take sufficient notice of the epistemological difficulties that confront individuals and society, or recognize that rules are an important means of overcoming these problems. There are limits to how far we can calculate the value of our rules of conduct because, first, there are limits to the extent to which our imperfect knowledge allows us to foresee the consequences of our actions; and, secondly, the rules themselves enable us to calculate and make predictions of the behaviour of other individuals. In effect, once rules are seen as embodying tacit or practical knowledge, it becomes difficult to judge or criticize rules on the basis of calculations of the putative benefits of particular (rule-defying) actions. If the knowledge embodied in such rules is unarticulated it cannot, although it must, enter into the calculations of the value of those actions.

For Hayek, the value of social rules is best tested, not by the theoretical calculations of the ends-utilitarian, but by the 'success' of those rules in co-ordinating the different plans of the individuals and groups in society. 'They serve not to make any particular plan of action successful, but to reconcile many different plans of action' (*MSJ* 22). When rules lead to conflicts, which arise when different individual plans are rendered incompatible and irreconcilable under the terms they establish, the rules themselves reveal their inadequacy. (The main shortcoming of this argument is that it is never clear what is to count as a '*successful*' reconciliation of plans. As we shall see later, it reveals a deeper problem in Hayek's thought.)

Hayek's critique of utilitarianism displays his anti-rationalism most clearly, for his arguments appear, at this point, to be most at odds with the views of Popper.[20] On several occasions Popper has

---

[20] I am assuming here that Popper is a rationalist; for a contrary view see D. Stove, *Popper and After: Four Modern Irrationalists* (Oxford, 1984).

argued that the value of criticism, and of theoretical and scientific enquiry generally, lies in the fact that the testing of theories often saves us from the risks and dangers inherent in the practical experiments of life. We allow our theories to be destroyed instead of putting ourselves at risk, and put them into practice if they defy falsification. Of course, Popper does not reject the idea that practical knowledge is also tested and modified in the course of human life but his emphasis on our theoretical powers is greater than Hayek's. We shall return to this contrast later (sect. 5) when we come to examine Hayek's epistemology more critically.

In spite of Hayek's criticisms of utilitarianism, it is tempting to label him as a utilitarian for, as we shall see, his defence of liberty and the liberal order relies heavily on consequentialist arguments. John Gray has, in fact, suggested that Hayek might best be regarded as an indirect utilitarian.[21] While Hayek does not, like Mill, accept the Principle of Utility as a maxim of practical reasoning, his defence of the framework often invokes claims about the securing of general welfare. To refuse to see Hayek as an indirect utilitarian is, it would appear, to argue against the possibility of rendering a coherent account of his system of ideas. Yet there are two reasons for not placing him in the utilitarian camp. First, he himself goes to some length to reject utilitarianism as a variant of constructivism and as a doctrine which ignores the epistemological claims at the heart of his political theory. Secondly, if Mill, for whom utility is a principle which guides practical reasoning, is to be seen as an indirect utilitarian, as Gray forcefully argues,[22] then it is unhelpful to so label Hayek, whose consequentialism aims at no determinate end-state such as one in which happiness is maximized. (Whether or not his political thought rests on any more coherent moral theory will be considered in ch. 5.)

Hayek's objection to utilitarianism is fundamentally that the only 'utility' that can be seen as a determinant of rules of conduct is not a utility that is *known* to social agents, or to any one individual, but a hypostatized 'utility' to society as a whole. Utilitarians are 'driven to interpret the products of evolution anthropomorphically as products of design and to postulate a personified society as the author of these rules' (*MSJ* 22). The indirect utilitarian is as guilty

---

[21] *Hayek on Liberty*, 2nd edn. (Oxford, 1986), 59–61; 'Hayek and the Rebirth of Classical Liberalism', *Literature of Liberty*, 5 (1982), 19–66.

[22] *Mill on Liberty: A Defence* (London, 1983).

of this charge as the direct utilitarian if he takes utility to refer to ends-utility rather than means-utility. The constructivistic nature of utilitarianism lies *not* in the fact that it seeks to justify rules or practices by appealing to the virtue of usefulness but rather in the fact that it does not acknowledge the limits imposed by ignorance. Our limited predictive powers make it difficult to justify existing practices, or the creation of new rules, on the basis of a view of the future end-state. (This is not to say that Hayek sees no way of dealing with ignorance, as we shall see in ch. 3.) While rules may thus be defended on the basis of their past and current effectiveness or compatibility with social life or with the community's 'sense of justice', they cannot be defended on the basis of a future end-state which comprises the 'total consequences' of those rules (*MSJ* 19).

Because Hayek sees the 'social problem' as an epistemological problem of a particular kind he argues against any attempt to solve it by holding up an ideal whose conception ignores this difficulty. He thus rejects not only utilitarianism but also social contract theory as another variant of constructivism. In numerous critical references to Hobbes and Rousseau (although he does not object *explicitly* to the contractarianism of Locke and Kant!) he levels the familiar charge of constructivism against the idea of a social contract providing 'a guideline for deciding whether or not existing institutions were to be approved as rational' (*RO* 10). Unfortunately, Hayek has devoted little space in his writings to contract theory and much of his argument against it lies implicit in his attack on constructivism generally. It would be worthwhile making this critique more explicit to make clearer Hayek's views on constructivism and the significance for political theory of the nature of knowledge. I propose to do this by comparing Hayek with Rawls, to see how the critique of constructivism bears upon Rawls's theory of justice.

4. HAYEK AND RAWLS

In his Dewey Lectures Rawls identifies four variants of what he also calls constructivism: utilitarianism, perfectionism, intuitionism, and 'Kantian constructivism' (*KC* 515). It is the fourth variant that he wishes to outline and defend as a means of justifying the principles of justice that were articulated in *A Theory of Justice*. While interesting in its own right as a contribution to moral theory,

Rawls's work is significant for us because it explicitly attempts to do what Hayek suggests is not possible. It must, however, be noted that Hayek has made no explicit critique of 'Kantian constructivism' and that Rawls's term constructivism is somewhat different from Hayek's 'constructivist rationalism'. The reason why Hayek may be contrasted with Rawls is not that the latter uses the *word* 'constructivism' to describe his approach to moral theory but rather that his very enterprise is one Hayek would question.

Rawls's initial concern in *A Theory of Justice* was to discover universally applicable principles of justice. Under the impact of extensive criticism, however, it became clear that the character of his theory did not justify Rawls's universalist aspirations and in the Dewey Lectures the entire project is recast to reflect his more parochial, if no less contractarian, concerns: 'We are not trying to find a conception of justice suitable for all societies regardless of their particular social or historical circumstances. We want to settle a fundamental disagreement over the just form of basic institutions within a democratic society under modern conditions' (*KC* 518).[23] Kantian constructivism is the preferred method of settling this disagreement. It does this by setting up 'a certain procedure of construction which answers to certain reasonable requirements, and within this procedure persons characterized as rational agents of construction specify, through their agreements, the first principles of justice' (*KC* 516). Put differently, Kantian constructivism 'specifies a particular conception of the person as an element in a reasonable procedure of construction, the outcome of which determines the content of the first principles of justice' (*KC* 516). Rawls's intention is thus to construct, first, a *procedure* for reaching agreement on what is the best set of principles of justice, i.e. a method which we would all accept as the best and fairest way of choosing those principles; and secondly, a *theory of the individual* who takes part in this procedure, which specifies those qualities of personhood which enable him to choose but do not distinguish him from other individuals to such an extent that the procedure secures not an agreement but a compromise. This

---

[23] See also Rawls's more recent article, 'Justice as Fairness: Political Not Metaphysical', *Philosophy and Public Affairs*, 14 (1985), 223–51. For a critique of Rawls's attempt to develop a more universal theory see B. Barry, *The Liberal Theory of Justice: A Critical Examination of the Principal Doctrines in* A Theory of Justice *by John Rawls* (Oxford, 1973); and also P. Pettit, 'A Theory of Justice?', *Theory and Decision*, 4 (1974), 311–24.

account of the choosing individual we may all recognize as ourselves. The construction does not enable us to view society from without so as to make choices unaffected by our history and traditions. Rather, it indicates how those traditions can be articulated, enabling us to make explicit those principles of justice which we would in fact accept. 'What justifies a conception of justice is not its being true to an order antecedent to and given to us, but its congruence with our deeper understanding of ourselves and our aspirations, and our realization that, given our history and the traditions embedded in our public life, it is the most reasonable doctrine for us' (KC 519).

The point of this articulation is to enable liberal democratic society to bridge the *impasse* in its political culture. The impasse suggests there can be no agreement on how social institutions should be arranged if they are to conform to the freedom and equality of citizens as moral persons, and it emerges in a conflict between the Lockean view and the tradition stemming from Rousseau (KC 519). If, however, we were able to 'find a suitable rendering of freedom and equality, and of their relative priority, rooted in the more fundamental notions of our political life and congenial to our conception of the person' (KC 519–20), to articulate that agreement embedded in our traditions, this conflict could be resolved as both parties would accept the principles of justice (or institutional arrangements) that flowed from their common tradition. The point of articulating the liberal democratic tradition is to show that the bases of agreement can be found, and justice in the arrangement of social institutions secured. The device that will articulate this tradition is a variant of the social contract.

Rawls's social contract takes place in the 'state of nature' he calls the Original Position (OP), and the constraints imposed in the OP, and the nature of the parties therein, represent the freedom and equality of moral persons in a 'well-ordered society'. (A 'well-ordered society' is one which is regulated by a public conception of justice and in which members view each other as free and equal moral persons (KC 521).) Persons in the OP will choose the principles of justice appropriate to a well-ordered society if decision procedures are *fair*, i.e. conducive to such a choice, and if they are the sorts of people who could reach such a choice because not encumbered by the interests which flow from such contingencies as social position, wealth, or natural ability not essential to moral personhood, and which make agreement more difficult to attain. Rawls secures both these conditions at one stroke by building into the OP a 'veil of ignorance' which turns the parties into solely *moral* persons and not persons advantaged or disadvantaged by the accidents of circumstance. They thus have rational autonomy (the essence of moral personhood) in contrast to the full autonomy of persons in a well-ordered society. The moral persons of the OP, ignorant of, and uninfluenced by, their potential social position, are able to choose, and agree upon, principles of justice because they have, first, a sense of justice, i.e. they can understand, apply, and act from principles of justice, and secondly, the ability to form, revise, and rationally pursue a conception of the good (*KC* 525).

The parties in the OP are concerned with the justice of the 'basic structure' of society and their reflections on this issue are informed by two considerations. First, they are aware of the objective circumstances of society in which goods are moderately scarce. Secondly, they recognize that conceptions of the good vary, and that people have different ways of evaluating arguments and evidence when they try to reconcile their differences (*KC* 536). Like the members of a well-ordered society which serves as their model of the just society, the parties of the OP are 'not indifferent to how the fruits of their social co-operation are distributed' (*KC* 536). Now, because the well-ordered society is one whose stability is founded 'not merely on a perceived balance of social forces the upshot of which all accept since none can do better for themselves' (*KC* 539), but is one in which citizens affirm their existing institutions because they believe them to satisfy their 'public and effective conception of justice', the parties of the OP are to be guided in their deliberations by these two considerations. They must seek not a compromise of interests but an agreement on a conception of justice which satisfies the demands of publicity.

Publicity ensures, so far as the feasible design of institutions can allow, that free and equal persons are in a position to know and to accept the background social influences that shape their conception of themselves as persons, as well as their character and conception of the good. Being in this condition is a precondition of freedom; it means that nothing is or need be hidden (*KC* 539).

The parties are thus required to assess conceptions of justice subject to the constraint that the principles chosen must serve as a public conception of justice. Three conditions must be met to fulfil the demands of publicity: (a) society must be effectively regulated by public principles of justice; (b) the general beliefs which sustain the first principles, i.e., the theory of human nature and social institutions, must be supported by methods of public enquiry: the procedures of science; (c) the full justification of the public conception of justice must be possible and whoever wishes to carry out the procedure must be able to find the justification reflected in public culture, law, political institutions, philosophical, and historical traditions (KC 537).

Rawls's well-ordered society, exemplifying all three levels of publicity, is much like Popper's Open Society in which social order is the product not of a superimposed ideology, or of 'historically accidental or institutionalized delusions, or other mistaken beliefs about how its institutions work' (KC 539), but of the free acceptance of social institutions open to criticism. Guided by this model, the parties in the OP must choose principles which would serve such a society and reject principles which, though they 'might work', are not publicly acknowledged, or not founded on generally understood beliefs, or recognized as fallacious (KC 540).

Given the conditions of the OP, its members, who represent us as purely moral (rather than fully social) persons, would choose principles of justice that best represented our shared understanding of justice. What is of crucial importance about the OP is that it specifies an epistemological state in which we know enough to choose principles of justice, but not enough to be able to distort them to our own advantage. The knowledge Rawls allows those in the OP, under the veil of ignorance, is sociological and psychological knowledge but not (complete) knowledge of themselves or of each other.

From Hayek's anti-constructivist perspective, however, Rawls's enterprise appears misconceived. What Rawls is attempting to do is to articulate what cannot be articulated. The assumptions made in this attempt are not only implausible but, in fact, presume the absence of problems whose solution is the product (rather than the pre-condition) of justice. The problem stems from the contractarian character of Rawls's theory and, more specifically, his answer to the question 'why should we take any interest, moral or otherwise, in the hypothetical contract?' It should interest us, he replies, because:

the conditions embodied in the description of this situation are ones that we do in fact accept. Or if we do not, then we can be persuaded to do so by philosophical considerations of the sort occasionally introduced . . . what we are doing is to combine into one conception the totality of conditions that we are ready upon due reflection to recognize as reasonable in our conduct with regard to one another. Once we grasp this conception, we can at any time look at the social world from the required point of view. It suffices to reason in certain ways and to follow the conclusions reached (*TJ* 587).

For Rawls's OP articulates what Hayek calls the 'sense of justice' or *Rechtsgefühl* and Hume called the sense of natural justice. While Hume stipulated simply that rules or laws must conform roughly to our sense of natural justice, and Hayek argues that this sense leads us to reject as unjust particular proposed rules, Rawls attempts to capture this sense in a formal theory. Yet for Hayek, the very nature of this sense defies such formalization for a number of reasons. First, as Hume also argued, the sense of justice is not fixed but changes over time. This sense, Hayek avers, is essentially 'that capacity to act in accordance with non-articulated rules' (*NS* 81). The capacity to act, and recognize if others act, in accordance with non-articulated rules, exists before attempts are made to formally state such rules. Most articulated rules are 'attempts to put into words what has been acted upon before, and will continue to form the basis for judging the results of the application of the articulated rules' (*NS* 81). Once particular articulations of rules of conduct are accepted they will serve to inform others of these rules. But their acceptance is not always certain or immediate, for in the course of articulation and promulgation, both articulated and unarticulated rules change: 'the development of articulated and unarticulated rules will constantly interact' (*NS* 81). This makes it difficult to give theoretical expression to our sense of justice, particularly through a theory which seeks to 'regard the human situation . . . from all temporal points of view' (*TJ* 587),[24] for that sense of justice is continually being modified by the explicit rules that develop in society.

Rawls is not unaware of these difficulties. Nevertheless, he thinks it worth attempting to provide an account of a person's sense of justice which, he claims, is not the one which fits his judgement prior to his examining any conception of justice, but one 'which matches his judgements in reflective equilibrium' (*TJ* 48). This

[24] See Ch. 5, n. 2.

equilibrium is reached after a person has weighed various conceptions of justice and revised or retained his judgements accordingly. While Rawls acknowledges that a *complete* account of the sense of justice (via reflective equilibrium) is unattainable, Hayek implies that the problem is even greater: we can never articulate this sense of justice sufficiently to construct a theory of justice. The background of unarticulated rules can never be captured to form the first premiss of a syllogism defining justice. It is not that argument about justice and equity is not possible; rather, the idea of criticizing the justice of the social structure as a whole from the perspective of a putative sense of justice elicited from that social structure is mistaken. (Where this leaves Hayek, however, is a question we must turn to when we come to consider the coherence and the consistency of his position.)

A second argument the anti-constructivist Hayek might present against Rawls's attempt to describe the sense of justice of a liberal democratic society is that the very idea of articulating a *common* sense of justice against which to test the justice of social institutions is untenable because no such *common* sense exists. Or at least, there is sufficient *disagreement* among individuals about what is just to make such institutions as laws, conventions, legislatures, and courts necessary. Institutions of justice do not reflect a shared *conception* of justice. Rather, they reflect man's epistemological predicament: he is able neither to articulate fully his understanding of right and wrong nor to know enough about his world to be certain about his (and others') judgements. Institutions make up for this lack because they embody rules of conduct which have been tested by experience. What individuals do share (to varying extents) is confidence in the appropriateness of the institutions serving this function. In this regard, Hayek's theory is strongly Humean: the sense of justice does not serve to *justify* particular social institutions, though no institution will survive if it conflicts with that sense.

Now, Rawls does not deny the existence of different conceptions of justice; but he does claim that there is, among persons in 'reflective equilibrium', an 'approximate' similarity in their principles, and that the divisions that do exist are 'along a few main lines represented by the family of traditional doctrines' (*TJ* 50). These differences are, however, reconcilable in theory (for they are reconciled in practice) by 'a suitable rendering of freedom and equality, and their relative priority, *rooted in the more fundamental notions of our political life* and congenial to our conception of the person' (*KC* 520, my italics). This theoretical reconciliation is Rawls's endeavour: 'The task is to articulate a public conception of justice that all can live with who regard their person and the relation to society in a certain way' (*KC* 519). The Hayekian anti-constructivist response, however, would be that the most that could be articulated is not a public conception of justice but the conception of one individual. This he sees as a feature of constructivism which, in regarding 'society' as the standard-bearer of shared values, turns 'society' into a *personified* pursuer of particular aims (such as 'social justice') (*NS* 13, *RO* 26–7). In Rawls's OP, Hayek's accusation is borne out by the fact that it contains, in effect, only one person. The veil of ignorance strips the members of the OP of their individuality leaving them with identical, featureless, personalities. The OP is less a device for producing *agreement* than one which expounds the moral reasoning of a single individual. As Rawls himself notes, it is 'a theory of the moral sentiments . . . setting out the principles governing our moral powers, or more specifically, our sense of justice' (*TJ* 51). Yet he does not see this as a problem, for his claim is precisely that the sense of justice of one individual, at its deepest level, is shared by the community and is thus, to some extent, representative of a shared sense of justice.

Moreover, Rawls argues that if social institutions embody and implement a conception of justice which we cannot express theoretically or formally, it becomes unclear how we assess our social institutions without some theory of justice. Indeed, if political philosophy cannot hold up an ideal, or at least a model, against which institutions may be evaluated, does political philosophy have any place in the life of the polity? The conclusion that, for us, there exists 'no reasonable and workable conception of justice at all' would spell the end of practical philosophical enquiry: 'This would mean that the practical task of political philosophy is doomed to failure' (*KC* 570).

What Hayek would dispute, however, is not the capacity of political philosophy but the nature of its task which, for him, is not to uncover and reconstruct the bases of our agreement but to *criticize* the existing social order. Although he has often been labelled a conservative, Hayek in effect repudiates the conservatism of Rawls's approach to political philosophy which defends a theory of justice that articulates the values of a particular society. Indeed, Hayek explicitly states that conservatives seeking comfort in his political philosophy will be disappointed because the 'proper conclusion from the considerations I have advanced is by no means that we may confidently accept all the old traditional values' and because, in his view, there are not '*any* values or moral principles, which science may not occasionally question' (*NS* 18–19). And he claims for the 'social scientist' the 'right critically to examine and even to judge, every *single* value of our society' (*NS* 19). The kind of philosophical undertaking Hayek denies is not that which questions the values implicit in social practices but that which seeks at one and the same time to question *all* social values (*NS* 19). Implicit in this attitude is the assumption that the task of political philosophy can never be completed, for criticism will always have a place in a society in which values change. That there is no single 'reasonable and workable conception of justice' which philosophers can identify or construct does not thus signify the practical irrelevance of political theory but, rather, explains why it will always be a vital part of any polity.

Yet how does political theory proceed to assess social institutions without a theory of justice to guide it? This assessment, Hayek argues, takes two forms which, together, constitute the method of 'immanent criticism' (*MSJ* 24). Such a form of criticism attempts to test or judge *particular* rules, within a given system of rules, for their consistency or compatibility with other accepted rules in the system of such rules to known specific effects that it will produce' legal rules once we recognize the irreducibility of the whole existing system of such rules to know specific effects that it will produce' (*MSJ* 24). Rules would thus be consistent with each other if they did not lead individuals who obeyed them into conflict.

Such conflict would emerge either because a rule led two people to take incompatible actions or because the precedence of one rule over another was unclear. For example, a rule which upheld a right to blockade and picket a workplace in the course of a strike could lead to conflict in a society which endorsed rules upholding a right to work. Here the mechanisms of justice would have to correct this conflict either by specifying which rule had priority and so should override the other, or by repudiating one of the rules. The political theorist, in such cases, would similarly be required to present reasons why one rule or set of rules was inadmissible or of subordinate importance. The ultimate test of the applicability or correctness of a rule is thus the 'compatibility of the actions of different persons which they permit or require' (*MSJ* 25). This test is, in the final analysis, one of whether the actions permitted or restricted by a rule are compatible with social life. For example, laws prohibiting the sale, and consumption of alcohol into, say, French society, would not endure if the mechanisms of justice prevailed, and courts were able to assess such legislation in the light of the way of life of the populace. Should a central legislature or executive enforce such laws in societies in which they interrupted ordinary practice the consequences would be social conflict which would be either tolerated or repressed.

Hayek's argument is that the absence of the mechanisms of justice, which enable people to submit rules to criticism, and their replacement by or subordination to central legislative authority threatens to lead to totalitarianism, simply because rules cannot be tested practically. The reason why central authority is unsuccessful in producing laws which are compatible with social life is that *knowledge* of the compatibility of rules with social practice is not available to it. (Although this argument, as we shall see, casts doubt upon the possibility of *any* legislation.)

If the political theorist requires a perspective from which to assess and criticize these social institutions, then the existence of a moral and political tradition is of great importance. While no part of a tradition of rules of conduct, or of philosophy, is sacred and exempt from criticism, 'the basis of criticism of any one product of tradition must always be other products of tradition which we either cannot or do not want to question . . . particular aspects of a culture can be critically examined only within the context of that culture' (*MSJ* 25). Political philosophers invariably draw upon a tradition or particular elements of a tradition of thought in presenting arguments to criticize existing institutions. It must be acknowledged, however, that there is no one perspective from which political theory presents its criticism, for it will draw from a variety of philosophical and cultural viewpoints.

The defect of Rawls's enterprise, for Hayek, would be not that he holds up an ideal or model conception of justice by which social institutions may be assessed, but rather that he claims to have articulated a perspective, from which to evaluate conceptions of justice, which is the real perspective of all moral persons. Moreover, the perspective of the OP is quite unlike that of any living person in so far as it is the viewpoint of an individual without interests or attachments and possessing a full knowledge of 'all the relevant and true beliefs concerning human nature and social theory' (KC 541). It is a perspective from which the most significant feature of the human condition (in Hayek's view) is eliminated; for the uncertainty which stems from human ignorance is assumed away. Yet it is not clear how we would know what conception of justice we would choose if we could see things from a perspective in which we knew what we do not know. It is not enough merely to say that the parties in the OP know all the relevant and true beliefs concerning human nature and social theory; what is needed if we are to know how we would judge from that perspective is not just the assumption that we do know: we need that true social theory before us. Rawls does not offer us any such social theory. Indeed he cannot; for it is not possible to present a social theory which is not, to some extent, influenced by the interests and assumptions which dominate the theorist. (And again, it is the task of the *institutions* of science to test and evaluate such theories.) Even Rawls's attempt to restrict the scope of this knowledge of social theory by excluding knowledge of the truths of religion and philosophy (arguing that 'long experience suggests, and many plausible reflections confirm, that on such doctrines reasoned and uncoerced agreement is not to be expected' (KC 542)) is problematic, for the divides between social theory, philosophy, and religion are differently drawn.

Finally, the anti-constructivist Hayek would disagree with Rawls's use of the perspective of the OP to construct principles of justice founded on a view of the distributive concerns of justice. For Rawls, the primary subject of justice is what he calls the 'basic structure of society' or the way in which the major social institutions distribute not only 'fundamental rights and duties' but also the 'advantages of social cooperation' (TJ 7). A just basic structure of society (or simply a just society) is one in which, given the fact that everyone's well-being depends upon a scheme of co-operation, the division of advantages is 'such as to draw forth the willing co-operation of everyone taking part in it, including the less well situated' (TJ 15). While he recognizes that no society can be one into which individuals enter voluntarily in the literal sense, a just society comes as close as is possible to being a voluntary scheme in so far as it is founded on principles which free and equal persons would assent to under *fair* circumstances (*TJ* 13). The principles they would accept are principles of distribution. Rawls is eager to note that this view of the question of justice tallies with tradition, and likens his approach to Aristotle's.

The more specific sense that Aristotle gives to justice and from which the most familiar formulations derive, is that of refraining from *pleonexia*, that is, from gaining some advantage for oneself by seizing what belongs to another, his property, his reward, his office, and the like, or by denying a person that which is due him, the fulfilment of a promise, the repayment of a debt, the showing of proper respect, and so on. . . . *Aristotle's definition clearly presupposes, however, an account of what properly belongs to a person and of what is due to him. Now such entitlements are, I believe, very often derived from social institutions and the legitimate expectations to which they give rise* (*TJ* 10, my italics).

In Rawls's view, Aristotle had a conception of social justice to account for such entitlements. Rawls's task is to say what just claims amount to in a liberal democractic society by outlining the basic structure of a just society.

Whether or not Rawls's interpretation of Aristotle is correct, Hayek would dispute the plausibility of the enterprise of identifying the entitlements of individuals in the abstract. Here he denies both Rawls and Nozick. He would reject Nozick's claim that individuals' holdings are just if they are justly acquired and if the original acquisition of the relevant goods was just. (Nozick, of course, left the problem of justice in initial acquisition unsolved; for Hayek the problem defies solution.) Rawls's approach is different in that he seeks to tie entitlement to society's members' conception of individual entitlement. Because he sees that human interests might distort any conception of individual entitlement he tries to present a conception in a situation in which these interests do not influence the construction. Hayek rejects this approach because no objective entitlements can be found. For Rawls this is not the case: 'Kantian constructivism holds that moral objectivity is to be understood in terms of a suitably constructed social point of view that all can accept' (*KC* 519). For Hayek, there is no such point of view; rather, there are many points of view. The argument that there is a single point of view from which we can identify a conception of individual entitlement which would match our 'considered convictions' about the matter is no more plausible than the medieval arguments that there existed just prices and just wages discoverable independently of, and different from, those arrived at in a competitive market (*MSJ* 75). Any construction of a point of view from which to outline entitlements would represent not a view of persons in society but the view of the single individual involved in that construction.

We can see how Hayek and Rawls differ, and hence Hayek's criticism, more clearly if we note the more profound difference between their approaches to the problem of justice. For Rawls, justice is a feature of the distribution of goods and bads which are the product of social co-operation. Institutions are just if distribution, which is their concern, is just. For Hayek, however, justice is the means of *securing* social co-operation and not *directly* concerned with the question of distribution. In this he follows Hume, for whom justice was the precondition of the existence of society. Rules of justice secure co-operation by *defining* our entitlements or property, for co-operation can more easily take place once entitlements are less uncertain. We can agree to use *my* horse to plough *your* field once we know what is mine and what yours. Without this knowledge such co-operation is still possible but, with the benefits more uncertain, less likely to take place. Rules of justice solve this problem by defining entitlements and so making it easier for the individual to assess the costs and see the benefits of co-operation.

But how should these rules determine entitlements in the first place? For Rawls this is a matter of (social) justice; for Hayek it is not. The rules defining property, Hayek argues, emerge over time in response to problems or disputes over possession: they are the product of convention rather than agreements reached after philosophical argument. Just as conventions establishing property boundaries emerge to resolve conflicts, so does justice emerge as a convention to secure individuals in their knowledge of the stability of these boundaries. Other institutions emerge because conventions alone are inadequate to secure this growing body of knowledge: of rules of justice. Following Hume, Hayek sees the result as the evolution of the institutions of law and government, whose concern is to identify and implement the rules of justice.

Rawls rejects this approach in his essay 'A Well-Ordered Society':

Suppose we begin with the initially attractive idea that the social process should be allowed to develop over time as free agreements fairly arrived at and fully honoured require. Straightaway we need an account of when agreements are free and the conditions under which they are reached are fair. In addition, while these conditions may be satisfied at an earlier time, the accumulated results of agreements in conjunction with social and historical contingencies are likely to change institutions and opportunities so that the conditions for free and fair agreements no longer hold.[25]

For him, the justice of the basic structure must be established first if social processes are to be just—and the principles governing this structure and its regulation and correction so as to be 'just over time', must be agreed to in fair and free circumstances in which no one can take advantage of social and natural contingencies and the results of historical accidents and accumulations.[26] For the anti-constructivist Hayek, however, such agreements do not, and need not, take place in circumstances that *all* would recognize as free and fair. In the world of real individuals, no such circumstances exist. The important thing is that agreements are made and conventions accepted despite the fact that the conditions that prompt the making of agreements usually favour one party over the other. For *rules* are adopted precisely because there is no single viewpoint regarding the fairness or equity of the circumstances in which agreements are made. Because no single common viewpoint exists, the equity of the rules adopted cannot be articulated in a way that all parties would immediately accept and the development of equitable or fair rules is, for Hayek, a process of trial and error. The absence of a viewpoint shared by all individuals makes this search for equity in rules a continuing *practical* task.[27] Thus: 'Conclusions derived from the articulated rules only will not be tolerated if they conflict with the conclusions to which yet unarticulated rules lead. Equity develops by the side of the already fully articulated rules of strict law through this familiar process' (*NS* 82).

[25] In P. Laslett and J. Fishkin (eds.), *Philosophy, Politics and Society*, 5th series (Oxford, 1979), 6–20, at p. 9.
[26] Ibid.
[27] Hayek quotes with approval Edwin Cannan's *History of Local Rates in England* (London, 1912), p. 173: 'The judgement of mankind about what is equitable is liable to change, and . . . one of the forces which cause it to change is mankind's discovery from time to time that what was supposed to be quite just and equitable in some particular matter has become, or perhaps always was uneconomi-cal' (*MSJ* 107). (But see *MSJ* 184 n. for Hayek's reservations about Cannan's term 'uneconomical'.)

While Hayek and Rawls both see themselves as liberals, the ultimate difference between them is that they represent two different theories of *individualism*. Rawls's philosophy rests on a constructivist account of the individual in which all individuals are held to share common moral elements. This is the basis of their moral equality. All non-moral elements, which include the individual's talents, appearance, and social position, are not part of his person but contingent and morally irrelevant circumstances. His individualist theory of justice seeks to be true to this conception of the person and, so, to offer a view of the kind of social structure which will continually return human relations to relations among individuals of this kind. The task of justice is thus to regulate and correct the work of history by redistributing, as far as possible, the goods that enable individuals fully to be individuals: the goods of liberty and opportunity, income and wealth, and the bases of self-respect (*TJ* 62).

Hayek's view of the individual, on the other hand, is a more historical one inasmuch as he sees the individual not in the essential moral character of man but, rather, as the product of the social process, to be identified by the very fact that he has talents, a distinctive appearance, and exists in particular circumstances in which he has interests, attachments, and obligations. The kind of social order required for individuals so conceived is, for Hayek, one which will co-ordinate the different actions stemming from their various purposes. (We shall look more fully at Hayek's individualism in the next chapter.)

5. SOME IMPLICATIONS OF HAYEK'S CRITIQUE OF CONSTRUCTIVISM

What does Hayek see as the implications of his view of knowledge for the problem of justice? Essentially, he wishes to argue that, because our knowledge is largely tacit knowledge, because we know more than we can say, and because the rules that govern our behaviour will always remain unarticulable in the final analysis since we shall never be able to specify the rule which governs our application of rules, there can never be an account of justice which specifies a social structure governed by explicit rules that conforms to our sense of justice. On this basis Hayek suggests that rules of justice cannot be constructed in the abstract but must be the outcome of the social process. Although the activity of theorizing is a part of that process, it is no more than that: a *part* of the process. There can be no blueprints produced by political theory, and all evaluation of the rules and social processes that dominate society must begin by acknowledging the existing tradition within which all social and moral discourse takes place.

The question is, how acceptable are the implications Hayek draws from this attitude? Moreover, need his sceptical, subjectivist epistemology lead him in this direction? These questions arise, in part, because Popper has argued from similarly sceptical premises for a far more critical attitude towards tradition than the anti-constructivist Hayek allows, and for a more important place to be given to theoretical enquiry. Popper's arguments do not deny that Hayek is right to caution against the excessive zeal of those who wish to change the world to accord with their own, often Utopian, visions. 'Too many social reformers have an idea that they would like to clean the canvas, as Plato called it, of the social world, wiping off everything and starting from scratch with a brand-new rational world. This is nonsense and impossible to realize.'[28] Blueprints, he notes, 'have no meaning in an empty social world, in a social vacuum'.[29] From this position, however, Popper argues that all traditions must be subjected to critical scrutiny, for just as there are dangers in the wholesale rejection of traditions, so are there dangers in their uncritical acceptance. People tend to cling to uniformities in behaviour and to be afraid to originate irregularities and change; and they often wish to assure others of their predictability in the hope of making them act in a similar way. In this way do traditional taboos arise, which explains 'the strongly emotional intolerance which is characteristic of all traditionalism'.[30] Traditions such as these must be challenged, and they are best challenged by the tradition of tolerance, which seeks critically to evaluate the merits and demerits of existing tradition.

Yet is this so different from what Hayek himself is saying? After all, does Popper not echo Hayek when he writes of traditions that

even if we ultimately reject them, in order to replace them by better ones (or by what we believe to be better ones), we should always remain

---

[28] 'Towards a Rational Theory of Tradition', in *Conjectures and Refutations*, pp. 120–35, at p. 131.
[29] Ibid. 132.
[30] Ibid.

CONSTRUCTIVISM AND JUSTICE 81

conscious of the fact that all social criticism, and all social betterment, must refer to a framework of social traditions, of which some are criticized with the help of others, just as all progress in science must proceed within a framework of scientific theories, some of which are criticized in the light of others.[31]

There is an important difference between what they are saying, one which poses problems for Hayek. First, it must be noted that, particularly in his more recent writings[32] but clearly throughout his work, Hayek is far more hostile to 'reason' than Popper is. Man, he argues, is 'often better served by custom than by understanding', for he invariably learns 'to do the right thing without comprehending why' it is the right thing (*EP* 157). Secondly, Hayek has emphasized not the role of reason in modifying tradition but the role of tradition in creating reason. 'Tradition is not something constant but the product of a process of selection guided not by reason but by success. It changes but can rarely be deliberately changed. Cultural selection is not a rational process: it is not guided by but it creates reason' (*EP* 166). This outlook had led Hayek to stress that we are severely limited in our capacity to criticize our traditions and that the development of successful traditions—of systems of rules of conduct—is the product not of rational selection but of *natural* selection. Those traditions which do not adapt but persist in maintaining harmful rules of conduct simply will not survive for the simple reason that its bearers will not survive.

This epistemological position, as we shall see in Chapter 5, has disturbing consequences for Hayek's moral theory. But what does it mean for his political theory more generally? What is implied by the claim that there exist these limits upon our powers of reason and that our political philosophy should accept that we must rely less on our capacity to reason and to calculate and accept the fact that traditions, networks of social institutions, are better chosen by the 'natural' processes of selection? Hayek sees implied in this position little more than the view that the ultimate, and so most important, test of the correctness of a rule is its compatibility with the system of rules. The process of natural selection will eliminate bad rules, rules which bear false knowledge and render some human actions incompatible with social practice.

But there is more at stake than that. This theory of knowledge

---

[31] Ibid.
[32] See his recent collection, *Knowledge, Evolution and Society* (London, 1983).

also implies that we can never know *when* reason can play a useful role in the evaluation of our practices or system of rules. If reason is to have some function in the development of rules of conduct, it must be able to identify the range of its powers; it must be able to specify the domain within which it can assert its powers, and thus *explain* why certain areas of social life, certain practices or institutions, will not be subject to rational reconstruction. For Hayek, reason is altogether incapable of such a task. This problem, because it remains unresolved, leads him into a number of contradictory and confused claims about how to deal with social rules: it leads him to make confused claims about *politics*. He argues, for example, that

> though we must constantly re-examine our rules and be prepared to question every single one of them, we can always do so only in terms of their consistency or compatibility with the rest of the system from the angle of their effectiveness in contributing to the formation of the same kind of overall order of actions which all the other rules serve (*EP* 167).

Yet his own epistemology immediately puts the question: how can we possibly know the overall order of actions which all these rules serve? If rules are the outcome of a spontaneous process, which reflects the plurality of ever-changing human values only a part of which any single individual or organization will be aware, how can we know in what direction any modification of these rules must take place? The very next sentence following this passage in fact notes that 'we cannot redesign but only further evolve what we do not fully comprehend', thus emphasizing this lack of understanding. The contradiction into which Hayek seems to be locked is one in which he is forced to claim that there can be no social theory that can guide our evaluation of the entire structure of our institutions, while conceding that a considerable social theory, explaining the purpose served by our institutions, is necessary for us to evaluate and alter our rules of conduct. At times Hayek appears to think social theory unnecessary: 'The only bases for judging particular rules is in their reconcilability or conflict with the majority of other rules which are generally accepted' (*EP* 171). Such claims are clearly untenable, for without some kind of social theory there can be no way of identifying rules, much less distinguishing between a majority and a minority of rules—even if one assumes (what is surely false) that all rules are of equal significance.

This is an important problem. It makes it hard, if not impossible, for Hayek to make any positive claims about the good society: about the principles which govern its operation or how we might move towards it. His anti-constructivist epistemology suggests that we can never articulate the principles of a liberal order for we can never comprehend the workings of society well enough to know what kind of rules would best sustain it.

Yet Hayek has sought both to develop a comprehensive social philosophy and to articulate the principles of a liberal order on the basis of that social theory. So before making any final pronouncements about the coherence of his endeavour, we must look more closely at that theory—at its strengths as well as its weaknesses—and also at the normative conclusions he tries to defend. This is the task of the next two chapters.

3
Individualism and Social Theory

Hume's politics, as we saw in Chapter 1, are grounded in a hostility towards a particular kind of rationalism. In his rejection of Whig contractarian doctrines he was distancing himself from that rationalist outlook which viewed society from an ahistorical perspective and judged the social order by contrasting it with ideal conceptions of rationally ordered societies. Hayek, as a critic of 'constructivist rationalism', clearly shares Hume's anti-rationalist, anti-Cartesian attitude. Just as Hume's philosophy is at odds with Kant's, so does Hayek's anti-constructivism set his own theory at odds with that of the most prominent modern Kantian: Rawls. Yet the similarities between Hume and Hayek do not end here. Hume's suspicion of all attempts to secure political values with abstract philosophical justifications also inclined him to present the case for rules of justice which preserve private property and contractual obligation in a social theory which drew attention to the possibility of economic and social order without external (political) direction, and which highlighted the danger to liberty posed by the extension of the scope of public authority. In this respect Hume's arguments anticipate Hayek's social theory which has been concerned to elucidate the nature of social order with a view to alerting others to the dangers attending any attempt to organize society in accordance with preconceived plans or ideals.

Many of Hayek's arguments are, like Hume's, largely negative. They do not so much establish a case for accepting particular liberal principles as show what problems face the critics of liberal individualism who wish to restructure society to ensure the distribution of benefits and burdens in accordance with, for example, preferred conceptions of desert or need or merit. Hayek's social theory, however, forms a more comprehensive and ambitious corpus than does Hume's, even though they share a concern to repudiate those who would judge (and reshape) society from some transcendental perspective. For this reason it is worthy of close attention. Despite the problems he encounters in trying to establish a set of normative liberal principles, his social theory offers an important challenge to the critics of liberal individualism. To show this is the primary concern of the present chapter.

Liberalism has long been derided as a political philosophy which lacks any theory of society,[1] the implication being that it can therefore contribute little to the discussion of questions concerning the nature of the good society and the place of the individual in the social order. This view has been repeated in recent years by those critics of Rawls who take his theory of justice to suffer from deficiencies most characteristic of liberal individualism. Thus Wolff suggests that, because Rawls's two principles 'abstract from the real foundations of any social and economic order', one cannot even properly ask whether his conclusions are right or wrong. Rawls's theory, he argues, 'is in the end a theory of pure distribution' and, consequently, could not but fail. Yet what this failure reveals, he insists, is not any lack of sophistication or imaginativeness on Rawls's part, nor any inadequacy of execution but, rather, 'the inherent weakness of that entire tradition of political philosophy'.[2] The most powerful criticisms of Rawls have indeed come from the notable tradition of social theory stemming from Hegel and Marx, embodied in the work of Wolff and, more recently, Michael Sandel.[3] But these critics have been wide of the mark when they have asserted that their objections apply to liberalism more generally. There is, as Hayek's work exemplifies, a tradition of liberal social theory which tries to meet the arguments of Hegelian and Marxist philosophy, a tradition which merits more serious attention.

Far from trying to present an answer to any 'pure problem of distribution', Hayek insists that questions about the correct allocation of resources in society cannot be answered in the abstract. Any theory defending particular distributive institutions must consider the nature of society and the ordering mechanisms that sustain it, and the implications of the limitations of human knowledge. While his is undoubtedly an individualist philosophy, it

[1] See C. Wright Mills, *The Marxists* (Harmondsworth, 1962), 28–9.
[2] R. P. Wolff, *Understanding Rawls: A Reconstruction and Critique of* A Theory of Justice (Princeton, 1977), 210.
[3] M. Sandel, *Liberalism and the Limits of Justice* (Cambridge, 1982). See also R. P. Wolff, *The Poverty of Liberalism* (Boston, 1968).

is also one which seeks to understand the individual as a social being. Individualism, for him, is a *social* theory. This chapter is concerned with Hayek's social theory of individualism.

The concept underpinning Hayek's social theory is the theory of spontaneous order, and the first part of this chapter elucidates that theory and explains how it informs Hayek's critique of 'social justice'. The individualism which is generally seen underlying the liberal theory of justice is one which radical critics of liberalism reject as based on an incoherent conception of the individual. The next part of this chapter outlines the radical challenge. This will afford us a firm critical standpoint from which to identify the distinctive elements of Hayek's individualism and so to reconstruct his rejoinder to liberalism's challengers. Then will we be able to evaluate the strength of Hayek's social theory and to anticipate the qualities that will be necessary in his theory of liberty if he is successfully to turn the projections of his theory of society into the foundations of a normative political philosophy.

2. SOCIAL JUSTICE AND THE THEORY OF SPONTANEOUS ORDER

'[S]ocial theory begins with—and has an object only because of— the discovery that there exist orderly structures which are the product of the action of many men but are not the result of human design' (RO 37). The theory of how such social structures arise is, in Hayek's thought, the theory of spontaneous order. It is important because it is the basis upon which he launches the strongest arguments against the idea of social justice. So it is important to see precisely what claims the theory makes. 'Spontaneous order' is a species of 'order', and by 'order' Hayek means '*a state of affairs in which a multiplicity of elements of various kinds are so related to each other that we may learn from our acquaintance with some spatial or temporal part of the whole to form correct expectations concerning the rest, or at least expectations which have a good chance of proving correct*' (RO 36). Order can be created by forces outside the system or it may be created from within as an equilibrium is generated by the interaction of elements whose natures impel them towards stable formations. This distinction is between an order that is 'made' and one that is formed spontaneously given the existence of particular elements in an environment. In the natural world, a crystal is a perfect example of a 'spontaneous order': it is an order which cannot be constructed, although it can be produced by creating the conditions in which crystals form. Crystals thus differ from microchips, which can only be made by deliberately arranging layers of chemically treated cells. This distinction between exogenously and endogenously created structures is not always clear cut since many structures that are 'made' could not be 'made' unless particular substructures will form spontaneously. A digital watch cannot be made without relying on the spontaneous orders formed by liquid crystals when an electric charge is generated. Nevertheless, the distinction between the *processes* of order formation can be sustained. Ultimately, this is a distinction between orders that are deliberately created and orders that are the unintended products of action or natural movement. The mind, society, and many social institutions, Hayek argues, should be understood as spontaneous orders.

Spontaneous order is produced by 'individual elements adapting themselves to circumstances which directly affect only some of them, and which in their totality need not be known to anyone . . .' (*RO* 41). In highly complex structures such as the mind or society, this means that, since we know, at most, the rules observed by the elements comprising the structure and not all the elements and the circumstances in which each is placed, our knowledge of the order will be restricted and highly general. This immediately limits the extent to which we can control such orders: we cannot control them in the way we can control the growth of less complex structures like crystals. These constraints are important for Hayek because they indicate that, in human society, in which we are able to alter *some* of the rules of conduct which the elements (i.e., individuals) obey, we can, to a limited extent, influence the general character and not the detail of the resulting order (*RS* 41). Hayek's concern is not to argue against any evaluation and correction of the rules which govern the operations of society, or to deny that the social structure can be extended in its scope or range to facilitate the completion of more complex and difficult tasks. Rather, his aim is to argue that, if we wish to solve any of a variety of social problems, we have to understand and make use of the spontaneous ordering forces which govern society. Just as Hume argued that '[s]overeigns must take mankind as they find them' and, indeed, must try to 'comply with the[ir] common bent' (*E* 266), so Hayek suggests that we cannot act against these forces; and ignore them at our peril. Socialist advocates of 'social justice' have done just this, and it is against their assumptions that his theory of spontaneous order is directed.

Society, for Hayek, is a spontaneous order made up of individuals and organizations. Crucially, it is not itself an organization, despite the fact that the elements which comprise it are often organizations. This distinction is important but not rigidly clearcut. The family, the farm, the firm, the court, and government are all organizations integrated into the spontaneous order of society but, in daily routine, may operate as spontaneous orders when conventional rules rather than central commands govern their operations. At other times, such associations may behave like organizations, when the commands of a chief or central authority maintain, and give direction to, that order—say, in time of war, or during family migration, or in a particular corporate decision-making process (*RO* 47). Society itself, however, is not an organization although the two types of order will often coexist within it. This reveals the most important fact about societies, or at least 'free' societies: 'that, although groups of men will join in organizations for the achievement of some particular ends, the co-ordination of the activities of all these separate organizations, as well as of the separate individuals, is brought about by the forces making for a spontaneous order' (*RO* 46). Hayek's notion of society, then, is one of a historical entity which is continuously evolving, rather than one of a structure within which various functions are performed. Society is not an organization but a *growth* which possesses its own impetus as an order that is more than the sum of its parts (though it can be analysed by examining its constituent parts).

Here the comparison with Hume's social theory is instructive, for Hayek's idea of the evolution or spontaneous growth of society is very close to Hume's account of the growth of social institutions such as law and justice. Hume saw society as the condition natural to man because of the circumstances which confronted him and the 'infirmities' (*T* 485) that burdened him. The two institutions which characterized society and, indeed, implied each other's existence, were justice and property. These institutions arose in response to the problems created by man's limited benevolence. Hayek's account of the nature of society follows Hume's to a considerable degree but with one significant development: he makes explicit what is implicit in Hume's theory: that the emergence of those rules which signify the existence of a social order occurs in the absence of any *knowledge* that the formation of society was a solution to the problems of the human condition. Society was not the product of any deliberately co-operative venture but an *unintended consequence* of individual action.

It should be noted, however, that the notions of 'spontaneous order' and 'unintended consequences' are not extensionally equivalent. Not all unintended consequences of human action result in the formation of spontaneous orders. The notion of unintended or unanticipated consequences is a far broader notion which refers not only to the stable patterns or formations which issue from human action, but to all unforeseen results which follow. The notion of a spontaneous order, however, refers more narrowly to those results which form complex orderings or patterns. While we may find that, within society, many human actions will have unintended consequences, only some of them will lead to the formation of regularized patterns of behaviour or orders.[4] Society itself, of course, as a stable formation which arises as the unintended consequence of human interaction, is a spontaneous order.

The 'accidental' nature of this emergence is strongly emphasized by Hayek, for whom society can exist 'only if by a process of selection rules have evolved which lead individuals to behave in a manner which makes social life possible' (*RO* 44). And he presents a more detailed account than Hume does of how such accidents can lead to the formation of a social order. An overall order may be produced only if individual responses to circumstances lead them to observe rules which would produce an order. Because all individuals adapt their behaviour to their *own* circumstances in their *own* way, not all will adopt precisely the same conventions or rules of

---

[4] Hayek himself seems to recognize this distinction for, in his essay 'The Results of Human Action but not of Human Design', in claiming that the task of social science is the explanation of phenomena as the unintended outcome of individual actions, he notes that his conception, although similar, differs from Robert Merton's conception of 'unanticipated consequences' (*S* 100 n.). Merton's view is expounded in his article, 'The Unanticipated Consequences of Purposive Social Action', *American Sociological Review*, 1 (1936), 894–904. On this point see also R. Hamowy, *The Scottish Enlightenment and the Theory of Spontaneous Order* (Carbondale, 1987), 3–4; A. Flew, 'Social Science: Making Visible the Invisible Hands', *Quadrant*, Nov. 1981, 24–9.

behaviour, even if their circumstances are very similar. The important question for social theory is: what properties must the rules possess for the separate actions of the individuals to produce an overall order (*RO* 45)? Hayek's response is that, in any society, the reason why rules are adopted vary: some rules all individuals obey because of the similar situations they find themselves in and which render particular rules (economically) advantageous; some are established as certain people impose rules upon others by force.

Three features of Hayek's theory of the spontaneous order of society should, then, be noted. First, it sees society as the product of human action based on a limited knowledge of the environment, but not the result of design. Secondly, it is conceivable that rules which evolved spontaneously, in the emergence of shared practices, may be deliberately acted upon by individuals seeking to improve them. Thirdly, spontaneous orders of society are orders of rules governing conduct. His emphasis on the rule-governed nature of human conduct in the spontaneous order of society is important because he has often been misinterpreted as a thinker concerned only to 'unleash' mysterious 'market forces' by removing laws restraining human action. Yet he does not see the market as independent of rules or laws, but sees law as defining the market in so far as it defines property and rights. Ultimately, he defends two Humean arguments: first, for the impartial maintenance of property distinctions and, secondly, for the prevalence of private or *several* property rather than extensive public property. And, like Hume, he sees that laws must be sensitive to individual perceptions of justice.

At the heart of Hayek's social theory, then, lies not a view of *homo economicus* but of man as a rule-following animal. Not all the rules he follows are followed consciously, for only a small proportion of those rules are articulated or, indeed, articulable. He offers no account of an unchanging *human nature* in the way that Hobbes and Hume do. In emphasizing that man is rule-governed, both in the operations of his intellect and in his co-operations with his fellows, he denies that there is a human nature independent of the circumstances of human history. This history has produced not merely scientific and political changes but also the 'spontaneous orders' of individual minds and of human cultures: orders which continually interact and modify each other so that neither remains unaltered. The 'categories' of human understanding change over time as the sensory order is transformed by the process of adapting to a changing cultural environment; and the legal, conventional— traditional—categories that distinguish cultural formations themselves change as the social order is (often unintentionally) transformed by human action.

The theory of spontaneous order is similar to Hume's account of the emergence of social institutions and also draws on the other Enlightenment Scots, notably Smith and Ferguson. Yet, philosophically, this theory has an older pedigree which rejects the claims of the Enlightenment in general and looks to Vico, whom Hayek quotes with approval as 'the only important parallel on the Continent to the anti-rationalist British tradition' (*CL* 429). Vico rejected the idea of a fixed human nature shared by all epochs and cultures, and denied the notion that there were 'eternal truths, and unalterable laws, rules of conduct which entail ends of life which any man might, in theory, have recognized in any time and in any place'.[5] In replacing the concept of a static human nature with a pattern of systematic change, Vico saw men as beings who could understand themselves as 'purposive beings whose modes of thought, feeling and action alter in response to new needs and activities, which generate new institutions, entire new civilizations, that incarnate man's nature'.[6] The implication of Vico's account of human civilization is that 'all classification, selection, interpretation is in the end subjective, that is, does not correspond with, or fit into, "objective" grooves in the external world'.[7] Each language, each culture, categorizes reality in different ways and, while there exist similarities and parallels between these different realms, there is no central identity which makes translation from one milieu to another wholly possible.

Hayek shares with Vico a theory of man as a creature whose 'nature' is embodied in the spontaneous order of his cultural milieu. Thus, while he draws consciously upon the Humean account of the evolution of property distinctions, laws, and justice, his theory of spontaneous order is even more process-dominated inasmuch as nothing, not even the 'categories' of human understanding, are held constant. 'It is probably no more justified to claim that thinking

---

[5] I. Berlin, *Vico and Herder: Two Studies in the History of Ideas* (London, 1976), 140.

[6] Ibid. 141.

[7] Ibid.

man has created his culture than that culture has created his reason' (*EP* 155). For Hayek, mind and culture developed concurrently and not successively (*EP* 156). The strikingly Viconian and Hegelian nature of this view emerges when he likens his theory of the spontaneous order of mind and culture to Popper's notion of 'World 3' (a notion which Popper himself likened to Plato's theory of Forms and Hegel's Objective Spirit[8]). He sees culture as something which is kept alive by the millions of brains participating in it and which is the outcome of a process of evolution distinct from the biological evolution of the brain—whose structure itself became useful when there was a culture to absorb. Mind, 'can exist only as part of another independently existing distinct structure or order, though that order persists and can develop only because millions of minds constantly absorb and modify parts of it' (*EP* 157).

When explained in this way, the idea of 'mind' bears some resemblance to Hegel's concept of *Geist*. Yet whatever the similarities between their respective accounts of the development of mind or of culture, they differ importantly in their views about man's capacity to apprehend and control the course of human development and, consequently, in their views about the demands of justice in modern society.

Hegel emphasized that, while I could, as an individual, alienate parts of my labour, if I alienate *all* of my time as crystallized in my work and in all my produce, I make myself someone else's property, thus causing the loss of my being, my actuality, my personality. The state was needed to intervene in the market to mitigate as far as possible the likelihood of such developments. And there was a considerable tendency for this to happen in the modern world because the 'cunning of reason' secured mutual interdependence in an imperfect and highly unpredictable way. Society, if not quite a spontaneous *dis*order, was too imperfect a spontaneous order without the rational intervention of the state to secure the welfare of those whose needs were not met by the market. (Needs, here, are not so much those goods biologically necessary for survival as those goods socially necessary for anyone to be an independent agent in society.) This interpretation has been defended by Raymond Plant both in his studies of Hegel and in his own political writings.[9]

---

[8] *Objective Knowledge: An Evolutionary Approach* (Oxford, 1981), 106.
[9] R. Plant, *Hegel: An Introduction*, 2nd edn. (Oxford, 1983), esp. ch. 9;

Hegel, in Plant's view, saw that in the market order not subject to *rational control,*

individuals are at the mercy of arbitrary changes in economic activity: 'whole branches of industry which supported a large class of people suddenly fold up because of a change in fashion or because the value of their product fell due to inventions in other countries: whole masses are abandoned to poverty which cannot help itself'. Only a constrained and controlled market, Hegel thinks, will be able to obviate these painful and irrational consequences of economic activity.[10]

This view of the imperfections of the spontaneous order of the market is bolstered in the twentieth century by Fred Hirsch,[11] and Plant draws explicitly upon his work to formulate his Hegelian critique of the Hayekian viewpoint. One of the unintended consequences of individual actions, Hirsch argued, was a set of outcomes which were in no way desired by those individuals. The 'tyranny of small decisions' lay in the fact that they resulted not in co-ordination but conflict between individual values and social outcomes.[12] Worse, dislocations caused by the operation of the market were often severe enough to create and sustain large-scale poverty and distress. Thus Hegel noted that, while the 'unimpeded activity' of civil society resulted in expansion of population and industry, this was only one side of the picture: 'The other side is the subdivision and restriction of particular jobs. This results in the dependence and distress of the class tied to work of that sort, and these again entail inability to feel and enjoy the broader freedoms and especially the intellectual benefits of civil society.'[13] Far from seeing the 'system of needs' as a Hayekian 'catallaxy', as a 'self-equilibrating system of production, distribution and exchange', Plant argues, Hegel insisted that the market had to be controlled by

---

Equality, Markets and the State, Fabian Tract 494 (London, 1984); 'Hirsch, Hayek, and Habermas: Dilemmas of Distribution', in A. Ellis and K. Kumar (eds.), *Dilemmas of Liberal Democracies: Studies in Fred Hirsch's* Social Limits to Growth (London, 1983), 45–64; R. Plant, H. Lesser, and P. Taylor-Gooby, *Political Philosophy and Social Welfare: Essays on the Normative Basis of Welfare Provision* (London, 1980), chs. 2, 4, 5, 9, and 10, esp. pp. 231–3.

[10] Plant, *Hegel*, p. 213.
[11] *The Social Limits to Growth* (London, 1978).
[12] Ibid. 79. See also Plant, *Equality, Markets and the State*, p. 11.
[13] Hegel, *Philosophy of Right*, trans. T. M. Knox (Oxford, 1978), sect. 243.

some sort of state intervention.[14] In expounding these views, Hegel was putting the first of two major arguments against liberal individualism.

The Hayekian response to the challenge posed by these claims emerges in his theory of spontaneous order generally, but more particularly in his explanation of the origins of discoordination in the market order. This explanation appears largely in Hayek's economics which, as Gerald O'Driscoll argues, is mainly concerned to present a theory of the *co-ordination* of economic activities.[15] The most important feature of his approach to the co-ordination problem is that, following Smith and Menger, Hayek does not see co-ordination taking place in a market which exists independently of the institutions (of law and justice) which define it. In sharing with Smith and, particularly, Menger the view of economics (and the social sciences generally) as the study of the unintended consequences of human action, his economic theory is unavoidably concerned with the social institutions which shape human action. The co-ordination of economic activity is not achieved simply by removing government from the economic arena but by developing the political, economic, and legal institutions which allow such co-ordination to take place. While for the most part, such institutions will emerge spontaneously as people try to solve co-ordination problems they encounter, there is an important role for government to play in the development of such institutions: 'while the rules on which a spontaneous order rests, may also be of spontaneous origin, this need not always be the case' (*RO* 45).

Although he is often identified as a defender of 'the free market' who argues simply against 'interference' by government, this view goes against what Hayek himself has identified as his (and liberalism's) main concerns. While he does argue for freer markets, defined by the institutions of private property and contract, he argues against the assumption that the formulas 'private property' and 'freedom of contract' solve our problems: 'Our problems begin when we ask what ought to be the contents of property rights, what contracts should be enforceable, and how contracts should be interpreted or, rather, what standard forms of contract should be

    [14] R. Plant, 'Hegel on Identity and Legitimation', in Z. A. Pelczynski (ed.), *State and Civil Society: Studies in Hegel's Political Philosophy* (Cambridge, 1984), 227–43, at p. 229.
    [15] *Economics as a Coordination Problem: The Contributions of Friedrich A. Hayek* (Kansas City, 1977), p. xx.

read into the informal agreements of everyday transactions' (*IEO* 113). That the operation of a market presupposes not only the prevention of violence and fraud but also the protection of rights is taken for granted, he observes, but it must not be assumed that this settles the issue, 'as if the law of property and contract were given once and for all in its final and most appropriate form, i.e., the form which will make the market economy work at its best' (*IEO* 111). If there is a task for public policy—and Hayek thinks there is—it is to improve those institutions which define the market or competitive order. The mistake of the nineteenth-century liberals was to give the impression that the abandonment of all harmful or unnecessary state activity was 'the consummation of all political wisdom' when it was equally important to ask '*how* the state should use those powers which nobody denied to it' (*IEO* 109).

Here, however, Hayek makes an important distinction between 'the competitive order' and 'ordered competition' (*IEO* 111),[16] for he wishes to emphasize that the aim of social policy should not be to order (i.e. restrict) competition so as to achieve *particular* economic or social goals but to define the rights and duties which make competitive markets possible. The ills that the critics of the market attribute to it stem from the failure properly to define the institutions necessary for its operation and the reliance on (macroeconomic) policy which hinders rather than helps the working of the 'competitive order'. So Hayek denies what Hegel and some of his modern defenders assert: that the 'system of needs' is responsible for the discoordination and dislocations evident in civil society. To see why Hayek does this we need to look a little more deeply into his economic and social theory as they are informed by his theory of knowledge.

The two most important points in Hayek's account of the market are, first, that it is, itself, a 'corrective' mechanism, adjusting or co-ordinating individual actions by informing people when their actions are *incompatible* with the intentions or purposes of others or with their own; and, secondly, that it is a dynamic social process which loses its co-ordinating effectiveness when attempts are made to arrest it. None of this implies that market outcomes are in any sense 'perfect': not only will individuals often be frustrated, but there will occasionally be dramatic failures. Yet the very fact that in this process expectations are continually and 'systematically'

---

[16] Or between 'planning for' and 'planning against' competition (*RS* 31).

disappointed is crucial to its successful operation (*NS* 185). Here we can see how Hayek's economic philosophy is grounded in his view of knowledge as pre-eminently practical. We acquire knowledge not merely theoretically but in the practical testing of hypotheses in the real world, and knowledge grows as we continue to make such tests in an attempt to adapt to our environment. The market is an order in which competition is the 'discovery procedure' which allows us to test our knowledge of the preferences of others, of our own future preferences, and of the *compatibility* of the various plans of actions. Our guides in this arena are the information generated in the market (through, for example, advertising), the information afforded by prices which signal the relative values attached to various commodities or services and, ultimately, the knowledge generated by the failure or disappointment of enterprises or expectations.

It is the knowledge thrown forward by such failures which is the most important. While prices, as bearers of information, help to guide adjustments to unforeseen changes (*NS* 187), adaptation of the whole order of activities to changed circumstances 'rests on the remuneration derived from different activities being charged without regard to the merits or faults of those affected' (*NS* 187). Activities which serve no demands or needs will thus be eliminated in the process of adaptation.[17] (One of the problems, however, is that some may be too poor to express their demands and so have their needs met in the market. We shall turn to this question presently.)

In portraying market processes in this way, Hayek was attempting to draw economists away from their tendency to characterize the competitive order as an *equilibrium* state, arguing that because equilibrium 'presupposes that the facts have already all been discovered and competition therefore has ceased' (*NS* 184), such a static concept was of limited theoretical use.[18] Like many Austrian (and Swedish) economists familiar with Menger's work, he wished to develop techniques of dynamic analysis, to recast economic theory 'so as to focus on the market *process*, by which the disparate

---

[17] For an application of this view of the role of loss-making see J. Burton, *Picking Losers . . . ? The Political Economy of Industrial Policy* (London, 1983). For a more general exploration of the role of knowledge, and the consequences of its suppression, see T. Sowell, *Knowledge and Decisions* (New York, 1980).

[18] See also A. A. Alchian, 'Uncertainty, Evolution and Economic Theory', *Journal of Political Economy*, 58 (1950), 211–21.

plans of individuals are equilibrated, rather than on equilibrium *states*.'[19] In this he was reacting against the tendency to present the individual in the market-place purely as an economizing or utility-maximizing agent, for concentrating exclusively on what Israel Kirzner calls 'Robbinsian maximizing behaviour'[20] inhibited the study of market processes. The significance of these concerns in Hayek's economics lies in the fact that they are an integral part of his theory of spontaneous order and of his individualist political theory which begins, not with abstract 'economic man' but with a *social* theory of human action.

This view of the 'system of needs' as a dynamic process involving concrete agents is important because it denies the often made criticism of liberalism that it begins with abstract, asocial individuals which it is unable to locate in the social context. While the Robbinsian account of human behaviour is of efficiency-seeking behaviour, the approach of Hayek and the Austrian school does not avoid but emphasizes the fact that the *identifying* of ends and means is equally important for the understanding of human action. As Kirzner puts it, 'Human action treats both tasks—that of identifying the relevant ends-means framework and that of seeking efficiency with respect to it—as a single, integrated human activity.'[21] Here is the significance of Hayek's view of knowledge; for in both his economic and sociological theory he emphasizes that we cannot assume that human knowledge is given independently of the social process. He thus locates rationality not in the isolated individual consciousness but in the network of social institutions. And he rejects the idea that each individual knows his interests best, since he rejects the assumption that human reason exists 'in the singular, as given or available to any particular person', arguing that it 'must be conceived as an interpersonal process in which everyone's contribution is tested and corrected by others' (*IEO* 15).

Ultimately, Hayek's defence of the spontaneous order of the market rests not on a claim that individuals, left alone, can best further their known interests through the market's efficiency in matching wants with goods, but on the stronger claim that, defined by the right institutions, market processes enable us to discover not only how to get what we want, but also what we do in fact want.

---

[19] O'Driscoll, *Economics as a Coordination Problem*, p. 8.
[20] I. M. Kirzner, *Competition and Entrepreneurship* (Chicago, 1978), 32–3.
[21] Ibid. 34.

He assumes man's initial ignorance in all areas of knowledge (including self-knowledge) and argues for the individualist political outlook as the best guide to establishing social institutions to enable men to flourish despite this ignorance. 'The true basis' of the individualist view 'is that nobody can know *who* knows best and that the only way by which we can find out is through a social process in which everybody is allowed to try and see what he can do' (*IEO* 15).

In defending the market by calling attention to the need to define such institutions as contract and private property, Hayek rejects the claims that public policy should be concerned with the problem of *correcting* 'market failures'. For the value of the market lies in the fact that it is itself a 'corrective' process. Indeed, it is a learning process which Hayek denies can be bypassed with the development of theoretical knowledge. An example supporting this view arises in Sam Peltzman's attempts to record the benefits of the 1962 US Drug Amendments intended to increase 'safety' and save consumers from buying drugs lacking real pharmaceutical value. In the unregulated market, elimination of ineffective drugs was carried out by doctors and patients through trial and error. The surprising conclusion reached was that laws intended to shorten or eliminate the learning process by preventing ineffective drugs going to market, resulted in little or no reduction in the proportion of such drugs available to the consumer (but a reduction in the number and a rise in the cost of drugs).[22] What this study would illustrate, for Hayek, is the way in which the corrective process of the market is difficult to supplant. Theoretical knowledge must ultimately be tested in practical application. Indeed, the whole process of matching goods with wants or needs can best take place in a market in which individuals discover not only what goods will satisfy their needs but also what their needs are. This view of the market as a discovery procedure is clearest in Hayek's criticisms of J. K. Galbraith.

In *The Affluent Society*, Galbraith argued that the price system did not serve the consumers' wants. Consumers' desires were not their own but created, largely by advertising and salesmanship, whose central purpose was to create wants that did not previously exist. Wants, he wrote, 'depend on the process by which they are satisfied': this is the 'Dependence Effect'.[23] He concluded that the

[22] See H. Lepage, *Tomorrow Capitalism: The Economics of Economic Freedom* (La Salle, 1982), 127–31.

[23] *The Affluent Society* (Harmondsworth, 1962), 136.

market process is wasteful because scarce resources are devoted to producing goods for which individuals have no desire, to be sold only after vast sums are spent persuading them to buy. Hayek's response, in 'The Non Sequitur of the "Dependence Effect" ', argued that wants 'created by the process by which they are satisfied' are no less important than others (NS 313–14). Indeed, most of our present wants and needs were engendered by the production processes of civilized life. 'Most needs which make us act are needs for things which only civilization teaches us that they exist at all, and these things are wanted by us because they produce feelings or emotions which we would not know if it were not for our cultural inheritance' (S 314). The needs that are 'created' should not be repudiated but, to some extent, welcomed, for they contribute not merely to material well-being but also extend the scope of our activity, our feelings, our aesthetic understanding and our self-knowledge. Thus, while the production process may 'create' desires which many think harmful (cigarettes?), they also create wants for things (such as music and film) which enrich human experience. What Hayek denies is that anyone should be able to restrict the growth of wants or needs merely because some wants are deemed artificial.

Here it is important to note that Hayek also differs from those who see consumption as the 'revealed preferences' of individuals. He does not claim that to find a person's real preferences we should consult his actual choices. Individuals do not always know what they prefer (let alone how to satisfy their preferences) and their activities must be seen, at least partly, as attempts to *discover* their wants. The problem with 'revealed preference', as Amartya Sen explains, is that it presumes too little and too much: 'too little because there are non-choice sources of information on preference and welfare as these terms are usually understood, and too much because choice may reflect a compromise among a variety of considerations of which personal welfare may be just one'.[24] It is unlikely that behaviour 'can be at all captured within the formal limits of consistent choice on which the welfare-maximization approach depends'.[25] Hayek has never adopted this approach

[24] 'Rational Fools: A Critique of the Behavioural Foundations of Economic Theory', in F. Hahn and M. Hollis (eds.), *Philosophy and Economic Theory* (Oxford, 1979), 87–109, at pp. 92–3. See also Sen's 'Behaviour and the Concept of Preference', *Economica*, 40 (1973), 241–59.

[25] Sen, 'Rational Fools', p. 93.

because of his emphasis on the market as a process in which knowledge is 'discovered'. This aspect of the Austrian approach has been most fully exploited by Kirzner who, drawing on Mises and Hayek, emphasizes that *entrepreneurship* is a feature of a great deal of decision making, and not just of the decisions of 'entrepreneurs'. The non-entrepreneurial element of decision making is that which involves *calculation*, but the calculational element in decision making is *not* the most important.[26] Entrepreneurship requires not the ability to calculate but *alertness* to opportunities, whether for profits (in the case of producers) or for 'satisfaction' (in the case of consumers). Crucially, neither producer nor consumer 'knows' beforehand if his decision to produce or purchase is the correct decision. Entrepreneurship is always risky.

Earlier we noted that, in his development of the Misesian critique of socialism, Hayek sought to show that the fundamental problem in economics was not a *calculational* problem but an *epistemological* one. We can now take this observation further. In his essays on 'Socialist Calculation' (*IEO* 119–208)[27] and his papers on economics and knowledge (*IEO* 33–56, 77–91) he tried to show that the centralization of *production* decisions would lead to discoordination between demand and supply of goods, as well as to production problems in the absence of prices allowing comparative cost calculation. This would happen because only by the decentralization of decision making 'can we ensure that the knowledge of the particular circumstances of time and place will be promptly used' and economize on the amount of knowledge necessary for successful decision making (*IEO* 84). The weakness of socialist planning was that it required *more* knowledge for decision making and yet was *less* able to ensure that knowledge of opportunities was utilized. Central planning used too few entrepreneurs.

[26] I. M. Kirzner, 'The Primacy of Entrepreneurial Discovery', in *The Entrepreneur in Society* (Sydney, 1983), 59–80, at p. 60. See also L. von Mises, *Human Action: A Treatise on Economics*, 3rd rev. edn. (Chicago, 1966), 253.

[27] For an account of the 1930s debate on economic calculation under socialism see the *Journal of Libertarian Studies*, 5 (1981), esp. papers by D. Lavoie, 'A Critique of the Standard Account of the Socialist Calculation Debate', 41–87, and D. R. Steele, 'Posing the Problem: The Impossibility of Economic Calculation under Socialism', 7–22. For some criticisms of Hayek's approach to the calculation issue see P. C. Roberts, *Alienation in the Soviet Economy: Toward a General Theory of Marxian Alienation, Organizational Principles, and the Soviet Economy* (Albuquerque, 1971), 99. A more recent historical account of the Calculation Debate is D. Lavoie, *Rivalry and Central Planning: The Socialist Calculation Debate Reconsidered* (Cambridge, 1985).

In his political theory, Hayek goes on to argue that it is the *epistemological* rather than the calculational problem which characterizes not simply the production process but the human condition generally. The market, defined by the institutions of justice, is to be praised not merely for making production cheaper; for what is discovered in the market process is not only 'economic' knowledge, but knowledge of the world, of others, and even of oneself. This is why in *The Constitution of Liberty* he stresses the importance of the social process remaining 'experimental': when experiments are forbidden because superior knowledge has rendered parts of the process of trial and error otiose, then the 'beliefs that happen to be prevalent at a given time may become an obstacle to the advancement of knowledge' (*CL* 37). For knowledge 'advances' not just with the growth of explicit or scientific knowledge, but 'with every adaptation to the environment in which past experience is incorporated' (*CL* 26).

This view of the spontaneous order of the market emphasizing its nature as a corrective process enabling individuals to adapt to circumstances through trial and error is the basis of Hayek's rejection of the Hegelian viewpoint. Although he accepts that the system of needs co-ordinates actions imperfectly and cannot prevent the distress resulting from the market's unpredictability, he denies that the solution is direct state intervention. The costs of such a solution greatly outweigh its benefits: 'while it is easy to protect a particular person or group against the loss which might be caused by an unforeseen change, by preventing people from taking notice of the change after it has occurred, this merely shifts the loss onto other shoulders but does not prevent it' (*IEO* 21 n.).[28] This argument is limited in so far as it does not show that it is illegitimate to shift the burden of loss in this way. It may be justifiable to do so on the basis of particular moral principles. Yet it is an important response to the concern expressed at the dislocations that appear in market societies, for Hayek has tried to show that the road to the reduction of the market's imperfections lies not in the way of centralist intervention but in that of institutional design. For

[28] 'If capital invested in an expensive plant is protected against obsolescence by prohibiting the introduction of such new inventions, this increases the security of the owners of the existing plant but deprives the public of the benefits of the new inventions' (*IEO* 21 n.).

it does not really reduce uncertainty for society as a whole if we make the behaviour of the people more predictable by preventing them from adapting themselves to unforeseen change in their knowledge of the world. The only genuine reduction of uncertainty consists in increasing its knowledge, but never in preventing people from making use of new knowledge (*IEO* 21 n.).

Clearly, Hayek is aware that poverty is an urgent problem, and, like Hegel, he sees it as 'a relative, rather than an absolute, concept' (*CL* 44). What is seldom noted is that he sees poverty as likely to be perpetuated in 'static' or 'stagnant' societies in which market processes are impeded by intervention inspired by egalitarian considerations (*CL* 49). He sees material equality as attainable in societies in which competition fosters greater *progress*. Invoking the claims of Adam Smith, he equates the society in which material progress has ceased with one in which the condition of the 'labouring poor' is most harsh and least likely to be alleviated (*CL* 42).

Yet 'progress' also has a more important meaning for Hayek, one which suggests that his defence of the market is not founded upon welfarist concerns. It refers to the 'cumulative growth of knowledge and power over nature' that is the result of the 'successful striving for what at each moment seems unattainable' (*CL* 41). This is important not for utilitarian reasons: the answer to the question 'would we be better off or happier', he argues, 'does not matter' (*CL* 41). What matters is the striving: 'It is not the fruits of past success but the living in and for the future in which human intelligence proves itself. Progress is movement for movement's sake, for it is in the process of learning, and in the effects of having learned something new, that man enjoys the gift of his intelligence' (*CL* 41). Hayek argues that the social process, continuing undirected by the limited understanding of individual reason, is essential for the growth of knowledge. To halt or redirect that process is to slow, not merely material advance, but the means by which individuals learn about their environment, about each other, and about themselves. (Indeed, it is to halt the growth of rationality. In this account, 'rationality' is not manifested in the minds of reflective, self-aware individuals but, more generally, in the social institutions which embody 'knowledge'. If freedom comes as Spinoza argued, from reflection and, so, self-understanding, Hayek's theory of the free society takes the process of acquiring this reflective self-understanding out of the mind of the Spinozistic *individual* and relocates it in the *social* process. We shall return to this idea in ch. 4.)

Hayek's views on the nature of spontaneous order, and of the importance of progress conceived as the continuing evolution of order as individuals seek to learn from their trials and errors, form the foundations of his case against the idea of 'social justice'— which he identifies as the idea that society be organized 'in a manner which makes it possible to assign particular shares of the product of society to the different individuals or groups' (*MSJ* 64). This view takes the main question to be 'whether there exists a moral duty to submit to a power which can co-ordinate the efforts of the members of society with the aim of achieving a particular pattern of distribution regarded as just' (*MSJ* 64). The conclusion of Hayek's theory of spontaneous order, informed as it is by his economics, denies that any one individual or group can acquire the knowledge to wield such a power with any prospect of success. Even if there were agreement on what distribution would be just, the fact that society is a spontaneous order makes it impossible for a 'social product' to be redistributed, for the mechanisms of redistribution in turn alter the nature and extent of the 'social product'. Any theory of social justice must specify not only the nature of the distributive entitlements but also what kind of society there would have to be for these shares to be distributed. The problem, however, would remain that the distributive outcomes of any spontaneous social order could *not* be guaranteed or even predicted. People will always seek to alter their circumstances, constantly changing the pattern of distribution. The cost of preserving distributive patterns is increased (but unsuccessful) intervention by the distributive authority in individual decision making.

Now, there are some difficulties with Hayek's social theory and the most obvious one concerns the nature of 'spontaneous order' and the claim that we cannot act in defiance of the spontaneous ordering forces which dominate society. The problem is: how is a 'spontaneous' order to be distinguished from non-spontaneous orders? Put differently, how are they to be distinguished from organizations? This is a problem because it is not clear in Hayek's social theory to what extent the spontaneous development of legal and political institutions is a part of the spontaneous development of order. As he is not an anarchist but sees a place for politics in the development of the institutions of justice, he does not present what might be termed a 'pure theory of spontaneous order'. Indeed the market can only flourish, in his view, if sound institutions of justice, law, and property are put in place. Yet it is obscure how far these institutions arise 'spontaneously', when it is permissible to alter them, or what criteria we may use to evaluate their functioning, since, in Hayek's terms, institutions embody knowledge of which we are otherwise unaware, and thus to seek to change them to fit requirements established by reason is the most dangerous hubris. In short, while Hayek has developed a theory of the spontaneous ordering forces of society, he has not come up with an explanation of the extent to which reason can criticize and try to alter the direction of social development. His claim that all criticism has to be 'immanent' criticism is inadequate if he is to criticize, say, the continuing development of the welfare state. The question left unanswered by his theory is: how can we know when an order is not a spontaneous order but an organization? And this is an important failing since the theory is the basis of his critique of social justice.

There is a greater danger still. Hayek wishes to argue through the theory of spontaneous order that there are limits to man's capacity to control the social environment. Because society is a spontaneous order, composed of rules and practices which have emerged over time, and whose value or function is seldom fully appreciated, attempts to direct social institutions may distort or destroy important social processes. Yet if 'reason' must be viewed as merely an *aspect* of the development of social order, severely limited in its capacity to comprehend the whole of which it is a part, not only does it become impossible to distinguish spontaneous processes from constructed organizations, but the very idea of criticism and social reform becomes illusory. The problem is well put by Ronald Hamowy in his discussion of the idea of spontaneous order in the Scottish Enlightenment.

The theory of spontaneous order, thus construed, inevitably militates against any program of comprehensive reform. If the social arrangements we have inherited are the result of a slow evolutionary process brought about by trial and error and if the reason embedded in these arrangements is beyond our comprehension, then we must accept them despite our ignorance of their purpose or our inability to appreciate their value. Even institutions that appear socially injurious or patterns that initially seem undesirable are theoretically exempt from sudden and extensive change. Thus suttee in India, the binding of feet in China, slavery in the southern states, all could claim the protective shield of tradition and of the wisdom Burke would have argued was contained in these traditional institutions.[29]

The theory of spontaneous order seems to cut both ways: it tells against the wisdom of planning for 'social justice'; but denies the possibility of reform once the damage has been done. Maybe this is simply the final, unpleasant truth. Yet, as we shall later see more fully, it is also deeply inconsistent with Hayek's critical endeavours over most of this century.

Leaving these difficulties aside for the moment, however, Hayek has an important point to put to those who argue that social justice requires institutions which constantly readjust the allocation of goods according to distributive principles. This most contentious point is that, even if morally admissible, the venture would fail on the distributors' own terms.

Just as Hume was criticized for the strictness of his conception of justice, so Hayek has been accused of 'harshness' for his attack on 'social justice'.[30] This charge, however, comes as a part of a wider (radical) critique of liberal individualism which stems, in part, from Hegel. While we have seen his response to criticisms of the ills of market society, it must be noted that these arguments reply only to the first part to the 'radical' critique. The second part, however, goes on to make more serious claims about the plight of the individual in market society, and the failure of liberal society, and liberal theory, to deal with such problems. We turn now to examine this critique, as it appears in the writings of Alasdair MacIntyre, Robert Paul Wolff, and Raymond Plant.

3. THE RADICAL CRITIQUE OF INDIVIDUALISM

There may be some confusion about the 'tradition' from which the radical critique of liberal individualism springs. Indeed, even to refer to 'the radical critique' may be to invite fierce contention because of the different views about who are the bearers of such a critique. Confusion stems from the fact that some critics claim to write in the tradition of Hegel and Marx, while others profess

[29] *The Scottish Enlightenment*, p. 35.
[30] See A. Arblaster, *The Rise and Decline of Western Liberalism* (Oxford, 1985), 345.

allegiance to an Aristotelian tradition (and to see the work of Hegel and Marx as criticism of individualism launched by dissenters from within a shared tradition), and yet others claim to draw upon an anti-individualist tradition which encompasses both Aristotle and Marx. The first set of critics would include such writers as Raymond Plant, the second, Alasdair MacIntyre, and the third, Robert Paul Wolff. Yet in spite of their differences I propose to examine their various views as constitutive of a radical critique of liberal individualism because they attack the same doctrine from a common, radical, perspective—understanding the word 'radical' in its etymological rather than its popular sense. They all seek to go to the root of liberalism, whose individualist premises they see to be destructive of the very possibility of attaining—or even understanding—human community. We shall look to see what criticisms have been put to liberalism and ask how plausible they are as objections to Hayek's individualist politics.

All these critics share a conviction that community is inadequately understood by liberal individualism. Community is *not* merely the summation of private interests or the unintended by-product of individual interaction. Raymond Plant elaborates this point when criticizing Hegel for not coming to terms with the fact that, if 'mutuality and interdependence' are a by-product of self-seeking activity, then this is not sufficient for a sense of community, fraternity, or *Sittlichkeit*.

Community is not just a matter of particular outcomes but of *intentional* relationships in which people *directly* work for one another, value one another and engage in benevolence and altruism. Self-seeking may generate interdependence, and we may, as Hegel implies, lack a sufficient appreciation of this, but unintended interdependence is not sufficient for *Sittlichkeit*. This sense of interdependence needs to be internalized so that self-seeking is diminished and action is for the sake of the whole.[31]

While Hegel, on occasion, recognized this, and suggested that our awareness of our interdependence would motivate us to work for the satisfaction of the needs of others, Plant argues, he did not fully realize that the changed motivations would pose problems for any capitalist economy in which, according to the classical economists,

---

[31] Plant, *Hegel*, pp. 229–30. Durkheim makes a similar point when criticizing the 18th- and 19th-cent. economists for seeing society as *no more than* an association characterized by spontaneously developed mutual interdependence. See *The Division of Labour in Society*, trans. W. D. Halls (London, 1984), esp. p. 320.

self-seeking was necessary for capitalist enterprise. Hegel's failure to think this problem through is evident in his assumption that state charity would not be able to overcome the problem of poverty generated by individualism: clearly he did not think human motivation would change *that* much.[32] Yet the inadequacy of Hegel's analysis, as Plant interprets it, does not deny the problem that is brought to light: if society cannot be sustained by the private norms generated by market relations, since the continuation of such relations presupposes some shared moral consensus, how is this consensus or 'social solidarity' to be understood and how might it be undermined? Here Plant argues that the minimal state defended by 'economic liberals' may lack the moral capital necessary for its sustenance.[33] Referring to Hayek's arguments that there is no agreement within society on the values of social justice and that the market does not reward merit but those who are lucky enough to be able to satisfy demands for particular values, Plant notes that such attempts 'to divorce the market from substantive moral principles may well render the market unstable' since luck is an inadequate base upon which to secure social solidarity.[34] Our problem in the modern world is that an entrenched individualism makes it hopelessly difficult to attain an agreed rational *Sittlichkeit* to yield the principles needed to constrain the market.

Alasdair MacIntyre also tries to show the inadequacy of liberal moral culture but suggests that 'the crucial moral opposition is between liberal individualism in some version or other and the Aristotelian tradition in some version or other'.[35] He argues against those who see the key intellectual conflict of modern times as one between liberal individualism and some version of Marxism drawing on Kant and Hegel. Indeed, he denies that Marxist philosophy might rescue the notion of autonomy 'from its original individualist formulations and restore it within the context of an appeal to a possible form of community'.[36] 'Secreted' within Marxism is a certain 'radical individualism' which Aristotelians

---

[32] Plant, *Hegel*, p. 230.

[33] Here he also draws on arguments put by I. Kristol, ' "When Virtue Loses All Her Loveliness"—Some Reflections on Capitalism and the "Free Society" ', in his *On the Democratic Idea in America* (New York, 1973), 90–106. See also Kristol's essay, 'The Shaking of the Foundations', 22–30.

[34] Plant, *Hegel*, p. 232.

[35] *After Virtue: A Study in Moral Theory* (London, 1981), 241.

[36] Ibid. 243.

would repudiate. The free individual for Marx is 'a socialized Robinson Crusoe', whose free association with others has no basis in his theory. Marxists trying to fill this lacuna in their social theory have subsequently been reduced to adopting the liberal approach, putting forward abstract moral principles and utility as principles of association.[37]

For MacIntyre, in the post-Enlightenment world, the central moral problems have come to be questions about how we know which *rules* to follow and the idea of virtue has become as marginal to the moral philosopher as it is to his society's morality.[38] The very notion of society has ceased to be one of 'a community united in a shared vision of the good for man' and a shared practice of the virtues.[39] We have, rather, a society ridden with fundamental disagreement, in which moral philosophy reflects the conflict which politics conceals beneath the rhetoric of pluralism.[40] Individualist moral discourse is unable to articulate, and its culture unable to provide, the requisite agreement to the particular practices regarded as necessary for political community. The result is an everyday life pervaded by basic controversies which cannot be *rationally* resolved.[41]

In short, the inadequacies of liberal individualism as moral theory and political doctrine stem from an impoverished conception of rationality (grounded in the fact/value distinction) which is unable to locate the individual in the moral and political community, and are manifested in the perpetual conflicts which plague its society. The abandoning of virtue is revealed most clearly in the political theories of Rawls and Nozick which reject the idea that *desert* is central to any account of justice.[42] The notion of desert 'is at home only in the context of a community whose primary bond is a shared understanding both of the good for man and of the good of that community and where individuals identify their primary interests with reference to those goods'.[43] Liberal discourse does not allow of any substantive theory of the human good and is so unable to secure the idea of justice in any social context or community: justice becomes an abstract relation predicated not of

[37] *After virtue: A Study in Moral Theory* (London, 1981), 243.
[38] Ibid. 219.   [39] Ibid. 219–20
[40] Ibid. 235.   [41] Ibid. 227.
[42] Ibid. 232.   [43] Ibid. 235.

real individuals but of artificial, undifferentiated individuals or atoms.

This is also the criticism Wolff has in mind when he stands against the 'liberal utilitarian conception of human nature' a 'much older tradition, going back to Aristotle and finding its most powerful expression in the writings of the young Marx'.[44] '[C]lassical liberalism', he writes, 'insofar as it assumes that all values are private values, portrays society as an aggregation of Robinson Crusoes who have left their islands of private value merely for the instrumental benefit of increasing their enjoyment through mutually beneficial exchange.'[45] Liberalism's mistake is that it conceives the relations among individuals as purely instrumental or accidental, rather than intrinsic and essential.[46] And this mistake is evident in liberalism's inability to provide an account of the nature of the individual or society which bears any resemblance to real individuals or societies. Thus classical liberal economic and political theory, and its formal models of game theory and welfare economics, 'presuppose that human beings are utility-maximizers, seekers after gratification whose reason is employed in finding the most efficient allocation of their scarce resources'.[47] This contrasts with the views of the young Marx who, correctly, recognized that creative, productive, rational *activity*, rather than consumption, is the good for man: to treat the expenditure of labour as a cost is a sign not of prudential rationality but of a 'warped and distorted personality'.[48] Wolff's critique of Rawls thus proclaims that, like all liberal theories, it relies on an impoverished conception of human rationality which does not recognize the rational nature of *all* human activity. Rationality is not simply an isolated faculty of instrumental worth, enabling us to choose how best to satisfy our preferences. Acting and having preferences are themselves rational activities (and can be criticized as such). This is why the models of bargaining, game theory, and welfare economics, on which Rawls relies, and which employ

---

[44] *Understanding Rawls*, p. 208. (MacIntyre, however, has criticized Wolff's equating of liberalism with utilitarianism, in *Against the Self-Images of the Age: Essays on Ideology and Philosophy* (London, 1971), 281.

[45] *Poverty of Liberalism*, p. 172.

[46] Ibid.

[47] *Understanding Rawls*, p. 208.

[48] Ibid. 209.

thinner notions of rationality, are bad models for analysing social and economic life.[49]

The poverty of the liberal conception of rationality, for Wolff, is also evident in its account of community and politics, for it fails to see that society is more than a by-product of individual relations. Drawing on Oakeshott, he points out that men are incapable of relating to one another except in the context of a 'tradition' embodied in a community. The kind of community he envisages is *not* the unintended consequence of economic transactions but an 'affective community, community characterized by the reciprocal consciousness of a shared culture'.[50] Community does not consist simply in culture itself, nor in the private consumption of that culture: '. . . it is the mutual awareness on the part of each that there are others sharing that culture, and that through such mutuality we are many together rather than many alone.'[51]

Mutual awareness is also possible because collective work involves reciprocity of awareness: man lives not only in affective community but also in 'productive community'. Men can come to know *one another* through co-operation and productive activity, and this is a form of community which is an important component of the public good.[52] Community reaches its fullest extent, in a way liberalism does not see, when there is collective deliberation upon social goals and determination of social choices: what Wolff calls 'rational community'.[53] Attaining such a form of community requires a form of discourse or 'public conversation' in which each member of society recognizes his fellow citizen as a rational moral agent with a right to reciprocal equality in the dialogue of politics, and in which that discourse is not just of instrumental value but the 'essence' of the political order.[54] The political dialogue of rational community has value not because it enables individuals to satisfy their private interests but because that dialogue has intrinsic value.[55] It is an end which is of greater worth than 'the liberal goals of distributive justice and the satisfaction of private interests'[56] for it is a richer

---

[49] *Understanding Rawls*, p. 204.
[50] *Poverty of Liberalism*, p. 187.
[51] Ibid.
[52] Ibid. 190–1.
[53] Ibid. 192.
[54] Ibid.
[55] A view B. Ackerman, *Social Justice in the Liberal State* (London, 1980), would surely accept as part of his defence of liberalism.
[56] *Poverty of Liberalism*, p. 194.

form of the human good that it seeks. Here is why Wolff criticizes Rawls's theory as one which, typically, focuses exclusively on distribution and which is, in the end, a 'theory of pure distribution'.

We can focus more sharply on his point if we note how Allen Buchanan's criticisms of Wolff go astray. Buchanan argues that 'Rawls's theory is *not* concerned exclusively, or even primarily, either with the distribution of the means of consumption or, more broadly, with distribution in any sense which contrasts profitably with production'.[57] None of Rawls's principles is exclusively distributive because '*any of these principles may require changes in basic productive processes*'.[58] But this misses Wolff's point. Rawls is concerned with the production process and, ultimately, with the basic structure of society, from the perspective of distributive justice. The question he asks is, 'how should goods and bads be distributed in the just society?' And this is, at least in *A Theory of Justice* and Rawls's earlier work, an abstract question about what constitutes a person's legitimate distributive share of the benefits and burdens produced in any society. For Wolff, this is the wrong question. Indeed, it is a question which cannot make sense, for one cannot consider distributive entitlements independently of the productive process. Any answer to this question would be a philosophically inadequate account of the human condition.

What these radical critics of liberalism share is a view of human society which emphasizes that community is not a by-product of individual relations or private choices but, rather, the crucial prerequisite to the existence of morality, of culture, and, indeed, of 'individuals'. Community is not merely the result, or even the manifestation, of human interdependence; it is the achievement of human *awareness* of this interdependence and of the *obligation* that it implies. The bonds that sustain human society are not simply epiphenomena of individual behaviour but reflect a solidarity that could not be the unintended product of unreflecting individual action. Within human society, reciprocal awareness or consciousness is of vital importance if individuals are to *share*, rather than merely *consume*, a common culture. And a shared culture is essential if there is to be any shared morality. The failure of liberal theory, for these critics, lies in its inability or unwillingness to recognize that, without a cultural community, moral discourse can

---

[57] *Marx and Justice: the Radical Critique of Liberalism* (London, 1983), 123.
[58] Ibid. 123–4.

have no content and conflict and disagreement can have no rational resolution. In practice, the breakdown of community and the disappearance of moral consensus, hastened as it has been by the poverty of the language of liberalism, has led to the isolation of the individual. If this isolation is to be ended and the conflicts which plague society are to be settled, we will need a reconstruction of the basis of community according to a vision of society as something more than 'a collection of strangers, each pursuing his or her own interests under minimal constraints'.[59] While the various critics of liberalism differ in their assessments of how to reconstruct community so as to recover the moral culture necessary for human flourishing, all agree that the recovery of moral community is vital if social life is to resolve its conflict and, indeed, sustain private relations among individuals.

Our question, now, is: how pertinent or damaging are these criticisms when held against Hayek's individualist political theory? And how far is liberalism generally susceptible to the same criticisms? I suggest that neither Hayek nor liberalism generally are as open to these objections as the critics imagine.

Hayek argues explicitly against this communitarian viewpoint in his critique of 'tribalism' and the attendant defence of the 'open society'. In doing this he appears to accept something like MacIntyre's account of the emergence of a society of strangers pursuing their own interests under minimal constraints but with the difference that he regards it as a welcome development rather than as symptomatic of moral and cultural decay. In his view, the growth in the size of societies has rendered the call for a return to the morality of the small community hopelessly implausible and, indeed, dangerous. Here, 'the morality of the small community' refers to systems of rules of conduct which emphasize that right conduct aims *directly* at the well-being of the community or particular persons within it. In such communities, *loyalty* appears in the forefront of the virtues.

MacIntyre, in fact, suggests that in modern liberal society patriotism has been displaced as a virtue because 'we lack in the fullest sense a *patria*'.[60] Patriotism is not possible in a society in which government does not represent the moral community of

---

[59] MacIntyre, *After Virtue*, p. 233.
[60] Ibid. 236.

citizens and in which political obligation is, consequently, un-clear.[61] The minimal character of the moral consensus in liberal society, as he sees it, appears clearly in the writings of Rawls and Nozick which 'exclude any account of human community in which the notion of desert in relation to contributions to the common tasks of that community in pursuing shared goods could provide the basis for judgements about virtue and justice'.[62]

For Hayek, the defenders of the communitarian viewpoint have not seen either the impossibility of (re)creating these forms of community in the large societies of the modern world, or the costs of attempting to do so. What distinguishes the Open Society is the fact that it 'indefinitely enlarged the circle of other people in relation to whom one had to obey moral rules'; but what this has also meant is that 'the extension of the scope of the moral code [has] necessarily brought with it a reduction of its content' (*MSJ* 146). Consequently, if we are to have the same enforceable duties towards all, we cannot have duties towards some which are greater than the duties which we owe others—except in so far as certain natural or contractual relations obtain (*MSJ* 146). Hayek's point is that the wider the extent of our moral obligations, the fewer and the lesser those obligations can be if we are to owe them equally to all. This is largely a consequence of our inability to comprehend the whole of the extended community of whose life we are a part. If we owe duties to the extended community this must attenuate what special duties we might have had to the smaller, local community. Aiming deliberately, in our actions, at the well-being of other members of the large community that is modern society is impossible because we cannot *know* the circumstances under which these members live.

The idea of treating them according to *desert* (rather than the morally sparser notion of entitlement or rights) becomes impracticable, for it requires some human beings to be able to determine what other persons deserve or are worth (*CL* 97). Hayek rejects this because he rejects the view 'that we can and do know all that guides a person's action' (*CL* 97). While this may be plausible in a smaller, closed society, in which relations are more personal, it cannot be so in an expanding society open to new members, in which the

[61] Ibid.
[62] Ibid. 233.

composition and beliefs of the community are open to change.

There is one criticism of Hayek to be made here. In bringing in the issue of size, arguing that distributive justice is possible in a small, but not an extended, society he seems to compromise his position unnecessarily. Since he wants to suggest that it is only in the open society that the individual is able to know (because free to seek) the good for man, why concede that in a small, closed society men can know what guides each other's actions? Here he might have drawn on Hegel, who argued that only in civil society can men know one another as men (as opposed, say, to master or servant); only in civil society can minds 'mediate' one another on a basis of equality. Hayek might very easily accept such a claim, without making the implausible concession that in a closed society men can know all that guides a person's actions.[63]

Hayek's arguments reveal the depth of his individualist commitments which lead him to emphasize the importance of the individual over the claims of community, although he does not deny that the individual's nature is, to a great extent, the product of his society. While acknowledging that the moral rules established by the community ought to be accepted, and never discarded without careful scrutiny because they embody knowledge of whose value we are often unaware (although, if not critically examined, they may be found to codify harmful practices), he continually returns to his individualist standpoint to stress the importance of considering all individuals equally, whatever their community membership. He thus insists repeatedly on the necessity for formal rules of conduct delineating the boundaries of individual liberty. This, again, is a position that MacIntyre rejects when he repudiates '[m]odern systematic politics, whether liberal, conservative, radical or socialist'.[64] While the rule of law ought to be vindicated, liberty defended, and suffering relieved, by governments appointed to the task, 'each particular task, each particular responsibility has to be evaluated on its own merits'.[65]

Hayek's response to this view is clear in *The Constitution of Liberty*, where he argues that the 'belief that collective action can dispense with principles is largely an illusion' which stems from the false assumption that present decisions have no implications for

---

[63] I owe this point to Brian Beddie.
[64] MacIntyre, *After Virtue*, p. 237.
[65] Ibid.

future ones (*CL* 111). Decisions create expectations that, at the very least, similar cases in the future will elicit the same responses. Eschewing 'systematic politics' or political principles does not diminish the demand for consistency in decision making: 'A government that claims to be committed to no principles and to judge every problem on its merits usually finds itself having to observe principles not of its own choosing and being led into action that it had never contemplated' (*CL* 111). In paying such importance to principles, liberal individualism recognizes most explicitly that it is not enough to seek to promote particular goods simply because they are goods. All goods carry *costs*, and the promotion of one form of good will, to some extent, affect the promotion of others. Equally important, every form of good has its own proponents who accord it a relative importance *vis-à-vis* other goods. If any one is to be promoted, it is not enough that it be judged on its merits; its *relative* merits must be assessed because not all goods can be promoted at the same time. MacIntyre cannot simply call for the task of relieving 'unwarranted suffering' to be evaluated 'on its own merits' because, in the absence of any principle of comparative evaluation, this offers no justification for tackling one task instead of (or before) another. To deny this is to threaten to make 'arbitrary' decisions which have no justification beyond the fact that they promote particular goods. This is the politics that Hayek, and liberals generally, repudiate.

It must be noted, however, that the Hayekian (liberal) conception of society as a collection of strangers free to pursue their own interests does not amount to a defence of egoism. Nor is it based on the claim that man is by nature an egoist. While Hayek contends that the rules or laws that define the relationships and practices within society ought to recognize the individual as the bearer of entitlements—and indeed ought to attach greater importance to individual entitlements—he nowhere asserts that the individual would or should always act in his own selfish interests. Individualism, in Hayek's view, does not regard society as *merely* a collection of strangers. Rather, it affirms the importance of the family, the community, and the group, and the value of collaboration (*IEO* 23). When he defends the individual's freedom to pursue his own interests, this in no way denies that the individual's interests encompass those of others or that his interests involve obligations to members of his family and community. What is rejected, however, is the view that all obligations ought to be legally enforceable, for Hayek repudiates the idea that society is or can be no more than a collection of egoists bound together *only* by the laws defining entitlements. It is a 'false individualism' which seeks to 'dissolve all these smaller groups into atoms which have no cohesion other than the coercive rules imposed by the state, and which tries to make all social ties prescriptive' (*IEO* 23). Groups and communities are not held together by the laws which define entitlements; rather, it is because of the fact that groups or communities have evolved traditions and conventions that such laws can be developed at all (*IEO* 24).

Hayek's individualist philosophy carries the response to several criticisms of liberalism put by MacIntyre and Wolff. When Wolff berates liberalism for portraying society as an aggregation of Robinson Crusoes who co-operate purely for mutual benefit, and accuses it of seeing people as simple utility-maximizers, his criticisms do not disturb Hayek, who also rejects the models of game theory and welfare economics as inadequate models of human rationality, and refuses to see society as a co-operative venture engaged in by agents whose rational activity consists primarily in the calculation of the costs and benefits of co-operative activity. But he does not then take the step that Wolff does to argue that social relations ought *not* to be defined by laws which make individuals the bearers of entitlement, and seek primarily to delineate the spheres of individual right and responsibility. In other words, he would reject Wolff's 'rational community', for he denies that 'collective determination of social choices'—or 'politics'—is the most desirable means of securing the human good.

Here he produces two closely related arguments. First, he challenges the assumptions about the nature of politics which underlie Wolff's argument. Wolff sees the participatory politics of a 'rational community' as a good in which each individual takes part in a public discourse or conversation which is itself of paramount value. Yet the 'dialogue' that takes place in the political process is by no means neutral or impartial with respect to all citizens or interests. On the contrary, the political process strongly favours existing, powerful, and well-entrenched groups which are better able to use the arena of public discourse to defend their interests, than those groups which lack such skills or resources. Drawing on the work of Olson, Hayek argues that, the greater the scope of politics and the larger the number of decisions taken 'collectively', the more likely it is that 'the non-organizable interests will be sacrificed to and exploited by the organizable interests' (*POFP* 97).[66] What Hayek denies is not Wolff's assertion that, for as long as the dialogue of politics is accorded merely instrumental value, it will be cherished no more highly than any other means to private ends.[67] Rather, he rejects the assumption that politics, as a mechanism for 'collective deliberation' can produce a dialogue that is more than an instrument which groups use to pursue their parochial interests.

This leads to Hayek's second objection to Wolff's argument: that, if there is to be any social dialogue, it is wrong to assume that politics will produce a public conversation which is co-operative rather than conflictual, fair rather than distorted in favour of the powerful. (This attitude makes it difficult, however, for Hayek to defend the idea of 'corrective legislation'—as we shall see in ch. 4.)

None of this is to suggest Hayek thinks there is no place for political dialogue in society. His intention is to stress that politics is only one aspect of public discourse, and to show that other institutions facilitate that all-important dialogue about the nature of the good. This dialogue takes place not only in the legal process, in which arguments about the nature of the good and harms constantly arise among citizens, firms, and other civil associations, but also in the 'market'. In characterizing the market, defined by the institutions of justice, as a mechanism which allows 'knowledge' to be tested, distributed, and co-ordinated, Hayek draws attention to the fact that there exists a continuing 'debate' about the nature of the good—albeit one that is not *articulated* in philosophical terms. The 'dialogue' takes place not only in verbal discourse, but also in practice as individuals adopt or reject ways of living according to their own experiments and their observations of the successes and failures of others. This is not to argue that 'the good' is a subjective value or to imply that individuals will always pursue different conceptions of the good. Rather, it is to suggest that 'the good for man' (as MacIntyre puts it) is not in any way given immediately to human perception but must be discovered. The process of

[66] M. Olson, *The Logic of Collective Action: Public Goods and the Theory of Groups* (New York, 1970). See also his more recent work: *The Rise and Decline of Nations: Economic Growth, Stagflation and Social Rigidities* (New Haven, 1982). Wolff might, of course, argue that this is true only of existing politics.

[67] *Poverty of Liberalism*, p. 193.

discovery, according to Hayek, has to be one in which the search is not confined by limits imposed by individual reason.

Herein lies the chief merit of the liberal concern for, and emphasis upon, *procedural* or formal justice rather than the justice of substantive outcomes, for a concern for procedural justice does not mean indifference to, or unwillingness to consider, the nature of the good for man. The concern for procedures betrays a recognition that it is largely because of the rules of justice, which seek to preserve the freedom to pursue the good, that the good can be discovered. Those who argue that the nature of the good for man can (and must) be identified and that justice requires that we secure or preserve this good thus face several objections.

First, if the human good has to be identified, which individual or institution is to take up the task of evaluating, and choosing from among, the various conceptions of the good people favour? Any comparative evaluation will prove even more difficult than central planning for not only are views of the good life numerous but many may not emerge except in conditions which leave it open for competing views to be tried and tested.

Secondly, in a society in which there is, allegedly, no shared understanding of the good for man—the problem facing modern individualist cultures, says MacIntyre—and, accordingly, no shared conception of desert, it would seem futile (if not bloody-minded) to attempt to erect a standard of justice which accorded with a particular conception of justice and its corresponding notion of desert. Both the size of modern liberal societies and their constantly changing ethnic and cultural composition make this problem even greater.[68] The most pressing need, in such circumstances, would seem to be for procedures to evaluate competing claims—procedures which recognize that the existence of conflicting claims calls for a dialogue in which all parties can take part. For Hayek, as we shall see in greater detail in the next chapter, such a dialogue about the nature of the good can only take place in a *free* society—provided freedom is understood as he would define it. For the moment, it should be noted that, for him, freedom allows the liberal dialogue to manifest itself not simply in the political and legal processes of society but in all social practices in which individuals pursue, and advocate ways of achieving, the good.

[68] See J. N. Gray, 'Classical Liberalism, Positional Goods, and the Politicization of Poverty', in Ellis and Kumar (eds.), *Dilemmas of Liberal Democracies*, pp. 174–84.

Yet MacIntyre, Wolff, and Plant may raise a fundamental objection to such a response to their arguments: that the Hayekian, and more generally, the liberal, reply misses their central point about the nature of *community*, which should not be regarded as the by-product or unintended consequence of individual action. If a genuine community is to exist individuals must both share the substantive moral principles which dominate that community and consciously recognize the fact of their membership—and so be aware that it is the source, and the focus, of their obligations. The importance of the development of community in this sense is expressed most clearly by Plant's argument that only when individuals grasp the fact that they are interdependent will they seek to promote the satisfaction of each other's needs in a self-conscious way and thus effectively promote community as an *intentional* relationship.[69] If market relations are to endure, there must be some degree of moral consensus—and this consensus cannot be contracted as it is the basis of all contractual relations. 'Truth-telling, promise keeping, fair play, integrity, etc. are fundamental moral prerequisites for capitalist economic relations to persist.'[70] Yet under capitalism subjectivism about morality is encouraged and the standing of these extra-contractual or pre-contractual values, which form the moral basis of capitalism, is undermined. It is not apparent, and economic liberals have not considered, how moral pluralism can secure even a minimal social solidarity in a liberal minimal state. In short, it seems unlikely that a society can cohere if its organizing principles support purely *procedural* moral principles rather than *substantive* ones for, in the absence of agreement on substantive moral issues, procedures will break down, having produced outcomes which did not accord with society's various moral expectations. Plant quotes Kristol who also argues to this effect: 'The distribution of power, privilege and property must be seen as in some profound sense expressive of the values that govern the lives of individuals. An idea of self-government, if it is to be viable, must encompass both the public and private sectors, if it does not you will have alienation and anomie.'[71]

Yet several points suggest that liberal individualism is not quite

---

[69] Plant, *Hegel*, p. 230.
[70] Ibid.
[71] Ibid. 232.

as vulnerable to such criticisms as it seems. First, the norms of truth-telling, promise-keeping, fair play, and integrity Plant mentions are quite different from 'norms' of social justice. While it is true they are important if contractual relations are to persist, it is not evident that a consensus about the importance or correctness of these values is undermined by liberal individualism. Although there may exist disagreement about norms of distributive justice in so far as people espouse different conceptions of the good society, it seems less likely that the norms of promise-keeping and truth-telling would be disputed—simply because they are essential for almost any conception of the good society. The critics of liberal individualism have not shown how or why these fundamental norms are undermined by that individualism—particularly since the modern 'capitalist' states instantiated are also 'welfare' states. Moreover, they have not shown—nor is it evident—that allegiance to these basic norms alone is not enough to sustain society.[72] While they claim that, without general allegiance to substantive norms of social justice, there will be alienation and anomie, this has been asserted, not shown.

The argument here is that the sparser moral notion of entitlement is inadequate for social cohesion in the absence of a shared understanding of the basis of desert. As Sandel explains, quoting Feinberg, ' "desert is a *moral* concept in the sense that it is logically prior to and independent of public institutions and their rules". Entitlements, by contrast, are claims that can only arise under the rules or qualifying conditions of institutions already established.'[73] Thus entitlement can be invoked to justify a distribution only after the rules which lead to it have been justified—and this cannot be by reference to entitlement because it is the rules defining entitlement which are themselves in question. Entitlement can be justified by appeal to a stronger moral notion like desert, but desert does not flow out of the (unsecured) notion of entitlement.

But is this, in fact, the case? Assuming that desert is indeed logically prior to the institutions which define entitlement, it still needs to be shown that people should be entitled to the goods they

[72] For some perceptive remarks on why societies, including liberal ones, persist, see M. W. Jackson, 'On Her Majesty's Service', *Bulletin of the Australian Society of Legal Philosophy*, 43 (1987), 298–301, at p. 301. See also Jackson's critique of liberal justice in his *Matters of Justice* (London, 1986), esp. ch. 7.

[73] J. Feinberg, *Doing and Deserving* (Princeton, 1976), 87, quoted in Sandel, *Liberalism and the Limits of Justice*, p. 99.

'deserve', or at least that they are likely to accept only that individuals should be entitled to the goods they 'deserve'. Individualism's critics have not done this, and a practical example suggests that people have no difficulty accepting that others can, and should, hold strong entitlements to goods they do *not* deserve. Football players and spectators, however much they might bemoan the influence of bad luck in a match, readily concede that, while their team *deserved* to win (they created more scoring chances, were unlucky to miss a penalty, played better football), their opponents were *entitled* to victory because they scored more goals. Almost all would accept that the practice of football playing could not continue without rules which made victory an entitlement flowing from those very rules, rather than a consequence of someone's evaluation of who deserved to win.

Raymond Plant, referring to Hayek's discussion of the misperception that the market's virtue is that it rewards the deserving, notes the implication that, without such mistaken beliefs, the defence of the market may collapse. Yet, elsewhere, Hayek also suggests that people are less concerned about the 'merits' of those who enjoy great success. Ordinary people, Hayek writes, seldom 'grudge the very high earnings of the boxer or torero, the football idol or the cinema star, or the jazz king—they seem often even to revel vicariously in the display of extreme luxury and waste of such figures compared with which those of industrial magnates or financial tycoons pale' (*MSJ* 77). While these observations are largely unsubstantiated, the same has to be said of the claims of the critics of individualism who offer little evidence that liberal society faces a 'legitimation crisis', or a decline of patriotism or of social solidarity.

A second response to the critics of liberal individualism emerges out of Hayek's critique of social justice, and particularly his observation that there exists no agreement within society about what substantive criteria of distribution social justice requires since there is great disagreement about the bases of desert or merit. Appealing for the elimination of social injustice, he says, will not resolve this difficulty.

There can be no test by which we can discover what is 'socially unjust' because there is no subject by which such an injustice can be committed and there are no rules of individual conduct the observance of which in the market order would secure to the individuals and groups the position which as such (as distinguished from the procedure by which it is determined) would appear just to us (*MSJ* 78).

In the absence of such agreement about what outcomes are just, and of the procedures which, by defining entitlements, identify those outcomes which are just, politics becomes the means by which distributions are determined. The result would be distribution, not according to a shared perception of social justice but according to the strengths of contending interests. Such a procedure would not strengthen the bonds of community, if the radical critics' assumptions are accepted, because distribution would still not be tied to desert but would depend, to a large extent, on luck. Indeed the critics of liberalism have generally neglected the contention that, in politics, interest and power, rather than reason and philosophy, hold sway.

To the extent that the divisive nature of politics is recognized, no alternative is proposed by these critics. MacIntyre, for example, noting that 'modern politics' ('civil war carried out by other means'[74]) cannot be a matter of genuine consensus, calls for 'the reconstruction of local forms of community within which civility and the intellectual and moral life can be sustained through the new dark ages which are already upon us'.[75] Yet, if no genuine consensus is attainable in modern politics, how are we to create new forms of community which are not subject to the vicissitudes of 'modern politics'? To say simply that 'our lack of consciousness' of this situation, in which morality and civility are threatened by the forces of darkness, 'constitutes part of our predicament'[76] seems less than adequate.

Furthermore, even if genuine community must be more than a mere unintended by-product of private relations, and can be sustained only by individual awareness of society as the source of obligations and rights acquired with membership and by a moral consensus about the nature of those rights and obligations, it could also be argued that social solidarity (or consensus) is more likely to arise if agreement is sought on procedural rather than on substantive questions. This in no way suggests that rules of procedure do not produce substantive outcomes or that procedures are not the subject of intense disagreement. Rather, it is to point out

[74] MacIntyre, *After Virtue*, p. 236.
[75] Ibid. 245.
[76] Ibid.

that it is precisely because it is difficult to reach a consensus about substantive questions concerning the worth of different goods or outcomes that decision procedures are adopted. As this argument would have it, if there is a serious lack of consensus in modern liberal democracies, the reason for it is that too much is on the agenda. If a legitimation crisis exists, it is largely because consensus is being sought on so many issues over which interests conflict. Thus Hayek's response to liberalism's critics has been to argue that the kind of moral consensus they seek is incompatible with the persistence of large, expanding, and changing societies. The first step MacIntyre would have to take to reconstruct 'local forms of community' which sustain, and are sustained by 'stronger' moral agreement, would be to produce a theory justifying secession from the wider body politic.

Ultimately, the Hayekian rejoinder to these critics of liberalism amounts to a claim that the emergence, and survival, of the good society requires, not institutions which serve a shared or common understanding of the good for man but, rather, institutions which recognize that man in society is constantly engaged in the pursuit of that understanding. His defence of an individualist theory of justice rests on the argument that knowledge of the nature of the good is not 'given' to human understanding and, indeed, cannot be discovered without institutions of justice which leave people free to seek it. The critique of 'social justice', as Hayek interprets the term, thus rests on the claim that it attempts too much. To construct a theory of the good society as one characterized by (or aiming at) a particular set of distributive *outcomes* is an improbable task for several reasons. First, to define the good society, and so the good for man, in terms of one individual's conception of the good is to constrain society's development within the limits imposed by a single mind. Secondly, no single mind is able to comprehend the operation of society sufficiently to arrange its institutions to produce particular distributive outcomes—particularly since every step in an attempt to do so produces unforeseeable responses which make redistributive measures more uncertain. Thirdly, in the absence of any shared conception of just outcomes, attempts to produce particular outcomes are unlikely to command universal, or even general, assent and are more likely to fuel existing conflicts of interest.

Yet this is not all of the argument but only an aspect, albeit an

important one, of Hayek's theory of justice. We should conclude by
asking again how this theory may be characterized, what are its
weaknesses, and what arguments are needed to sustain a fuller
defence of liberal justice.

4. INDIVIDUALISM AND SOCIAL THEORY

Hayek's theory of justice is an individualist political theory. This
chapter has tried to show that it is not open to many of the
criticisms often levelled against individualism. Two questions now
lie before us. First, how might Hayek's individualism be characterized and distinguished from others which are, perhaps, more
vulnerable to these criticisms? Secondly, what does it *accomplish*:
how does his individualist social theory contribute to his defence of
liberalism?

The most important point is that, for Hayek, 'individualism'
offers a social theory rather than a set of claims about individual
rights, or any set of assumptions about the nature of the individual
as a rational agent. We might make this point clearer by developing
a distinction between two kinds of individualism which I shall label
'atomistic' and 'molecular'.

'Atomistic' individualist political theories begin by assuming that
the individual is an isolated, asocial creature who joins with others
to form society and, so, the polity. The individual is thus seen as the
source of the moral and political obligations which are incurred in
the formation of the polity because those obligations are held to
have force only in so far as they would have been incurred
voluntarily by the individual who enters into agreement with his
fellows. For this type of individualist, social arrangements are
justified only in so far as the principles which govern relations
among individuals are consistent with those which would have
been voluntarily accepted by individuals entering into a 'social
contract'. In recent years, Rawls and Nozick have presented
different variations of this social contract argument which illuminate the different reasons for thinking that individuals owe some
obligation to the rules (of justice) which govern society. In Rawls's
theory, the individual incurs obligations to respect the rules of
justice which he would have agreed to in fair circumstances—and
he would have agreed to such rules *in virtue of his nature as a
rational, self-interested moral agent*. In Nozick's theory, the
individual incurs obligations to obey the laws which arise in a

process *which does not, at any stage, involve a violation of his (natural) rights as a moral agent.*

'Molecular' individualist political theories differ from 'atomistic' ones inasmuch as they do not begin with undifferentiated, pre-social individuals but with society, composed as it is of individuals. Rather than attempting to show how individuals would come together to form society and so create their obligations, the molecular individualist approach asks what rights and obligations there must be if society is to be sustained and the security or freedom of the individual preserved. Hume was such an individualist who, starting from the assumption that man's first condition was social, argued that the preservation of society required rules of justice preserving individual *entitlements*.

We can sharpen this distinction between 'atomistic' and 'molecular' individualism if we inquire briefly into the definitions of 'atom' and 'molecule'. The *Shorter Oxford*[77] defines chemical atoms as 'the smallest particles in which the elements combine, or are known to possess the properties of a particular element'. The molecules of an element, however, represent 'the smallest portion into which the substance can be divided without losing its chemical identity'. Atomistic individualists take the individual to be the smallest *original unit which combines with others* to form the structure called society. Molecular individualists, on the other hand, take the individual to be the smallest *unit into which society can be differentiated without that unit losing its social characteristics*. Thus for the molecular individualist, society cannot be differentiated into units which are isolated individuals who are without interests and attachments (to families, friends, associations). A molecular individualist like Hayek thus founds his political theory on a *social* theory: the theory of spontaneous order. An atomistic individualist like Rawls, on the other hand, grounds his political theory on a conception of individuals who, behind the veil of ignorance, are effectively without interests or attachments. And Rawls offers no social theory because the nature of man and of society are irrelevant to his argument: the just society is one whose rules would have been chosen, by individuals acting not as interested, *human* beings, but purely as distinterested *moral* beings.

Finally, it should be noted that not all social contract theorists are atomistic individualists. Hobbes, for example, who would seem

[77] *The Shorter Oxford English Dictionary* (Oxford, 1959).

at first to be such an individualist, is not because the account of human nature upon which his theory rests, presents man as an undeniably social creature governed by passions which could only exist in the social context: notably by his desire for reputation and glory.[78] Equally for Locke, the social compact is concluded, not among previously isolated individuals, but among already social-ized men. The individualist who most decisively rejected any reference to human nature or circumstance in defending his moral and political philosophy was Kant. The rules of justice that must be accepted are those which would apply to all *rational* beings and not just to human beings: thus social theory is irrelevant to the problem of identifying rules of justice. Rawls's individualism is of a similar kind for his concern is to develop 'a viable Kantian conception of justice'[79] by detaching Kant's doctrine from its metaphysical surroundings and locating it in an understanding of the circum-stances of justice. Although he claims to be recasting Kant's theory within the 'canons of a reasonable empiricism'.[80] this involves little more than making the parties in the Original Position aware that they cannot assume that there will be no conflicting preferences in society, since there will be scarcity rather than a limitless supply of goods. It does not involve the presentation of any social theory. Rawls, like Kant, has a theory of rationality but not a theory of human nature. (Nozick, although he criticizes Rawls because his account of the person makes it impossible to distinguish individuals as 'thick with particular traits', retains the Kantian structure of Rawls's theory since no feature of the external world, or human nature, has any direct bearing upon the nature of individual rights or entitlements.[81])

The question which now arises, is, granted that Hayek is a

[78] So to a limited extent C. B. MacPherson is right to suggest that Hobbes's *Leviathan* describes not natural man but social man. See *The Political Theory of Possessive Individualism* (Oxford, 1962), 17–29. But see D. Herzog, *Without Foundations: Justification in Political Theory* (Ithaca, 1985), 37–8.

[79] Rawls, 'The Basic Structure as Subject', *American Philosophical Quarterly*, 14 (1977), 159–65, at p. 165.

[80] Ibid.

[81] See R. Nozick, *Anarchy, State and Utopia* (Oxford, 1980), 228. As Sandel observes, 'It is one thing simply to assert what is in some sense undeniable, that we are "thick with particular traits", and quite another to show how this can be true in a way not subject to the rival incoherences associated with a radically situated self, indefinitely conditioned by its surroundings and constantly subject to transformation by experience.' See Sandel, *Liberalism and the Limits of Justice*, p. 101.

molecular individualist, what does his social theory help him to accomplish? As John Gray has argued, the theory of spontaneous order is a value-free explanatory scheme which accounts for the character of complex phenomena found in nature and society but lacks any definite moral content.[82] The most obvious way in which the theory of spontaneous order contributes to Hayek's political theory is negatively: by showing that any political doctrine which seeks to justify a pattern of distribution must either come to terms with the nature of the social process or resign itself to being of practical irrelevance. Again as Gray points out, Hayek's demonstration that, even if clear principles could be determined for 'correcting' market distributions, no governmental authority could know enough reliably to implement and enforce them, presents 'a fatal blow even to Rawls's apparently attractive Difference Principle'.[83] This is an important aspect of his defence of his particular theory of liberty and of strict procedural justice. More significantly, however, by starting with an extensive social theory rather than with abstract individuals, Hayek is able to avoid several criticisms often made of individualism.

First, he is not forced to endow abstract individuals with 'natural' or pre-social characteristics in order to justify a theory of association or agreement and so is not open to the charge of arbitrariness in his definition of the individual. At no stage in the argument need he present the individual as anything less than a social creature.

Secondly, he is not open to the charge of making the unwarranted and misleading distinction between production and distribution. Marx argued in the *Critique of the Gotha Programme*, 'Any distribution whatever of the means of consumption is only a consequence of the distribution of the conditions of production themselves. The latter distribution, however, is a feature of the mode of production itself.'[84] Distributive questions cannot be considered independently of considerations about the nature of production or, indeed, about the nature of society, for what can actually be accomplished by a society will have great bearing on what kinds of distributions can be effected. Marx's social theory

---

[82] *Hayek on Liberty*, 2nd edn. (Oxford, 1986), 120–1.
[83] Ibid. 75.
[84] Quoted in Wolff, *Understanding Rawls*, p. 210.

correctly recognized that distribution according to need was impracticable in a world of scarcity and was possible only when scarcity had been overcome and conflict was no longer fostered by the relations of production themselves. This is a point that, for Wolff, Rawls ignores in treating distributive questions in the abstract. Hayek, however, beginning with a consideration of the nature of the social process, does not view justice as a problem of 'pure distribution'. Like Marx, he sees that justice cannot be considered apart from questions about the nature of society— although he does not go on to make the less defensible claim that there can be a society in which scarcity has been overcome (rendering justice redundant). Rather, he argues for a conception of justice which, he thinks, would co-ordinate, or bring harmony into, productive relations within the world of scarcity.

Thirdly, Hayek cannot be accused of grounding his political theory in a conception of man as a being whose rationality consists primarily in the capacity to calculate the means to satisfy his non-rational or given preferences. Here he departs from the model of rationality endorsed by Hobbes (for whom reason was the scout to the desires), Hume (for whom it was the slave of the passions), and Rawls (whose representatives in the OP, constrained by the demands of 'reasonableness'[85] embodied in that structure of choice, embrace a welfare-economic conception of rationality). He does not see man as a utility-maximizer and does not regard the process of preference formation as non-rational. The notion of rationality he employs is, rather, that view which underlies the Austrian approach to the explanation of economic phenomena. In this view, rationality does not consist in the capacity to calculate how particular goals may be attained, but is embedded in the social process which involves both goal selection and the testing of practical solutions to goal-satisfaction. Hayek makes clear, particularly in chapters 2 and 3 of *The Constitution of Liberty*, that political theory must see man not merely as a utility-maximizer but as a being who is engaged in the pursuit of knowledge of the good life. Thus his own political theory attempts to argue for a system of social institutions which does not restrict this process of discovery by giving too great a power to individual reason so that some individuals may claim to have identified both the form of the good for man and the

---

[85] See J. Rawls, 'The Basic Liberties and their Priority', in S. M. MacMurrin (ed.), *The Tanner Lectures on Human Values*, 3 (Cambridge, 1982), 1–89, at p. 14.

conditions of its achievement. His defence of individualism rests not on the claim that the individual knows best what he wants or where his interests lie and is most likely to satisfy those wants and interests if left alone; rather, it rests on the claim that individualist institutions alone can supply the lack when individual reason proves inadequate to solve the problems created by the human condition—that is, by the circumstances of justice.

Yet in the context of his project of justifying a *liberal* social order, Hayek's social theory alone cannot accomplish enough. While it offers an account of social processes which is both subtle and powerful, the most it can do is disarm those critics of liberal individualism for whom social justice requires distribution in accordance with desert or need, rather than entitlements or rights. It cannot specify the kinds of rights individuals should have in a liberal order. Put differently, it cannot specify the proper *scope* of individual liberty in the polity. To outline the nature of social institutions and of the market, and the process of their development, is not enough to defend any political prescriptions.

If Hayek's theory is to have any prescriptive force, he also needs, first, a theory of liberty defining what he means by leaving the development of society to the spontaneous ordering forces of the market (thus making clear what constitutes 'interference' and 'coercion') and so what kinds of institutions and laws will be needed to sustain this conception of liberty; and secondly, a moral theory justifying the assumptions upon which the defence of liberty and spontaneous order are based, for without a moral philosophy, the theory of spontaneous order might be used to justify any of a variety of political arrangements. Hayek has attempted to deal with this problem in his theory of liberty and the rule of law. What now requires examination is the coherence of his theory of liberty and the compatibility with his social theory of the moral theory which underlies it. These are the concerns of Chapters 4 and 5 respectively.

4

The Theory of Liberty

I. INTRODUCTION

Hayek's social theory, as we have seen, plays an important part in his political theory, for it is the basis of his rejection of arguments for seeing justice as a matter of substantive distributive *outcomes* rather than distributive *procedures*. The nature of society as a spontaneous order tells against the possibility of maintaining distributive patterns and so against the wisdom of trying to distribute goods according to conceptions of desert or need. The nature of politics suggests that it is not only difficult to secure agreement on conceptions of need or desert, but also hard to ensure, through political processes, distributive outcomes that reflect needs or desert rather than the power of contending interests. Hayek thus concludes that justice should aim simply to protect individual entitlements. Like Hume, he believes that entitlements should be defined by the conventions of ownership or property that society has developed, rather than seen as rights which can be identified in natural law. In Hume, the fundamental laws of nature, which were the laws of justice, enjoined the maintenance of the stability of property, the principle of its transfer by consent, and the 'obligation of promises'. In Hayek, the same principles are defended in his assertion that 'Rules of just conduct protect only material domains' and 'merely lay down the principles determining the protected domain of each on which nobody must encroach' (*MSJ* 123). To defend this notion of justice, he draws upon many of the economic and political arguments Hume invokes in defending a similarly narrow conception of justice.

Having put the case for tying justice to entitlement rather than to need or desert (or, indeed, any other patterning principle), however, Hayek still has to present a theory explaining the nature and scope of the domains to be protected by justice. As we noted in Chapter 3, he insists that it is not enough simply to invoke 'private property' and 'freedom of contract' as if the law of property and contract were given once and for all in its final and most appropriate form

(*IEO* 111). His response to this aspect of the problem of defending a theory of justice is to develop the *Kantian* notion that the just society is one governed by the 'laws of freedom'. This notion lies behind his insistence that justice aims at an 'abstract order' rather than at any distributive outcomes for, like Kant, he sees justice as concerned with the distribution, not of material benefits and burdens, but *freedom*. To aim at more than such an abstract order is to aim at a system in which laws seek to produce particular distributive outcomes. This would be impossible to achieve because of the nature of society as a spontaneous order; but, more than this, such a system of law would not be universalizable. The question now becomes: what is an abstract order and what are its principles?

Here Hayek becomes involved in arguments about the definitions of freedom, coercion, and law; the relations among freedom, law, and justice; and the nature of the institutions necessary to preserve justice. Our concern now is to identify and evaluate these arguments, to see if they can sustain the conclusions of his social theory. This will, in effect, lead us to assess the adequacy of his theory of liberty and his claim that liberty is sustained by the rule of law. But first we must turn to the question of why social theory leads him to develop a theory of liberty.

2. THE ARGUMENT FOR LIBERTY

In *The Constitution of Liberty* Hayek maintains that, while he would not deny the value of individual liberty as 'an indisputable ethical presupposition' (*CL* 6), it is important to show why liberty is an important value, indeed, 'that it is the source and condition of most values' (*CL* 6). His social theory thus offers a defence of this claim in three major arguments. The first asserts that liberty is not incompatible with order. Following Hume, Smith, and later Menger, Hayek tried to show how predictable and stable formations can result from the free, undirected actions of individuals. This concern is evident not only in his philosophical works but also in his 'technical' contributions to economics in the fields of monetary theory, trade cycle theory, and capital theory.[1] The

---

[1] N. Barry, 'Hayek on Liberty', in J. N. Gray and Z. A. Pelczynski (eds.), *Conceptions of Liberty in Political Philosophy* (London, 1984), 263–88, at p. 263. For Menger's influence see J. Shearmur, 'The Austrian Connection: Hayek's Liberalism and the Thought of Carl Menger', in B. Smith and W. Grassl (eds.), *Austrian Economics: Philosophical and Historical Background* (London, 1986), 210–24.

second purports to show that interference with individual liberty in an attempt to reconstruct the social order, and modify distributive patterns, would be counter-productive as the benefits of a spontaneous order would be lost while the likelihood of ever increasing infringements of liberty would rise. This claim received its first sustained defence in *The Road to Serfdom*. The third goes further still, for the most complex of his claims is that freedom is not only necessary for man's well-being, inasmuch as it enables him to enjoy the benefits only free markets will see produced, but essential for his development as a holder of so far undiscovered capacities. Indeed, freedom is necessary to make man (more) rational.

To see precisely how Hayek's social theory contributes towards the argument for liberty, we should first note briefly what he means by liberty or freedom. (In the next section we shall look more critically at his definition of liberty in the light of these arguments for liberty.)

An individual is free, according to Hayek, if he is not subject to unjustifiable coercion. To recognize that he is free is to acknowledge that there is a domain, defined by rules, within which he may 'use his knowledge for his purposes' or 'pursue his own aims' (*RO* 56). This domain of freedom is also the domain of individual *responsibility*. Freedom, here, 'refers solely to a relation of men to other men, and the only infringement on it is coercion by men' (*CL* 12). Not all obstacles men face infringe freedom. Equally, the lack of ability or power to perform an action does not, in itself, constitute unfreedom. (Here his definition parallels Felix Oppenheim's notion of 'social freedom'.[2]) Finally, he distinguishes his use of 'freedom' from the notion of 'inner' or 'subjective' or 'metaphysical' freedom or the idea that freedom consists in self-mastery or control of one's 'temporary emotions, or moral or intellectual weaknesses' (*CL* 5).

The main argument for liberty thus conceived is what Hayek calls the 'argument from ignorance'. This argument arises out of his social theory and its emphasis that the individual's pursuit of his ends depends on a co-ordination of human knowledge which cannot be effected by any single person or group. The value of freedom is that it facilitates the co-ordination of this knowledge and, indeed, enables individuals to discover 'knowledge'. The knowledge Hayek is concerned with here is not the individual's

---

[2] *Political Concepts: A Reconstruction* (Oxford, 1981). See also M. Levin, 'Negative Liberty', *Social Philosophy and Policy*, 2 (1984), 84–100.

'generic' knowledge but his 'concrete' knowledge of particular circumstances and opportunities. The chief value of freedom is that it provides 'both the opportunity and the inducement to insure the maximum use of the knowledge an individual can acquire' (CL 81). While Hayek puts the case a little too strongly when he argues that if we were omniscient there would be 'little case for liberty' (CL 29)—if that were so there would be little case for anything—his concern is to show that liberty is essential in a world of change and uncertainty, in which complete foresight is impossible. When the individual is not directed in his efforts to cope with such an environment he is more likely to adapt to changing circumstances. This is not because the individual in a free society is likely to develop better foresight but because his freedom permits him to adjust his actions or plans as his expectations are disappointed (CL 30, 32–3).

This adaptation takes two forms: (a) an emergence of new arrangements or patterns 'in which the efforts of different individuals are coordinated', and of 'new constellations in the use of resources, which will be in their nature as temporary as the particular conditions that have evoked them' (CL 33); (b) the modification of tools and institutions in response to new circumstances (CL 33). A by-product of this 'spontaneous' process of adaptation and the 'cumulative embodiment of experience in tools and forms of action' is the growth of *explicit knowledge* in formal generic rules which are communicable by language (CL 33).

The fact that this 'spontaneous' process does generate articulable knowledge also goes to emphasize that the argument for liberty is not an argument against organization or co-operation. While the social process under the system of liberty Hayek conceives is a *competitive* process, this does not preclude co-operation among those wishing to use the knowledge acquired in the course of adapting to the environment. It is only when 'such exclusive rights are conferred on the presumption of superior knowledge of particular individuals or groups that the process ceases to be experimental and beliefs that happen to be prevalent at a given time may become an obstacle to the advancement of knowledge' (CL 37). It is then that the argument for liberty becomes an argument against 'organization'—'against all exclusive, privileged, monopolistic organization, against the use of coercion to prevent others from trying to do better' (CL 37).

It is because Hayek sees society as characterized by uncertainty and the difficulty of correct foresight that he emphasizes the *instrumental* value of liberty understood as a protected sphere of individual action. This emerges most clearly in his claim that the value of the 'delimitation of protected domains' is that it allows the maximal coincidence of individual 'expectations' (*RO* 106–10). When facts and circumstances are constantly changing the most that can be held constant in an order which continually adjusts itself to such changes is a system of abstract relationships (*RO* 106). This means that such an order must be governed by rules which lead to the systematic (and so more, but not wholly, predictable) disappointment of particular expectations. What the rules would have to specify, then, is a way of distinguishing 'legitimate' expectations. The most effective method of defining a range of expectations which will be thus protected is to demarcate for each and every individual a range of permitted actions. This, he thinks, means delimiting property: 'rules are required which make it possible at each moment to ascertain the boundary of the protected domain of each and thus to distinguish between *meum* and *tuum*' (*RO* 107). What should be noted about Hayek's argument here is that his emphasis is on the importance of *maximizing* the satisfaction of expectations, rather than distinguishing *legitimate* expectations. Yet, as we shall soon see, this is not a line he pursues consistently.

Hayek's arguments for the delimitation of protected domains may be usefully contrasted with what Barry has called the 'rationalist case for liberty'.[3] What is distinctive about Hayek's position is the claim that only a small part of human experience can be controlled or accurately predicted because of the dispersal of knowledge among innumerable actors, and the fact that what is regarded as useful knowledge will depend upon the individual's liberty to take advantage of opportunities—either to produce or to consume—which he might discover. 'Rationalists' who defend liberty, however, use quite different arguments: the 'system of liberty' is valued, not as a discovery procedure, but as a most effective mechanism for matching preferences with goods, or production techniques with available resources. In this sense, those economists, such as Friedman, who argue from the principles of the

---

[3] Barry, 'Hayek on Liberty', p. 279.

general equilibrium system of neo-classical economics, are rationalists. They argue that, given man is a utility maximizer, the system of
liberty is most likely to result in the matching of individuals' known
desires with production goods. (This is not, of course, to deny that
Friedman also defends liberty on other—moral—grounds.)

Arguments beginning with a view of rational economic man
often finish as utilitarian defences of liberty. Hayek's case for
liberty, however, is not consistently utilitarian even though he
constantly points out the *instrumental* value of freedom. He does
not argue that we should try to maximize individual well-being or
happiness by maximizing preference satisfaction. Thus, as Barry
notes, Hayek should not be regarded as an 'orthodox utilitarian';
for him, because of the 'immeasurability of utility, and the
illegitimacy of interpersonal comparisons, the attempt to define a
"social utility" function is a rationalist delusion; liberty cannot be
justified because it contributes to this in some crude empirical or
quantitative sense'.[4]

Yet even Barry does not get to the heart of Hayek's defence of
liberty in arguing that, for him, the value of liberty 'is located in its
long-term, inherently unquantifiable advantages'.[5] The problem
with such an interpretation is that to identify Hayek as an indirect
utilitarian, concerned with long-term consequences, is still to
portray him as more consistently a utilitarian than he is.

The reason why Hayek is often regarded in this way may be his
somewhat obscure discussion, in *The Constitution of Liberty*, of
the nature of 'progress'. Here he identifies progress as a value which
liberty secures. Thus P. Dasgupta, in claiming that the value he
attaches to individualism 'is entirely instrumental in origin'[6] and
that his defence of individual liberty is 'based on instrumental
considerations',[7] points to his view of progress to indicate the end
Hayek seeks. The problem is that there are two different senses of
'progress' which are not clearly distinguished.

In one sense, 'progress' denotes the advance in material well-
being that can be seen in societies enjoying economic growth. The
value of progress here lies in the higher living standards and

---

[4] Ibid. 278.
[5] Ibid. 279.
[6] 'Utility, Information and Rights', in A. K. Sen and B. Williams (eds.),
Utilitarianism and Beyond (Cambridge, 1983), 199–218, at p. 214.
[7] Ibid. 215.

reduced distributive inequality it brings (*CL* 45, 48). If liberty were defended solely because it brought this kind of progress, then the argument for liberty would be a purely (indirect) utilitarian one.

In a second sense, however, 'progress' refers not to material advance towards welfarist goals but to the very existence of the conditions of individual freedom: freedom to experiment and to learn, for the individual to use his knowledge for his own purposes. In thus characterizing progress as that 'process of formation and modification of human intellect, a process of adaptation and learning in which not only the possibilities known to us but also our values and desires continually change' (*CL* 40), Hayek rejects the idea that happiness or pleasure or utility is what matters. What is important, he argues, is the '*striving*', for it is in the '*living* in and for the future in which human intelligence proves itself'; it is 'in the *process* of learning . . . that man enjoys the gift of his intelligence' (*CL* 41). In regarding progress in this (second) way, Hayek's outlook is decidedly *not* utilitarian, for he is suggesting that liberty is valuable not because the end-state or goal it enables us to reach is preferable but because the very condition of liberty is desirable. Indeed, Hayek (inconsistently with some earlier claims) questions whether one can say that new states of affairs brought about by progress can be 'better states'—'since our wishes and aims are also subject to change in the course of the process' (*CL* 41).

Here it may be worth comparing Hayek's view of 'progress' with that of J. S. Mill. While the idea of progress plays a large role in Mill's social theory, and particularly in his ethics, it is also the case, as Alan Ryan has shown,[8] that Mill's notion of progress is ambiguous. Progress is on occasion equated with improvement, but on other occasions not. Mill himself notes the distinction in his *System of Logic* when he writes that the 'words Progress and Progressiveness are not here to be understood as synonymous with improvement and tendency to improvement'.[9] While the advance of human history brought with it *change* which saw cumulative increase in human knowledge and power, this did not mean that it always brought *improvement*, since men themselves were changed in the process, moulded by the environment which they had

---

[8] See Alan Ryan, *The Philosophy of John Stuart Mill* (London, 1970), esp. pp. 179–85; Alan Ryan, *J. S. Mill* (London, 1974), esp. pp. 46–7 and 193–9.

[9] Bk. iv, ch. 10, in G. Williams (ed.), *John Stuart Mill on Politics and Society* (Glasgow, 1976), 58.

themselves transformed.[10] It is quite clear that what Mill valued was progress understood as the 'improvement of men's moral and intellectual qualities',[11] although all too often, he thought, society could be described as 'civilized' only because they had 'progressed' in the accumulation of wealth and power.[12] There is a sense in which all change, or historical development, is 'progress'; but change as such is not to be valued unless it brings improvement. And, consistent with his (indirect) utilitarian outlook, Mill argues that this improvement will come only under a regime of liberty: while the obstacles to human progress are great,

an indispensable condition of their being overcome is, that human nature should have freedom to expand spontaneously in various directions, both in thought and practice; that people should both think for themselves, and should not resign into the hands of rulers, whether acting in the name of a few or the majority, the business of thinking for them, and of prescribing how they shall act.[13]

Clearly, there is much that Hayek holds in common with Mill. Both are convinced of the importance of progress; and both connect progress with individual liberty. Yet there is an important difference between them. Mill emphasizes the value of liberty in paving the way to human improvement, which is realized when man is able to take advantage of the opportunity to explore his nature, and find or invent new ways of expressing it. This, in the end, is what 'happiness' consists in. And this is what Mill intends when he argues that the Greatest Happiness Principle appeals not to *mere* utility, but to 'utility in the largest sense, grounded in the permanent interests of man as a progressive being'.[14] Hayek, however, rejects the idea that happiness is in any sense an important concern. What he lays much greater stress on is the very engagement with the world in which man exercises his capacities and, so, produces what is called 'civilization'. What 'satisfactions' or 'pleasures' are produced in the course of all this are of little moment. What matters is the engagement, the 'striving': the

---

[10] Ibid.
[11] Ryan, *Philosophy of John Stuart Mill*, p. 184.
[12] See ibid.
[13] Mill, 'Chapters on Socialism', in *Fortnightly Review* (1879), in Williams (ed.), *John Stuart Mill*, pp. 335–58, at p. 347. See also Mill, *On Liberty*, ch. 3, in Mill, *Utilitarianism, Liberty, and Representative Government* (London, 1962).
[14] See Mill, *Utilitarianism*, p. 74.

'movement for movement's sake' which Hayek equates with progress (CL 41) (which is, in turn, equated with 'civilization'[15]). While Hayek and Mill share in common a notion that human life exhibits its worth only in the course of *activity*, they differ inasmuch as Mill stresses that this is because of what may *unfold* in the course of this activity, while Hayek seems to emphasize that the activity is its own point.

Yet if progress is interpreted in this (second) sense, and liberty is defended because it secures progress, is Hayek not then presenting a circular argument? Progress is defined as a process characterized by liberty and liberty is defended because it secures progress. This seems not to be a utilitarian argument for liberty; just a poor one. Yet what Hayek is trying to do is a little more complex. He is attempting to argue that what is valuable about human life is manifested in individual *activity*, in the *striving* in which the individual extends his capacities to the full. Value resides in his seeking after, rather than in his achievement of, particular goals. The condition in which such activity is possible is one of 'progress' (an odd word to use to describe such a notion). This appears to be a roundabout way (if not an illuminating one) of saying that the value of liberty resides in its being the condition of human flourishing. More simply, as Robert Paul Wolff might have put it, freedom is itself an individual value.[16]

This interpretation of Hayek's defence of liberty takes issue, then, with critics such as Barry, who argues that 'While Hayek does value liberty for its own sake, as a *theorist* of liberty he is clearly less concerned to celebrate the virtues of individuality and self-development than were, for example, Mill or von Humboldt.'[17] Despite the predominance of consequentialist arguments for liberty, his writings reveal a Kantian strain which asserts the value and dignity of the individual. He writes:

The recognition that each person has his own scale of values which we ought to respect, even if we do not approve of it, is part of the conception of the value of the individual personality. . . . A society that does not recognize that each individual has values of his own which he is entitled to

---

[15] 'In one sense, civilization is progress and progress is civilization' (CL 39).

[16] *The Poverty of Liberalism* (Boston, 1968), 193: 'The free society is good as an end in itself for it is itself a social value.'

[17] Barry, 'Hayek on Liberty', p. 277.

follow can have no respect for the dignity of the individual and cannot really know freedom (CL 79).

What Hayek offers, when compared with Mill, is not any *less* of an appreciation of individuality, but a different understanding of it. Unlike Mill, he does not define individuality against a notion of social conventions or norms which Mill took to be suppressive of individuality. Indeed, he criticizes Mill for precisely this attitude (CL 146).[18]

To see Hayek simply as a utilitarian is to emphasize the rationalist elements in his thought when so much of his argument is anti-rationalist.[19] The case for liberty is not simply that it will lead to superior consequences which we can predict, and still less that the individual as a rational being is better able to identify his interests if left free to do so (CL 76). Rather, freedom is valued more because it facilitates the development of human rationality (CL 38, EP 166). For it is only when the individual is not confined in his actions by limits imposed by others who wield the power to determine what is rationally permissible that his own rational powers can be extended. This view comes out most clearly in Hayek's discussion of the notion of 'individual responsibility' which he regards as an 'inseparable' part of liberty (CL 71). The assigning of responsibility does presuppose 'the capacity on men's part for rational action' but, more importantly, it also 'aims at making them act more rationally than they would otherwise' (CL 76). Rationality, here, means 'some degree of coherence and consistency in a person's action, some lasting knowledge or insight which, once acquired, will affect his action at a later date and in different circumstances' (CL 77). In fact, he argues, reason plays only a small part in determining human action; the point is 'to make that little go as far as possible' (CL 77), which requires the allocation of responsibility—i.e., the delimiting of domains of freedom.

This account of the relation between freedom and reason is very much in accord with Hayek's conception of the mind as a system of abstract rules guiding individual behaviour—rules which have

---

[18] On this see J. N. Gray, *Hayek on Liberty*, 2nd edn. (Oxford, 1986), 99–101.

[19] Though many have noted the tension between rationalist and anti-rationalist elements in Hayek. On this see J. N. Gray, 'F. A. Hayek on Liberty and Tradition', *Journal of Libertarian Studies*, 4 (1980), 119–37, at p. 120; N. Barry, *Hayek's Social and Economic Philosophy* (London, 1979), 64–5.

developed in response to the changing environment. Freedom is necessary if these rules are to be modified or replaced in response to changes in the environment, and this process of adaptation constitutes the development of reason. The individual who is not held responsible for his actions is less likely to learn the relationship between action and consequence, and so less likely to learn to act rationally and 'considerately' (*CL* 77). Hayek sees the mind, as we noted in Chapter 2, not as guided by fixed rules or categories for interpreting the world but as a developing structure whose growth is determined, in part, by the nature of the world it interacts with. This interaction takes place not simply through the mind's passive reception of stimuli but also through human actions which transform the (cultural) environment. To place limits upon individual action is to limit the interaction between mind and society and so retard the development of reason.

There is an interesting comparison to be drawn here between Hayek and Spinoza. In his *Ethics*, Spinoza argues that the development of the individual's rational powers should enable him to overcome the dominance of his passions or emotions and so to become free. There he equates 'the mind's power over the emotions and the mind's freedom', observing: 'how potent is the wise man, and how much he surpasses the ignorant man who is driven only by his lusts . . . distracted in various ways by external causes without ever gaining the true acquiescence of his spirit . . .'[20] We become free, he argues, when we acquire clear and distinct ideas of the causes of our own physical and mental states, i.e., when we acquire a more complete knowledge of nature and, so, of ourselves. For in acquiring this knowledge we cease to be ruled by our desires, or loves, or hates of particular things, by the emotions which arise out of our ignorance of the real causes of our 'pleasures' and 'pains'. In this sense, we begin to rule ourselves.[21] This contrasts with Hayek's view which emphasizes not that reason will bring man to freedom but that freedom is necessary to make man rational. Indeed this appears to result in a very clear distinction between Hayek's negative libertarian account of freedom and Spinoza's positive libertarian view of freedom as autonomy.[22]

[20] *The Ethics*, Part v, Prop. XLII, in B. Spinoza, *On the Improvement of the Understanding: The Ethics; Correspondence*, trans. R. Elwes (New York, 1955), 270.

[21] See S. Hampshire, *Spinoza* (London, n.d.), 121–76.

[22] See I. Berlin, 'The Concepts of Liberty', in his *Four Essays on Liberty* (Oxford,

Yet is this really the case? The difficulty of drawing so clear a contrast stems from Hayek's claim that, as long as the individual acts according to the rules that society has 'spontaneously' evolved—i.e. as long as he acts according to the law—he is free. The conception of freedom under the law, he writes, 'rests on the contention that when we obey laws, in the sense of general abstract rules laid down irrespective of their application to us, we are not subject to another man's will and are therefore free' (CL 153). For Hayek, whether or not these abstract rules are 'arbitrary'—and so coercive or freedom-limiting—depends upon how they have evolved: if they are the result of a 'spontaneous process', if they are the product of human adaptation to changing circumstances, if they are not the product of individual commands aimed at directing society towards particular purposes, then they are not 'arbitrary' and do not invade freedom. In short, rules do not infringe freedom when they emerge through this social process. As we observed earlier (and in ch. 3, sect. 5), however, Hayek also sees rationality as embedded in this social process—and in the rules which govern human action. Reason, like freedom, is an 'artifact of civilization' (CL 54) which does not guide but is created by cultural evolution (EP 166). Man came into the world in which there existed a 'repertoire of learnt rules which told him what was the right and what was the wrong way of acting in different circumstances' (EP 157). It was when the individual began to learn these rules, and so learnt to classify objects, construct models of the environment, and predict or anticipate external wants, that 'reason' appeared. And yet, Hayek insists, there was 'probably much more "intelligence" incorporated in the system of rules of conduct than in man's thoughts about his surroundings (EP 157). Indeed he further suggests that 'mind can only exist as part of another independently existing distinct structure or order' (EP 157) composed of many other minds absorbing and modifying that structure. In short, reason can only exist in so far as it is part of a rational environment. (Note also that Hayek suggests that the individual acts rationally when he is guided by habitual obedience to learnt rules rather than by deliberate reflection.)

In arguing that the individual is free when he is forced to submit

1976), 118–72, for a discussion of Spinoza as a positive libertarian. See also G. Parkinson, 'Spinoza on the Freedom of Man and the Freedom of the Citizen', in Gray and Pelczynski (eds.), *Conceptions of Liberty*, pp. 39–56.

to evolved rules (for he is not then subject to the arbitrary will of another), Hayek, in effect, claims that the individual is free when he acts rationally. The rules which guide his action are rational and he acts both rationally and freely when he follows them. And he would not be free were it not that he was a part of the civilization which created these rules and so produced reason. If that is the case, however, Hayek is clearly not a negative libertarian but, like Spinoza, a positive libertarian, for he sees the individual as free only in so far as he acts according to rules which are rational—i.e., rules which have evolved spontaneously. As Gray observes, Hayek comes close to endorsing a Rousseauesque or Kantian thesis about law and liberty in which it is held that 'true law' cannot limit freedom because it expresses a general will. Freedom is obedience to laws which a rational agent would prescribe to himself and these would be laws satisfying standards of generality and equality of application. In Hayek, Gray notes, 'we have the thesis, reiterated in the three volumes of *Law, Legislation and Liberty*, that "true law" must pass a test of universalizability'.[23]

If Hayek is not a negative libertarian, this raises the question of what the argument for liberty is an argument for. Is it an argument for the protection of individual domains (defined independently of the law) or is it one for a particular theory of law? To answer this question requires a closer look at Hayek's theory of liberty and its relation to law.

3. THE DEFINITION OF LIBERTY

Liberty, for Hayek, 'describes the absence of a particular obstacle— coercion by other men' (*CL* 19). And by 'coercion' he means 'such control of the environment or circumstances of a person by another that, in order to avoid greater evil, he is forced to act not according to a coherent plan of his own but to serve the ends of another' (*CL* 20–1). Coercion is an evil rejected for reasons which are strikingly Kantian: coercion 'eliminates an individual as a thinking and valuing person and makes him a bare tool in the achievement of the ends of another' (*CL* 21). But coercion may not be altogether unavoidable. It may be necessary to use it to prevent coercion. The important question for Hayek, as it was for Kant, is: when is coercion justifiable? Kant was quite clear that coercion was justified

[23] 'Hayek on Liberty, Rights, and Justice', *Ethics*, 92 (1981), 73–84, at p. 76.

only in so far as it was used to prevent invasions against freedom. For freedom was the only value which could be used to limit freedom. As Murphy puts it, Kant sought to establish 'the paradoxical claim that some forms of coercion ... are morally permissible because, contrary to experience, they really expand rational freedom'.[24] Hayek's answer is very similar as he states that the only justification for the use of coercion is 'the prevention of more severe coercion' (CL 144) and that the prevention of coercion is a demand of freedom. And, like Kant, he sees this right to coerce to prevent coercion as the monopoly of the state.

But how should unjustified coercion be distinguished from justifiable coercion and how should it be prevented? Kant's answer, as we saw in Chapter 1, is that right actions are to be distinguished by the principle that 'every action is just (right) that in itself or in its maxim is such that the freedom of the will of each can coexist together with the freedom of everyone in accordance with a universal law' (MJ 35). For Hayek, Kant's is the correct answer which, in his interpretation, asserts that rules of just conduct draw the boundary between justifiable and unjustifiable coercion by delimiting individual domains (MSJ 37). Both agree that the rules which delimit these domains are rules which specify *property* rights.

The recognition of private property, in Hayek's view, is 'an essential condition for the prevention of coercion' (CL 140), and he emphasizes that rules of just conduct aim to 'protect only material domains' (MSJ 123). Rules of property define the individual's protected range of expectations and thus reduce the 'mutual interference of people's actions with each other's intentions' by 'designating ... ranges of objects over which only particular individuals are allowed to dispose and from the control of which all others are excluded' (RO 107). He places great emphasis on the role of property in any just society for property is unavoidably linked to liberty (and also, as we shall see, to law).[25] Property is certainly important because we are seldom able to carry out a 'coherent plan of action' unless we are sure of our exclusive control

---

[24] J. G. Murphy, *Kant: The Philosophy of Right* (London, 1970), 109.
[25] 'Law, liberty, and property are an inseparable trinity. There can be no law in the sense of universal rules of conduct which does not determine boundaries of the domains of freedom by laying down rules that enable each to ascertain where he is free to act' (RO 107).

of some material objects; and if we do not control them we need to know who does so we may collaborate with others in pursuing those 'plans of action'. More importantly, it is essential that the material means necessary to pursue such plans not be controlled by a single agent. If this condition is met, freedom can be enjoyed by those with very little property (*CL* 140–1).

The crucial point about Hayek's position here, however, is that he asserts that liberty is not to be disaggregated. Freedom to dispose of one's goods (whether by gift or exchange) is no less important a freedom than the freedom to speak or to associate (or to dissociate). This view stands in clear opposition to that taken by liberals such as Rawls and Dworkin who, like Mill, distinguish different liberties, some of which are more important than others. To focus better on the nature of Hayek's contention we should examine more closely the arguments of his challengers.

Ronald Dworkin, in his essay 'We Do Not Have a Right to Liberty', rejects the idea that the freedom to use property is as important a freedom as, say, the freedom to speak, and further argues that the idea of a general right to liberty is 'incoherent'.[26] This position also implies that freedom of contract is not one of the more important freedoms, and Dworkin makes this clear in his suggestion that minimum wage laws do not in any way 'offend the right of those whose liberty is curtailed to equal concern and respect'.[27] The case for these putative freedoms, he suggests, might have force if the case for all liberties depended on the more general proposition that we have a right to liberty as such.[28] But since such a proposition is, at best, 'misconceived',[29] we can safely set out to distinguish the more important liberties which may not be violated.

But what makes the idea of a single, undifferentiated liberty, to which all individuals have a right, 'incoherent'? Before examining Dworkin's answer, we should note two features of his argument. First, and most obviously, the argument is expressed in the language of 'rights'—a language generally eschewed by Hayek. Secondly, and more importantly, it assumes a conception of 'rights' as 'trumps'.[30] To see rights as 'trumps' is to see them as

---

[26] In R. L. Cunningham (ed.), *Liberty and the Rule of Law* (London, 1979), 169–84, at p. 181.

[27] Ibid.

[28] Ibid.

[29] Ibid. 173.

[30] See R. M. Dworkin, 'Rights as Trumps', in J. Waldron (ed.), *Theories of Rights* (Oxford, 1985), 153–67.

entitlements to override or to 'trump' proposals which, even if beneficial socially, injure particular claims of the rights bearer.[31] Thus: 'If someone has a right to something, then it is wrong for the government to deny it to him even though it would be in the general interest to do so.'[32] Rights keep utilitarians in check for, while the vast bulk of laws which diminish liberty are justified (and justifiable) on utilitarian grounds, rights specify those areas where the social welfare maximizer may not tread.

Once this understanding of rights is clear, it readily becomes apparent why Dworkin rejects the right to *liberty* as 'incoherent'. If we are granted 'a general right to liberty as such' the idea of rights as trumps becomes incoherent. If I have a right to any or all the actions I could take, and everyone else has such a right, then everyone has a *trump* in every circumstance. And when all cards are trumps, no cards are trumps. The problem, however, is that there is no prima facie reason why we should regard the idea of a general right to liberty as incoherent rather than the idea of 'rights as trumps' as incoherent. Dworkin reaches the conclusion that a general right to liberty makes no sense only by assuming that rights *should* be seen as trumps; but the idea of a right to liberty is not inconsistent with a view which does not see rights as trumps to be used in a context in which actions are also (generally) justified on other (utilitarian) grounds, but which recognizes rights as serving to delimit the legitimate spheres of individual and group action. Such a view can (coherently) assert that I have a right to liberty in so far as I do not violate anyone else's (equal) right to liberty.

Dworkin's example of my lack of any right to drive uptown on Lexington Avenue does not pose any great difficulty here. He argues that 'it would be ridiculous for me to argue that' government would be wrong to choose to make Lexington Avenue one-way downtown because 'it is sufficient justification that this [choice] would be in the general interest'.[33] Yet to argue for a right to liberty, he claims, is to argue both that I have a right to drive uptown while agreeing that the government is justified in overriding that right. This difficulty only arises, however, because of the assumptions (A) that rights are trumps, and (B) that it is *equally* possible morally to justify actions on general interest grounds. Yet if A holds, then the *scope* of B must be reduced (to less than the

---

[31] See J. Waldron, 'Introduction' to *Theories of Rights*, esp. pp. 16–19.
[32] Dworkin, 'We Do Not Have a Right to Liberty', p. 170.
[33] Ibid. 171.

whole set of possible actions) if *A* is to remain a coherent notion. The theorist who defends the right to liberty can be coherent if he claims that that right exists only in so far as it does not involve violating another's (equal) right to liberty. For him, in the Lexington Avenue debate, the government wins *because it has the right to decide* who goes which way on one-way streets, and *not* because it is in the general interest that a decision be taken one way or the other.

While Hayek does not generally express his arguments in the language of 'rights', there is little doubt that he would see rights, not as trumps to be used in a utilitarian context but as serving to draw the boundaries of individual freedom. This is clearest in chapter 9 of *The Mirage of Social Justice*, in which he observes that 'so far as rules of conduct delimit individual domains, the individual will have a right to his domain' (*MSJ* 101). These 'negative rights', he argues, 'are merely a complement of the rules protecting individual domains' (*MSJ* 103). Rights thus identify protected domains by imposing constraints on all individual action.

Simply asserting (or assuming) that rights operate in this way is not, however, sufficient to defend the view that liberty should not be disaggregated into more and less important liberties. And Dworkin produces independent arguments to suggest why there exist 'basic liberties' and 'other [less important] liberties'.[34] Underlying his arguments is a claim that 'an assault on basic liberties injures or demeans us in some way that goes beyond its impact on liberty'; and it is from this assertion that he moves to the claim that, since 'liberty' cannot be coherently understood as a 'commodity', we cannot have a right to 'liberty' but only to 'the values or interests or standing that this particular constraint defeats'.[35] The idea of a general right to 'liberty' is thus dangerous for two reasons: first, it creates a false sense of necessary conflict between liberty and other values when social regulation is proposed; and secondly, it provides too easy an answer to the question of why we regard certain kinds of restraints (say, on speech or religious practice) as especially unjust. By thinking in terms of 'liberty' rather than 'liberties' we avoid the question of what is really at stake—which is something deeper than 'liberty as such'.[36]

[34] Dworkin, 'We Do Not Have a Right to Liberty', p. 173.
[35] Ibid.   [36] Ibid.

Hayek is not defenceless against this argument for he does not deny that there are values people seek which are 'deeper' or more important than 'liberty'. Observing that freedom of action (or 'liberty as such') is often equated with 'economic liberty', he argues that the concept of freedom of action is much wider than that of economic liberty and questions whether there are any actions which are merely economic, and whether any restrictions can be confined merely to 'economic' aspects: 'Economic considerations are merely those by which we reconcile and adjust our different purposes, none of which, in the last resort, are economic' (CL 35). While there exist values deeper than 'liberty as such', it is in no way clear that we can safeguard our liberty to seek them while denying liberty to perform other actions. The laws which uphold freedom of speech but deny the freedom to broadcast (by conferring monopoly powers on one or two radio networks) may not hinder the woman on a soap-box in Hyde Park from exercising her freedom to advocate her views, but may hinder those who speak more confidently from behind a microphone. While heavy taxes which prevent me from saving to go on my pilgrimage to Mecca injure my freedom to worship only *indirectly*, they injure me (even if not every Muslim) no less than a law *directly* forbidding me to travel there. Dworkin's charge that certain kinds of restraint are especially unjust misses the point Hayek is making in seeing liberty as whole. The argument is not that constraints on speech or religious practice are wrong because they violate liberty; it is that constraints on liberty are undesirable because they constrain our engaging in such particular activities.

Nor is it accurate to say that the idea of a right to liberty creates a false sense of conflict between liberty and other values when social regulation is proposed. Many, like Hayek, who see rights as delimiting individual domains, wish to show that conflicts among different pursuers of values are best regulated according to principles which respect (the right to) liberty. Plainly, some form of regulation is necessary and Rawls, noting that when 'liberties are left unrestricted they collide with one another', puts the matter clearly when he observes that

certain rules of order are necessary for intelligent and profitable discussion. Without the acceptance of reasonable procedures of inquiry and debate, freedom of speech loses its value. It is essential in this case to distinguish between rules of order and rules restricting the content of speech. While rules of order restrict our freedom, since we cannot speak whenever we please, they are required to gain the benefits of this liberty (*TJ* 203).

The Hayekian position does not dispute this but argues that the best method of regulation, which secures freedom most effectively, is one which specifies a protected domain within which the individual is free to act.

Yet, whether or not Hayek's arguments against the disaggregation of liberty into an ordering of liberties, and for seeing the delimitation of individual protected domains through rules of property as the most effective safeguard of liberty, can be sustained against other objections, it is certain that the problem does not end here. There remains the very large question of what principles should determine how that domain is to be delimited. Here Hayek finds himself on trickier ground. He is quite clear that this 'sphere belonging to each individual is determined, not by the demarcation of a concrete boundary, but by the observation of a rule'—indeed, a rule 'that is not known as such by the individual but that is honoured in action' (*CL* 149). Such rules are, of course, rules of just conduct, and they do not directly specify the protected domain but set down the conditions under which that domain can be created:

they leave it to the individuals under these rules to create their own protected domain. Or, in legal terms, the rules do not confer rights on particular persons, but lay down the conditions under which rights can be acquired. What will be the domain of each will depend partly on his actions and partly on facts beyond his control. The rules serve merely to enable each to deduce from facts he can ascertain the boundaries of the protected domain which he and others have succeeded in cutting out for themselves (*MSJ* 38).

But what are these rules of just conduct which enable us to delimit these domains? Hayek's answer leads him to elucidate further the relationship between liberty, coercion, and law, and it is to the problems that this raises that we must now direct our attention.

4. LIBERTY AND THE RULE OF LAW

Kant's theory of justice, as we saw earlier, falters when it claims that justice is served by delimiting a protected sphere of individual freedom because his moral theory does not produce any substantive principles by which such a sphere can be identified. Justice is seen as that condition in which the exercise of each person's will is compatible with everyone's exercise of his will in accordance with a universal law of freedom. Put differently, justice can be represented as the condition in which the general reciprocal use of *coercion* is consistent with the freedom of everyone according to universal laws (*MJ* 36). Such a condition is one in which the boundaries of individual liberty are specified, and Kant thinks that the individual has an *ethical* duty to enter such a *juridical* condition. This juridical condition is one in which there exist institutions—notably a legislature and a judiciary—that would specify the scope of individual domains and so limit coercion such that it remains consistent with the freedom of everyone. These institutions uphold the rule of law. Yet the rule of law does not specify how its upholders are to identify an individual's domain, and in Kant's philosophy, since they are owed unconditional obedience by all citizens, the rulers of society can effectively limit the range of the subject's freedom according to almost any consistently applied principle they may choose.

Our question is: does Hayek's attempt to defend the idea of a protected domain of freedom make any advance on Kant's scheme or does his own defence of the rule of law simply lead him to the same inconclusive results? This is an important question because, if his defence of liberty through the rule of law fails to secure certain substantive liberal conclusions, it would cast doubt upon the plausibility of seeing justice as the protection of entitlements through the enforcement of property rights. To evaluate his attempt to delimit the spheres of individual freedom we must return to his theory of coercion and the attendant defence of the rule of law.

There are two approaches one might take to the definition of 'coercion'. The first would assert that all coercive actions are morally wrong and that acts that are *not* morally wrong cannot be coercive in this sense of the term. For example, when Tibor insists that Fritz repay a loan when it falls due, despite the fact that Fritz now has to sell his family heirlooms to raise the money in time, Tibor is *not* coercing anyone because he is not acting wrongly. He is simply enforcing a contract.

The second approach would assert that actions that are morally sound can be coercive and that coercion is not to be regarded as a word that applies only to wrong actions. In this case, Tibor's actions coerce Fritz although they are not morally wrong. This distinction is essentially a verbal rather than a substantive one; it need not greatly matter whether all morally justifiable actions are defined as non-coercive or whether a moral theory seeks to differentiate between justifiable and unjustifiable coercion. What is important is that the moral theory be sound and that one definition of coercion is employed consistently. The difficulties in Hayek's account of coercion stem from a failure to decide which definition of coercion to use, for he uses both. This makes it hard for him to specify the individual's protected domain in terms of freedom (from coercion).

Hayek uses the word coercion in the first of these two ways when he observes that a hostess, who invites someone to a party only on condition that he conform to certain standards of dress and conduct, does not coerce him (CL 135–6). On Hayek's own definition it appears, at first, that this *is* a case of coercion because coercion 'implies both the threat of inflicting harm and the intention thereby to bring about certain conduct' (CL 134). Quite clearly, 'the alternatives are determined for him by the coercer so that he will choose what the coercer wants' (CL 134). This first impression is misleading, however, because Hayek wants to distinguish between 'coercion' and 'the conditions or terms on which our fellow men are willing to render us specific services or benefits' (CL 135). The distinction made here is clearly one between morally illegitimate actions, such as threats, which are coercive, and morally legitimate actions such as conditional offers, which are not coercive.[37]

Yet, having established his position that legitimate actions are not coercive, Hayek then goes on to argue that the state is justified in using coercion in certain circumstances—to raise money through taxation or to force individuals to provide 'various compulsory services' to society (CL 143). Here he uses 'coercion' in the second of the two ways discussed, for he asserts that there is a distinction to be observed between legitimate and illegitimate, or 'justifiable' and 'unjustifiable' coercion (CL 143–7).

This conceptual inconsistency is important because, if the protected sphere is to be identified by arguing that actions do not infringe that sphere only when they are not coercive, there can be no distinction between justifiable and unjustifiable coercion—

---

[37] I ignore here the question of the plausibility of such a distinction between 'threats' and 'offers' in terms of *coercion*. See, however, H. Steiner, 'Individual Liberty', *Proceedings of the Aristotelian Society*, 75 (1974-5), 33-50.

unless it is conceded that it can be justifiable to invade the protected sphere. If this latter concession is made, the whole point of specifying a protected sphere would be lost. In any event, unless the concept of coercion is clearly elucidated, it will become extremely difficult to develop a coherent argument for liberty through the rule of law. Hayek's concept of coercion is not consistently employed and two important arguments, which he develops to clarify the concept, serve only to create more confusion.

The first argument is that the use or 'threat of physical force is not the only way in which coercion can be exercised' (*CL* 135). This qualification, as Barry notes, opens up the possibility that certain kinds of market exchanges might also be coercive.[38] For example, if I know that you are desperately trying to raise money by selling your car but are unwilling to part with your autographed first edition of *The Constitution of Liberty*, I might 'coerce' you into selling me your prize possession by threatening to put all five of my cars up for sale at bargain prices. In a small town like ours, a large increase in the number of second-hand vehicles would send car prices plummeting—at least significantly enough to induce you to part with your first edition. Although I do not invade anyone's rights or protected domain here, my actions could be construed as coercive according to Hayek's definition. I *threaten to inflict harm* with the *intention* of bringing about certain conduct which will worsen the coerced person's situation, though I never threaten to use physical force or violate any rights.[39] Now Hayek wants to claim that market exchanges are not coercive; but in this case exchange results from coercive action despite the fact that no rights or protected domains have been violated. If he wishes, therefore, to defend this kind of coerced exchange, he would have to fall back to

---

[38] Barry, 'Hayek on Liberty', p. 271.

[39] This difficulty in Hayek's position was initially noted by R. Hamowy, 'Hayek's Concept of Freedom: A Critique', *New Individualist Review*, 1 (1961), 28–31, at pp. 28–9. Hayek responded by adding that for an action to be coercive it was also necessary that the action of the coercer put the coerced in a position which he regards as worse than that which he would have been in without the action. Thus simply adding to the range of a person's choices could *not* be coercive (*S* 349). But in my example this qualification does not seem to work because the owner of the first edition is clearly put in a worse situation by my attempt to force him to sell it. I have forced him to consider an option he regards as abhorrent (selling his copy of *The Constitution of Liberty*) by deliberately (but legally) making it harder for him to raise the money he needs. See also Murray Rothbard's critique in his *The Ethics of Liberty* (Atlantic Highlands, NJ, 1982), 219–28.

the position that some coercive acts are legitimate. Ironically, he does not do so in cases such as this, for the only kind of coercion he tries to justify is coercion by the state. This is odd because, in effect, he does not justify private coercion which does *not* violate anyone's domain, but does try to justify some kinds of state coercion which *do* violate the individual's protected domain.

The second of Hayek's arguments qualifying his definition of coercion also suggests that certain market exchanges can be coercive for he asserts that I am coerced by someone who refuses me goods or services which are 'crucial to my existence or the preservation of what I most value' (*CL* 136). Any monopolist in a position to withhold an indispensable good—Hayek's example is the owner of the only spring in an oasis—is thus able to exercise coercion. Here some obvious difficulties arise. First, how do we specify what is crucial to an individual's existence, especially since individuals rank their preferences differently: a Hindu at an oasis might never allow his cow to be slaughtered to save everyone perishing from hunger. Secondly, how do we determine the price to be charged for a good or service that is 'crucial to my existence', since, as Hayek reminds us, there is no such thing as a just price? Thirdly, in the case of all three owners of the different springs in the oasis independently refusing to sell their water to me at an affordable price, *who* is coercing me? If all three are, that clearly means that a trader on the free market acts coercively if he charges a high price even if he does *not* charge a monopoly price. Yet, again, we cannot solve this problem without a theory of just pricing.

The inadequacy of both of the arguments Hayek invokes to amplify his definition of coercion illustrates the inconsistency that plagues his use of the term. Moreover, it renders his definition of liberty unclear, since liberty is defined as non-subjection to unjustifiable coercion. The theory of coercion does not help to delimit the individual's protected domain, as it might have done, if Hayek had specified clearly and consistently what constituted coercion and stipulated that the individual's protected domain was that domain which could not be violated without coercion. The question now is: does the theory of the rule of law enable Hayek to find his way out of these difficulties? This means asking whether this theory enables us to specify the individual's protected domain, as Hayek thinks it does.

Law, for Hayek, does not limit freedom—because freedom consists in the absence of arbitrary coercion—but secures it, since it is law which enables us to distinguish individual domains. Here he is at pains to emphasize that by 'law' he means a general rule that everybody is bound to obey but which is not necessarily a command issued by a particular person. It differs from a command by its generality and abstractness. Ideally, he writes, law 'might be described as a "once-and-for-all" command that is directed to unknown people and that is abstracted from all particular circumstances of time and place and refers only to such conditions as may occur anywhere and at any time' (CL 149–50). While laws become more like commands as their contents become more specific, he argues, it must be noted that as we move from commands to laws 'the source of the decision on what particular action is to be taken shifts progressively from the issuer of the command or law to the acting person' (CL 150). Law, conceived as general, abstract rules, in effect delineates the sphere of free action of each individual while commands tend to assign particular things and particular times the individual may reserve for his own ends (CL 151). 'Primitive rules of conduct', embodied as they may be in customs, Hayek sees as having the character of commands as they often prescribe how an individual must behave in particular times and places to achieve particular ends. And while an individual following these rules is not obeying another man's will, the crucial point is that his choice of actions is restricted 'more than is necessary to secure freedom to others' (CL 151).

Hayek's conception of law is thus very much a Kantian one. This is made even clearer by his insistence that 'true law' is composed of 'abstract rules' and that 'In observing such rules, we do not serve another person's end, nor can we properly be said to be subject to his will' (CL 152). And, as is the case with Kant's legal theory, the notions of freedom and coercion are closely bound up with the idea of law: 'The conception of freedom under law ... rests on the contention that when we obey laws, in the sense of general abstract rules laid down irrespective of their general application to us, we are not subject to another man's will and are therefore free' (CL 153). Hayek thus shares with Rawls a recognition of the importance of the Kantian idea that liberty is acting in accordance with a law that we give to ourselves. But there is an important difference between Rawls and Hayek here. For Hayek, this Kantian idea of justice as freedom under law is secured by the establishment of the rule of law. For Rawls, however, the principle of the rule of law protects the rights of the person, those rights having been identified by the principles of justice (*TJ* 235). So the rule of law helps to provide a secure basis for liberty because it provides for the impartial and regular administration of rules but, in the end, it imposes only 'rather weak constraints on the basic structure' (*TJ* 235) of society: it is not enough to secure the justice of the social order. For this, principles of justice are needed, and these are to be identified through a process guided by the Kantian idea that we are free when we act according to laws we give to ourselves. Kant is the inspiration of the moral theory which identifies the principles of justice which are only then secured by the rule of law.

Hayek, however, does not perceive a need for a *separate* moral theory to justify particular principles of justice: justice is secured directly by the rule of law. The idea of the rule of law, regarded in the Kantian spirit, yields a freedom-maximizing rule and so yields the right to a protected domain.[40] According to this proposal the idea of seeking separate principles of social or distributive justice through a moral theory is simply otiose: justice is secured completely through the rule of law.

But is it? To answer this we will have to trace Hayek's theory of the rule of law more closely. The first point to note is that by 'the rule of law', Hayek means something more than the impartial enforcement of the law: 'The rule of law is therefore not a rule of the law, but a rule concerning what the law ought to be, a meta-legal doctrine or a political ideal' (*CL* 206). It is not merely a constitutional requirement, for a constitution can, ultimately, be amended by the legislators whom it binds; rather, it is a meta-constitutional doctrine about what a constitution should be. Once this is recognized, it becomes clear that the theory of the rule of law occupies the same place in Hayek's theory of justice as the Original Position does in Rawls's account of justice: they argue at the same level of abstraction. Ultimately, Rawls's theory of justice and Hayek's theory of the rule of law are both theories about what the laws ought to be; and both argue that the only acceptable laws are *just* laws. For Rawls, laws are just if they conform to or uphold the principles of justice established by his moral theory. For Hayek,

----

[40] On this point see Gray, *Hayek on Liberty*, p. 68.

laws are just if they conform to or uphold the rule of law. This is a point Raz fails to recognize in his critique of Hayek's theory for he takes Hayek to be using the term 'rule of law' in the same (weak) sense that Rawls uses it. Thus Raz claims that, since 'the rule of law is just one of the virtues the law should possess, it is to be expected that it possesses no more than prima facie force. It is always to be balanced against competing claims of other values.'[41] Raz does note the tendency of Hayek's theory to identify the rule of law with 'the rule of the good law'[42] and observes that to make this equation 'is to propound a complete social philosophy', but he does not see that this is a concern which Hayek explicitly acknowledges.[43]

In stressing the importance of the rule of law in this wider sense, Hayek remarks, some may imagine that he has 'put the cart before the horse'; but what he wishes to emphasize is that, important as the procedural safeguards (such as *habeas corpus*) which make up the rule of law may be, 'they presuppose for their effectiveness the acceptance of the rule of law' more broadly defined (*CL* 218). It is this broader notion or ideal of the rule of law which he thinks in greatest need of philosophical defence.

The rule of law, in Hayek's political theory, thus requires that the law itself possess three main attributes: (1) that its rules be general and abstract; (2) that they be known and certain; (3) that they respect individual equality before the law (*CL* 207–9). To be general and abstract, laws should be 'long-term measures' which refer to yet unknown cases and never to particular persons, places, or objects—and they must always be prospective rather than retrospective in outlook (*CL* 208). To be 'known and certain', laws need not all be explicit or codified. What is required is that there exist a set of judicial procedures such that the decisions of courts which articulate these laws become 'predictable'. Here Hayek emphasizes that while not all 'rules' can be put into explicit form, many will be recognizable as rules 'only because they lead to consistent and predictable decisions and will be known to those

---

[41] J. Raz, 'The Rule of Law and Its Virtue', in his *The Authority of Law: Essays on Law and Morality* (Oxford, 1983), 210–32, at p. 228.

[42] Ibid. 227.

[43] Ibid. 211. Gottfried Dietze correctly recognizes that Hayek's theory of the rule of law is a meta-legal doctrine but fails to further indicate or discuss what this implies for the structure of Hayek's political theory. See Dietze, 'Hayek on the Rule of Law', in F. Machlup (ed.), *Essays on Hayek* (London, 1977), 107–46, esp. pp. 112–13.

whom they guide as, at most, manifestations of a "sense of justice" ' (*CL* 209). In legal reasoning, he observes, the major premisses of any syllogism are not always explicit and often the principles upon which a decision might depend will have to be discovered by the courts. Ultimately, he argues (as we saw in ch. 2), 'all generalizations that we can formulate depend on still higher generalizations which we do not explicitly know but which nevertheless govern the working of our minds' (*CL* 209).

The third requirement of the law, if it is to conform to the ideal of the rule of law, is harder to define. The idea that law should apply equally to all is meant to give content to the idea of law as composed of general rules. Hayek sees that law may have the formal characteristics of generality while singling out particular persons by its categories of classification and to avert this tendency, suggests it should be guided by the ideal of equality. The problem is that there is no criterion that would always tell what kind of classification is compatible with equality before the law (*CL* 209). Hayek himself suggests two guidelines: that all classifications should be as acceptable to those they single out as to those outside the group; and that the law aim at improving the chances of yet unknown and not at benefiting or harming known persons (*CL* 210).

To appreciate the difficulties Hayek creates for himself in this account of the rule of law, a number of features of his theory should be brought out more clearly. First, he explicitly claims that, if law can satisfy these criteria, the requirements of justice will also have been met. In an important passage in *The Constitution of Liberty* he writes:

It is sometimes said that, in addition to being general and equal, the law of the rule of law must also be just. But though there can be no doubt that, in order to be effective, it must be accepted as just by most people, it is doubtful whether we possess any other formal criteria of justice than generality and equality—. . . so far as its compatibility with a reign of freedom is concerned, we have no test for a law that confines itself to regulating the relations between different persons and does not interfere with the purely private concerns of an individual, other than its generality and equality (*CL* 210).

Secondly, Hayek's emphasis on the law's abstract and general character leads him to stress the importance of the development of common law and to argue against the growth of legislation.[44] For the law which evolves through the judicial process, in his view, is necessarily abstract (*RO* 86) while the law created by command (as is legislation) need not be so: 'Abstract rules are not likely to be invented by somebody concerned with obtaining particular results' (*RO* 88). Legislators are more likely to be so concerned since they possess the power to seek particular outcomes. If the rule of law is to be maintained, Hayek avers, legislation should be concerned only to 'correct' certain developments in the common law. (Although, as we shall see, he is far from clear about how far we can say when these 'corrections' should be made.)

Finally, it should be noted that the ideal of the rule of law can only be pursued in a 'spontaneous order'. Only in a spontaneous order can the role of the judge be restricted to that of upholder of an abstract order or system of rules. In an order which is, like an organization, geared towards achieving particular aims or securing certain outcomes, principles of generality and equality will be subordinated to, or overridden by, those purposes. In a spontaneous order in which there are no 'social goals' the function of the judge can only be to 'maintain and improve' the working of that abstract order (*RO* 119). This is not to say that the judge must seek to maintain any status quo in the relations among particular persons. 'It is, on the contrary, an essential attribute of the order which he serves that it can be maintained only by constant changes in the particulars; and the judge is concerned only with the abstract relations which must be preserved while the particulars change' (*RO* 120).

These features of Hayek's ideal of the rule of law draw attention, however, to several fundamental problems which cast doubt upon the coherence of that ideal. These difficulties stem from the claim that the only criteria of justice are generality and equality. It is not clear that the abstract and general rules which conform to the ideal of the rule of law will always accord with principles which Hayek,

---

[44] This is more evident in *Law, Legislation and Liberty* than in *The Constitution of Liberty*. Arguably, Hayek changed his views because of criticisms made by Bruno Leoni in *Freedom and the Law* (Los Angeles, 1972), who argued that central legislatures faced the same problems that central planners did in the economic realm and that legislation had the same kind of discoordinating effects that economic planning produced.

and liberals generally, would find morally acceptable—unless those other principles are explicitly endorsed. Hayek seems both to assume that there do exist such principles (of justice) and to deny that they can be identified.

That he assumes that they exist is evident in his claim that legislation may be necessary to 'correct' the common law. There are three main reasons why common law may need correction in his view. First, 'case law' is, in some respects, a one-way street and may not be able to retrace its steps when some of the implications of earlier decisions are seen to be undesirable. Indeed, common law may produce some 'bad laws' which require correction through legislation (RO 88).

Secondly, because the process of judicial development of law is necessarily gradual, it may prove too slow to bring about 'rapid adaptation' of the law to wholly new circumstances.

Thirdly, if the correction of rules which turn out to be 'downright wrong' (RO 88) were to be undertaken by a judge this could lead to many expectations being disappointed as judicial decisions render some transactions, which took place when different rules were in force, illegal. 'In such situations it is desirable that the new rule should become known before it is enforced; and this can be effected only by promulgating a new rule which is to be applied only in the future' (RO 89).

The need for such radical changes may arise for either of two reasons: first, 'the recognition that some past development was based on error or that it produced consequences later recognized as unjust'; and secondly, the recognition that the earlier development of law was guided largely by members of a particular class whose views of justice did not meet the more general requirements of justice (RO 89). (Law governing relations between landlord and tenant, creditor and debtor, or master and servant, Hayek notes, was often shaped by the views and interests of one of the classes.)

But the question then arises: how do we identify a bad or unjust law? If the legislators are to correct the development of common law, by what principles are they to evaluate the justness of the laws which have evolved? This is never spelt out by Hayek; indeed he cannot do so because he has committed himself to the claim that the generality and equality of rules, in satisfying the requirements of the rule of law, have also satisfied the requirements of justice. Yet this idea sits uncomfortably with his view that *consequences* can be unjust (*RO* 89)—particularly if he also maintains that justice is an attribute of human conduct and not of outcomes. Furthermore, it is difficult to see why, if the development of common law can lead to laws which favour particular interests, legislation will not also lead to certain interests being similarly advantaged by the law. While Hayek has attempted to show how his 'model constitution' would overcome the difficulties posed by the legislature's susceptibility to pressure from political interests (*POFP* 105–27), he has not presented any clue as to how the legislators are to distinguish between a just and an unjust law. Nor does he indicate how they are to identify, or even estimate, the correct rate of adaptation of the law to new circumstances. And it is far from apparent how they are to know when judicial decisions 'correcting' the law would lead to so many expectations being disappointed that legislation would become necessary.

Perhaps this omission is not so surprising, for Hayek is never explicit about the principles by which judges should be guided when seeking the solutions to adjudication problems. While he does not deny that judges may err in seeking to discover 'what is required by the rationale of the existing order' (*RO* 119), he does claim that the judge, in each case he confronts, has to solve a problem which in most instances will admit of 'only one right solution' (*RO* 120). He appears to accept Dworkin's thesis that, in hard cases, the judge is obliged to seek the 'one right answer'[45] and that this search requires him to reach a decision which he can 'rationally defend ... against all objections' (*RO* 120). He fails, however, to specify the theory of justice—or the moral theory—which should inform such a rational defence.

A more fundamental problem stems from the absence of such a moral theory. The constraints imposed by the requirements of generality and equality are not sufficient to define the scope of the individual's protected domain in any substantive way. Hayek is not entirely unaware of this problem and anticipates the criticisms of writers like Samuel Brittan[46] when he notes that 'classification in abstract terms can always be carried to the point at which, in fact, the class singled out consists only of particular known persons', and

[45] R. M. Dworkin, *Taking Rights Seriously* (London, 1978), ch. 4.
[46] See his *The Role and Limits of Government: Essays in Political Economy* (London, 1983), 64–6. Brittan also fails to note that Hayek's theory of the rule of law is a meta-legal doctrine.

concedes that 'no entirely satisfactory criterion has been found that would always tell us what kind of classification is compatible with equality before the law' (*CL* 209). Yet the problem is more serious than he admits. In *Rules and Order*, after noting the concern that even rules which are general and abstract may place serious and unnecessary restrictions on individual liberty, and recognizing that rules requiring religious conformity would infringe liberty, he goes on to claim that: 'the fact is simply that such rules are not rules limiting conduct towards others or, as we shall define them, rules delimiting a protected domain of individuals' (*RO* 101). What this assumes, however, is that it is clear what kind of conduct constitutes 'conduct towards others' and what constitutes the individual's domain. Yet this is precisely what is *not* clear in Hayek's theory. Abstract, general rules requiring religious conformity may be construed as 'limiting conduct towards others' once it is recognized that even (otherwise private) religious practice may be regarded as action which affects other individuals—even if only to the extent that others are annoyed by the fact that someone might choose not to conform to the dominant faith. Hayek needs to explain why laws requiring religious conformity infringe an individual's domain by indicating the principles by which this domain is to be identified.

In the absence of such principles, no 'natural' domain can be identified: these principles are necessary if we are to distinguish between 'internal' and 'external' preferences. Unless the domain is clearly identified, the rule of law is not always going to produce liberal rules. The nature of this problem is drawn out by Sen in 'The Impossibility of a Paretian Liberal', and by Nozick's response to it.[47] Sen's paper demonstrated that a principle of collective choice reflecting liberal values even in a mild form 'cannot possibly be combined with the weak Pareto principle, *given an unrestricted domain*'.[48] What is of interest here, for our purposes, is not the Pareto principle, or Sen's suggestion that it is a 'prime candidate for rejection' in considerations involving social choice,[49] but the idea that social choice should be constrained by the individual's

---

[47] In A. K. Sen, *Choice, Welfare and Measurement* (Oxford, 1983), 285–90. See Sen, 'Liberty, Unanimity and Rights', in *Choice, Welfare and Measurement*, 291–326, for a discussion of the critical response to the first article.
[48] 'Impossibility of a Paretian Liberal', p. 290 (my italics).
[49] 'Liberty, Unanimity and Rights', p. 317.

protected domain (or rights). This is Nozick's solution to the liberal dilemma posed by Sen—a solution which involves relaxing the assumption of an unrestricted domain of social choice and construing rights as side constraints on individual action. For Nozick, the exercise of rights 'fixes some features of the world' and a social choice mechanism can make choices only within these constraints—'if there are any choices left to make'.[50]

While acknowledging the neatness of Nozick's solution, Sen correctly points out that it turns on the interpretation of a social ordering purely as a mechanism for choice rather than as reflecting a broader view of social welfare (or what makes for a better society). If a social ordering is understood in the latter, wider sense, however, there is a sense in which Nozick's rights can come within the domain of social choice, for it could then be argued that a society is better if it is one in which rights acted as side constraints. Nozick would, undoubtedly, remain unmoved by this observation inasmuch as his deontological view makes individual rights paramount. That a society in which rights were side constraints may also be a better society is, for Nozick, irrelevant. Sen's observation points to the possibility of an (indirect) utilitarian justification for such rights. For Nozick, however, the utilitarian perspective 'gives deontological considerations insufficiently fundamental weight'.[51]

Yet while Nozick establishes the scope of the individual's domain by positing (albeit, not justifying) certain fundamental rights, Hayek's attempt to establish that domain through the rule of law is more problematic. Hayek does not begin with 'fixed' individual rights but sees rights more as *variable* side constraints' generated by the rule of law (and so by the requirements of the generality and abstractness of legal rules). Thus: 'the free sphere of the individual includes all action not explicitly restricted by a general law' (*CL* 216). But the side constraints generated in this way are of limited strength since they cannot be side constraints on the (meta-legal theory of the) rule of law which determines what is to count as a protected domain. Indeed, what we find in Hayek's theory is a view of the protected sphere not as 'fixed' domain but as a domain continually redefined by the law. And, of course, if this is not stable

---

[50] R. Nozick, *Anarchy, State and Utopia* (Oxford, 1980), 166.
[51] *Philosophical Explanations* (Oxford, 1984), 495.

but variable, what constitutes 'conduct towards others' will not remain stable either because the scope of the other's domain will determine whether or not certain forms of conduct will encounter that domain.

What this means is that, in spite of Hayek's attempt to give the notion greater substantive content, the theory of the rule of law remains very much open-ended, and still unable to impose any stronger requirement of justice than consistency among general rules. In fact, Hayek places such great significance on the generality and abstractness of the rule of law that he condones many kinds of laws which most liberals would reject. If laws are expressed in general rules the individual, in many cases, need never be coerced for he will be able to foresee the circumstances in which he would be coerced and so avoid coercion. Indeed, Hayek goes so far as to claim that 'Coercion according to known rules, which is generally the result of circumstances in which the person to be coerced has placed himself, then becomes an instrument assisting the individuals in the pursuit of their own ends and not a means to be used for the ends of others' (*CL* 21). On this view, general laws forbidding Buddhist practices are not unjustifiable since one could avoid coercion by avoiding Buddhism.

Because the theory of the rule of law is not sufficient to justify or forbid any substantive practices, Hayek is, on many occasions, driven to present 'ad hoc' justifications for certain rules or institutions. Conscription, for example, is justified with the argument that such forms of compulsion 'are at least predictable and are enforced irrespective of how the individual would otherwise employ his energies; this deprives them largely of the evil nature of coercion' (*CL* 143). Taxation is also justified on similar grounds. Yet this is, in effect, to argue that a little coercion cannot do too much harm: 'a predictable limited period of military service certainly restricts the possibility of shaping one's own life less than would, for instance, a constant threat of arrest resorted to by an arbitrary power to ensure what it regards as good behaviour' (*CL* 143). Hayek commits the same mistake Kant did in so far as he goes on to grant the state various powers which do not follow at all from his legal and political philosophy. Unlike Nozick's minimal state, Hayek's state can legitimately engage in mild forms of redistribution by providing a welfare 'safety-net' for the poor or helping potential scholars or scientists without means to pursue their studies. It is not apparent from his theory why this mild redistribution is permitted; nor, indeed, is it clear how the level of the 'safety-net' is to be set. Also unlike Nozick, Hayek would deny trade unions freedom of contract in so far as he would declare illegal all closed shop agreements—even when voluntarily contracted—which he regards as agreements restraining trade and, hence, unjustifiable (*CL* 278).

There is, however, one important difference between Hayek and Kant here, despite the fact that both confer upon the government the right to actions which are not justified by their legal and political philosophies. While Hayek follows Kant in seeing justice as that condition in which coercion is regulated according to universal laws, he also goes on to argue that the government is justified in using coercion in order to prevent more severe coercion from emerging (*CL* 144). Thus while Kant stresses that the individual should enter a juridical state in which the right to coercion is *universalized* and so distributed such that no one has a greater right to coerce than anyone else, Hayek departs from this by conferring upon some individuals a greater right to use coercion in order to *minimize* coercion.

The fact that Hayek does have such a principle behind some of his seemingly arbitrary concessions to state authority cannot, however, rescue him from inconsistency. The idea of minimizing coercion, if it allows the state to act in violation of the principles of the rule of law, is an idea that then goes against the central contention of Hayek's political philosophy. On the other hand, if the state may not act against the principles of the rule of law, the minimization of coercion can only be otiose as a justification of any state action.

This brings us back to the question raised at the beginning of this section: whether or not Hayek's attempt to defend the idea of a protected domain of freedom represents any advance upon Kant's scheme. Our conclusion can only be that his argument for freedom through the rule of law is as unsatisfactory as Kant's argument for individual freedom under universal laws. In the absence of a separate principle delimiting individual domains, the meta-legal theory of the rule of law could endorse laws which seriously invade individual freedom by redefining individual domains.

Moreover, Hayek falls into more serious difficulties when he tries to extricate himself from such problems. In defending the view that coercion is justified when used to prevent greater coercion, he moves away from the Kantian notion of justice as the condition in which coercion is regulated by universal laws. In this view, the state, governed by the rule of law, *exemplifies* freedom. The view Hayek moves towards is a much more broadly consequentialist one, in which the state becomes an agency concerned to *promote* or maximize freedom.[52] These two standpoints are quite clearly inconsistent. And, indeed, this points to a deeper, more persistent conflict in Hayek's political philosophy.

5. CONCLUSION

We can return, now, to the questions raised at the beginning of this chapter and at the end of the previous one: what kind of a theory of liberty does Hayek defend and is it adequate to sustain the claims developed by his social theory? Clearly Hayek's theory of liberty is one which argues, not for the protection of individual domains as they are identified by any moral theory, but for general laws which enable individuals to define their protected domains. Individuals are free, according to Hayek's theory, in so far as the laws which delimit freedom are abstract, general, and apply equally to all, for in such circumstances the individual is *not* subject to the arbitrary will of another. In short, they are free if the laws which have evolved are not laws given to them by others but laws which they would give to themselves. In spite of his claim that the liberty he is defending is 'negative liberty', Hayek clearly endorses a positive libertarian thesis.

But the theory of liberty under law remains inadequate. It does not secure, as it should, the claims of Hayek's social theory: that the nature of the social process requires laws which allocate responsibility and entitlements to *individuals*. The theory of liberty does not secure these claims primarily because it does not establish how the domain of individual responsibility is to be determined. Or at least, in so far as the theory of liberty does indicate how the domain of individual freedom is to be delimited, it leaves open the possibility of so many kinds of rules fulfilling the demands of liberty under law that its value as a theory diminishes—or disappears.

---

[52] This distinction is made by Philip Pettit in 'The Freedom of the City: A Republican Ideal', in P. Pettit and A. Hamlin (eds.), *The Good Polity* (Oxford, forthcoming).

Before a final judgement can be passed on Hayek's political philosophy, however, we still need to ask whether any other aspects of his philosophy might make up for the lack in his theory of liberty. Does Hayek, anywhere in his theoretical writings, present a set of clear and compelling criteria by which to choose from among different institutions which satisfy the demands of liberty under the rule of law? To answer this question we will, once again, have to look closely into Hayek's writings. And our task, on this occasion, will be to discover whether he has developed a moral theory which will securely ground his political prescriptions.

5

Ethics and the Liberal Order

I. INTRODUCTION

Throughout his political writings, Hayek's primary concern has been to elucidate and defend the principles of a liberal social order. And, as we saw in Chapters 2 and 3, he holds that the need for liberal principles stems from the nature of order in social life. His political philosophy thus has its roots in his social theory:

> Liberalism ... derives from the discovery of a self-generating or spontaneous order in social affairs (the same discovery which led to the recognition that there existed an object for theoretical social sciences), an order which made it possible to utilize the knowledge and skill of all members of society to a much greater extent than would be possible in any order created by central direction, and the consequent desire to make as full use of these powerful spontaneous ordering forces as possible (*S* 162).

This philosophy argues that in liberal society people are most likely to achieve their various purposes because it is a society in which the protection of individual domains by rules of just conduct leaves them free to use their knowledge to pursue those purposes. In effect, he brings a substantial sociology to defend the claim that the good society must be one in which rules of justice seek to preserve *entitlements* (or rights) rather than to distribute benefits and burdens according to desert or merit or need.

Yet, as we discovered in Chapter 4, while Hayek is persuaded that questions of distribution cannot be decided in the abstract, and that social theory suggests that distribution be effected according to rules protecting entitlements, he is not so clear in his formulation and justification of liberal principles. This is most evident in his failure to articulate a satisfactory conception of liberty and in the inadequacy of his theory of the rule of law. As we noted earlier, it is, at best, uncertain whether the theory of the laws of liberty that accompanies his social theory can supply an account of how to identify the nature of individual entitlements in a liberal order. Put differently, it is not clear that he has offered any moral theory which would enable us to specify the kinds of rules of entitlement, or identify the rights, which should characterize the liberal order. This is the problem taken up in this chapter, for our question now is: what are the ethical foundations of liberal justice in Hayek's political theory?

It is difficult, however, to present an uncontroversial answer to this question, for Hayek himself never examines it in this form. He has been variously interpreted as a utilitarian, as a Kantian, and even as a traditionalist with conservative leanings who is both a sceptic and an evolutionary ethicist in moral philosophy.[1] To uncover what underpins Hayek's liberalism we should, therefore, consider these various interpretations of his thought with two primary concerns: first, to discover whether any of them, singly or in combination, account for the ethical basis of his liberalism; and, secondly, to see if there is a satisfactory moral theory grounding that liberal philosophy.

2. HAYEK AS A KANTIAN LIBERAL

While Hayek differs from Kant inasmuch as his is a view which, disavowing Kant's deontology, justifies justice by emphasizing its importance in the world of human experience, he nevertheless shares with him certain ideas about the demands of justice. What Hayek finds most compelling in Kant's legal philosophy is the idea that *universalizability* is a crucial test of the justice of a law, a principle, or an action; and for this reason he endorses Kant's view of justice as that condition in which the freedom of each is compatible with the freedom of all under universally binding laws. Hayek is also very much a Kantian when he argues that we are free when we are not subject to the arbitrary will of others for, in making this claim, he in fact asserts that we are free when we obey laws which we would give to ourselves. In this respect, his account of justice is contractarian, for he argues that just laws are laws which we would give to ourselves. The question is: to what *extent* can his theory of justice be regarded as a Kantian contractarian theory, particularly since, as we saw in Chapter 2, his arguments

---

[1] On Hayek as indirect utilitarian see J. N. Gray, *Hayek on Liberty*, 2nd edn. (Oxford, 1986), 59–61. On Hayek as a conservative see J. N. Gray, 'Hayek as a Conservative', *Salisbury Review* (Summer 1983).

often deny the contractarian constructivism of Rawls's political theory? In his attack on the idea of 'social justice' he appeals to arguments which might be seen as contractarian, yet his social theory presents many consequentialist arguments against the idea of justice in distribution. We need to establish whether the Kantian contractarian nature of his theory is more fundamental than his consequentialism or whether contractarian and consequentialist arguments are combined in a single (distinctive) moral theory.

There are three major claims in Hayek's account of justice which suggest that his is a fundamentally Kantian moral philosophy. The first is that the most basic and important test of justice lies in the principle of universalizability. The second is that laws are just in so far as they are not arbitrary commands imposed by others (but laws we would give to ourselves). The third is that justice is concerned with the distribution not of benefits and burdens but freedom. These assertions, along with the ensuing contentions that justice is *not* concerned with welfare or outcomes but is served by the delimitation of individual domains, form the basis of the critique of social justice as an ethical ideal. A look at the arguments against social justice Hayek derives from these claims should give us a better idea of the Kantian and contractarian nature of his moral theory, and make clear why this moral theory provides an inadequate basis for his defence of a liberal social order.

Hayek presents three main objections to the idea of social justice: first, that the demands of social justice, and the laws it requires, cannot be universalized; secondly, that these laws place us under the command of others, rendering us subject to arbitrary laws rather than laws we would give ourselves; thirdly, that social justice seeks to distribute benefits and burdens when, in fact, all that justice distributes is *freedom*.

The critique of social justice stems from Hayek's insistence that justice is an attribute of individual action rather than of substantive outcomes, and from the requirement that any rule of just conduct apply equally to all. Rules commanding particular *distributive* procedures, however, cannot satisfy the demand of universalizability.

Now, Hayek understands the universalization requirement in two closely related but different ways. On the one hand he says that, 'as a test of the appropriateness of a rule, the possibility of its generalization or universalization amounts to a test of consistency or compatibility with the rest of the accepted system of rules or values' (*MSJ* 28). On the other hand, he also states that when we ask whether it is 'possible' that a rule be generalized the 'appropriate interpretation is suggested by the manner in which Immanuel Kant approached the problem, namely by asking whether we can "want" or "will" that such a rule be generally applied' (*MSJ* 28). While Hayek does not recognize it, he is considering 'universalizing' a rule in two different contexts, each producing its own distinctive result.

If universalization takes place in the context of a system of accepted rules and the problem is regarded as one of deciding whether or not the rule in question can also be accepted as consistent and compatible with existing rules, the test of universalization does not exclude rules of distribution if the accepted system is a system of distributive procedures. All that would be required of the new rule is that it not come into conflict with existing (distributive) arrangements. If, however, universalization does not take place in the context of a system of accepted rules but is a test that is applied to every rule, and so is not a test concerned to reconcile a new rule with an established system but a test of whether the rules of conduct within any system can be universally willed, then universalization would (in Hayek's view) render rules of distribution unjust. Certain rules cannot apply equally to all since some would be required to obey laws (of taxation, for example (*CL* 314)) that others were not. This argument is unsound since there is no reason why a conditional principle or rule ('if you are rich you must pay more tax') cannot be universalized. It is clearly this second understanding of universalization that Hayek has in mind when criticizing the idea of social justice from the perspective of Kant's claim that ' "Welfare . . . has no principle . . . because it depends on the material content of the will, which is dependent upon particular facts and therefore incapable of a general rule" ' (*MSJ* 62). When universalization is regarded in this way Hayek's theory appears to be most contractarian in nature for he looks to be seeking an *external* perspective from which to evaluate rules of justice.

Yet the contractarian nature of his view of justice emerges even in the first account of universalization as a negative test of justice. Here Hayek comes closer to the approach taken by Rawls. In arguing that, while we have no 'positive criteria of justice' (*MSJ*

42), we do have criteria, stemming from 'our sense of justice' (*MSJ* 41) by which we reject unjust rules, he claims that the process of eliminating unjust rules can serve to develop an existing body of law so as to make it more just (*MSJ* 42). He then states:

In such an effort towards the development of a body of rules, most of which are accepted by the members of society, there will therefore also exist an 'objective' (in the sense of being inter-personally valid, but not of universal validity—because it will be valid only for those other members of the society who accept most of its other rules) test of what is unjust (*MSJ* 42).

In claiming that the 'objectivity' of justice is the product of a process in which individual senses of justice are tested and eliminated or reconciled, he seems to adopt Rawls's view of justification. Rawls states:

Ideally, to justify a conception of justice to someone is to give him a proof of its principles, from premises that we both accept, these principles having in turn consequences that match our considered judgements. Thus mere proof is not justification. A proof simply displays logical relations between propositions. But proofs become justifications once the starting points are mutually recognized, or the conclusions so comprehensive and compelling as to persuade us of the soundness of the conception expressed by their premises (*TJ* 580–1).

For Rawls, it is 'perfectly proper' that 'the argument for the principles of justice should proceed from some consensus' as this is the nature of justification (*TJ* 581). Though for Hayek justification does not take place in the realm of the hypothetical contract, the justificatory procedure is the same. And objectivity is its product. While he does not seem to seek to view the world *sub specie aetern-itatis*, he certainly does seem, like Rawls, to be seeking a perspective which 'is not a perspective from a certain place beyond the world, nor the point of view of a transcendent being', but 'a certain form of thought and feeling that rational persons can adopt within the world' (*TJ* 587).

In *A Theory of Justice* Rawls insisted that such a perspective is one from which we can 'regard the human situation not only from all social but also from all temporal points of view' (*TJ* 587).[2] For

---

[2] Note, however, that in his 1980 Dewey Lectures Rawls effectively abandons the idea of constructing a theory of justice which would hold for all societies and restricts himself to uncovering the principles that would be acceptable to liberal

Hayek the tests of consistency and compatibility (with existing arrangements) applied to new rules do not seek to render rules consistent with some viewpoint shared in all societies or in one society at all times. Rules are tested for their justice by being examined for their compatibility with rules in the society in which they are actually proposed. They are not tested in a hypothetical situation which abstracts from actual societies so as to isolate the essential conditions of moral choice. Yet this perspective retains its contractarian character because of two concerns (about justification) Hayek shares with Rawls: first, the idea that for rules to be justified they must be generated by processes characterized by individual choice (similarly, Nozick's emphasis on 'Invisible Hand Processes' enables us to identify the contractarian nature of *his* theory[3]); secondly, the idea that *agreement* is largely what justice, and morality generally, are concerned to secure.[4]

Can they both be regarded as contract theorists, however, when Hayek's contractarian premises lead to the critique of social justice while Rawls ends with a defence of a particular theory of social justice? The answer lies in Hayek's understanding of the problem of justice. To the extent that they are concerned with commutative justice, Hayek and Rawls are in substantial agreement: justice consists in respecting entitlements. But, as Rawls sees, respecting an individual's entitlements clearly presupposes an account of what an individual is entitled to (*TJ* 10). It presupposes an account of distributive (or social) justice. As Steiner puts it: 'Distributive considerations are logically prior to the rest because until we know what justly belongs to an individual, until we have formulated some conception of what is rightfully "his own", we are logically unable

democratic ones. But this makes it difficult to see how he can also hold on to the idea of uncovering principles of justice which are not valid only for the current generation(s) of his (Western) society since its future generations may well hold different values and priorities. It seems that Rawls cannot abandon the idea of uncovering principles of justice which are interspatially valid without also abandoning the idea of uncovering principles which are inter-temporally valid.

[3] But see H. Steiner, review of *Anarchy, State and Utopia*, *Mind*, 86 (1977), 120–9. See also Steiner's 'Can a Social Contract be Signed by an Invisible Hand?', in P. Birnbaum, J. Lively, and G. Parry (eds.), *Democracy, Consensus and Social Contract* (London, 1978), 295–316.

[4] T. M. Scanlon, in defending 'contractualism', notably against utilitarianism, claims that the idea of general agreement is 'in a more fundamental sense, what morality is about'. See his 'Contractualism and Utilitarianism', in A. K. Sen and B. Williams (eds.), *Utilitarianism and Beyond* (Cambridge, 1984), 103–28, at p. 128.

to know whether or to what extent an action of another individual constitutes an injustice to the first.'[5] For Rawls, individual entitlements are derived from social institutions and the 'legitimate expectations to which they give rise' (*TJ* 10). In theorizing about the basic structure of a just society he thus tries to develop an account of individual entitlements which just social institutions would uphold. The just basic structure is comprised of redistributive arrangements because preserving individual entitlements requires that legitimate expectations of distributive shares of social goods be met.

Hayek, however, refuses to concede that there is a genuine question about distributive justice. In this he is plainly mistaken; for his attempt to defend the liberal order leads him to articulate principles which either assume the acceptability of existing distributions or which have particular distributive implications. It is in his Kantian or contractarian guise that he denies that distribution is a matter of justice, and he insists that the classical formula of justice (*suum cuique tribuere*) should not be interpreted 'as referring to what is called "distributive justice" ', arguing that the aim of the rule of law 'is merely to prevent as much as possible, by drawing boundaries, the actions of different individuals from interfering with each other' (*MSJ* 108). Yet while he recognizes that the drawing of these boundaries must not be arbitrary (*MSJ* 109), he does not acknowledge that it is this very question of how (or where) boundaries should be drawn that forms the substantive problem of distributive justice.[6] Thus it is inadequate, as we saw in Chapter 4, to claim that the only criteria we can have of the justice of laws are the purely formal criteria of generality and equality, for this doctrine of the rule of law presupposes an answer to the prior question of social justice. In so far as Hayek follows Kant alone he faces the same, insoluble difficulties that beset Kant's enterprise. The principles generated by the (contractarian notion of the) rule of law are able to impose only the formal requirement of consistency among the laws. To put this criticism slightly differently, it is not enough for Hayek to demand only that laws effect an equal

[5] 'The Concept of Justice', *Ratio*, 16 (1974), 206–25, at p. 218.

[6] At least in so far as it is conceded that justice is about preserving entitlements. Of course, not all theorists would accept that justice is about preserving entitlements rather than rewarding desert or satisfying needs. See D. Miller, *Social Justice* (Oxford, 1979).

distribution of *freedom* if he wishes to defend a liberal social order, since freedom can be equally distributed among individuals who hold severely restricted entitlements in a non-liberal order.

The universalization requirement may be a *necessary* condition of the liberal order as Hayek conceives it, but it is not a *sufficient* condition. John Gray's explication of the complexity and severity of the test of universalizability does not rescue Hayek from the difficulties he incurs in making this test the fundamental test of justice. Following Mackie,[7] Gray notes that the universalizability test imposes upon the law not only a demand of consistency in the treatment of similar cases (or the merely formal requirement of non-discrimination) but also the demands of *impartiality* between agents and *moral neutrality* between the preferences of others regardless of tastes or ideals of life. When the test is fleshed out in this way, he contends, Hayek's reliance on it seems 'less misplaced' for it then rules out 'most if not all policies of economic interventionism and will fell all policies of legal moralism. Two large classes of illiberal policy supposedly allowable under a Hayekian rule of law, thus turn out to be prohibited by it.'[8] The problem which Hayek fails to tackle properly, however, is that even if *intervention* in individual 'economic' or 'moral' action is ruled out (and it is not clear that it is), such a test says nothing about the scope of individual freedom of action within which such intervention is impermissible. The boundaries of individual freedom, Hayek notes, are identified by the application of a rule; universalizability commands that these rules be consistently obeyed: intervention in an individual's life is forbidden because it involves breaking such rules which identify the individual's domain. But there is nothing in the universalization test to say that it is forbidden to change the rules to expand or, more importantly, to contract the scope of individual freedom.

Two other difficulties flow from these considerations. First, even if we grant that the universalization test is a test of the compatibility of rules not in every possible world but only in the world we happen to inhabit, the demand of compatibility cannot establish the kinds of rules which ought to be endorsed. If the world, or a society

---

[7] J. L. Mackie, *Ethics: Inventing Right and Wrong* (Harmondsworth, 1979), 83–102. But see D. Locke, 'The Trivializability of Universalizability', *Philosophical Review*, 77 (1968), 25–44.

[8] Gray, *Hayek on Liberty*, p. 64.

which Hayek has criticized, is one in which many incompatible rules coexist, what we need to know is which rules ought to be changed and rendered compatible with unchanged rules. Secondly, were the universalization test strictly applied, this would rule out many of the proposals Hayek makes: proposals which can only take effect if some institutions—such as government—are authorized to exercise discretionary power. This would be necessary to provide a welfare safety-net for the poor, or if the government is to perform certain 'service functions' Hayek favours (*CL* 365–6). The justification for such discretionary power is not to be found in any contractarian principles which deny the existence of the problem of distributive justice. Just as Kant's assertions about the role of government are inconsistent with the principles of his legal and moral philosophy, so do Hayek's views on the tasks of government appear as arbitrary pronouncements bearing little relation to his own, or indeed any, moral theory.

While Hayek's arguments, particularly those he uses to reject social justice, are strongly Kantian and contractarian, it must also be recognized that many of his claims stem not from this perspective but from other sources. Despite what he has said to reject social or distributive justice, there is no doubt that he has a good deal to say about the structure of the good society. What he refuses to recognize is that he is dealing with the question of social justice.

It would clearly be wrong to characterize Hayek's as a wholly Kantian enterprise. What must be established, however, is the part Kantian arguments play in his thinking and how they relate to the other kinds of argument in his political theory. To do this we should turn to consider other accounts of the (moral) foundations of Hayek's political thought.

3. HAYEK AS A CONSERVATIVE

The first alternative we shall examine contends that Hayek's is primarily a conservative political theory and that the Kantian considerations he invokes, at best, supervene this more fundamental feature of his outlook. There are several reasons why Hayek may be regarded as a conservative. First, as his social theory indicates (see ch. 3), he does not see the individual as a natural, self-generating entity but as a social achievement: the product of the spontaneous order of human culture. Philosophically, this not only puts him at odds with Kant's metaphysics of the self, and with Rawls's attempt to recast the Kantian project in arguments more congenial to an empiricist audience, but also (as we shall see) draws him closer to the ideas of Michael Oakeshott. Secondly, Hayek places great emphasis on the importance of *order* and, more specifically, the need to maintain existing order. The latter emphasis stems from his distinction between 'spontaneous order' and 'made order'. For him, social order is the product of the (inter-) actions of many men but cannot be the product of human design. He is often suspicious, therefore, of those who would reconstruct society according to principles of social justice. Thirdly, his account of the nature of the individual and society leads him to espouse a view of the importance of tradition which at times, conflicts with, if not undermines, the liberal principles he seeks to defend. So we must now consider how dominant are these elements in Hayek's thought: whether they reveal a fundamental conservatism and whether the conservative elements strengthen or weaken that theory as a whole.

To understand how Hayek, whose contractarian concerns are now evident, can be regarded as a conservative, we should look (again) to compare him with Rawls. On this occasion our concern will be to draw out the different roles they assign to individual reason in ethics.

In his discussion of 'Autonomy and Objectivity' (*TJ* sect. 78) Rawls claims that autonomy is the product of moral education (*TJ* 516). In asserting this he recognizes that the individual secures this education in society, and he emphasizes that, in an important sense, the individual cannot exist without others: 'Only in the social union is the individual complete' (*TJ* 525 n.). It is thus undeniable that *tradition* has an important role to play in our development as *moral* individuals. Yet Rawls wants to emphasize that, when it comes to adopting the principles of justice his theory defends, 'we are *not* influenced primarily by tradition and authority, or the opinions of others' (*TJ* 516, my italics). While it is our moral education as it is afforded by tradition and authority which may cultivate that capacity to grasp the principles of justice as principles that are *reasonable* for us, so does that education allow us to become autonomous and rational beings. 'However necessary these agencies may be in order for us to reach complete understanding, we eventually come to hold a conception of right *on reasonable grounds that we can set out independently for ourselves*' (*TJ* 516, my italics). On this view, he thinks, there is no antinomy between freedom and reason (for the contract theory he defends is able to characterize autonomy and objectivity in a consistent way through the device of the Original Position) (*TJ* 516–17). The individual achieves autonomy when he is able to grasp that conception of right and set out the terms of its reasonableness for himself: his understanding sets him free. As Sandel suggests, there lies at the heart of Rawls's theory a Spinozistic view that the achievement of this capacity to understand one's place in the world from the perspective of reason is the condition of individual freedom.[9]

In so far as Rawls accepts the power of reason to grasp substantive truths about the (social) world, he is, like Spinoza, a rationalist. For Spinoza, the mind possesses 'the power of conceiving things under the form of eternity . . . because it is the nature of reason to conceive things under the form of eternity'.[10] Rawls, while he concedes that human understanding, which enables the individual to grasp the principles of justice, is cultivated by social practices, 'by practices of moral instruction that inculcate a sense of justice' (*TJ* 515), nevertheless maintains that reason eventually grasps these principles independently. Tradition and authority thus fall away as justifications of right action. Principles of justice receive their justifications from the fact that, with the aid of the thought experiment afforded by the Original Position, we can see the world (or at least, in Rawls's later work, our society) from the perspective of eternity (*TJ* 587) and grasp the regulative principles this rational and reasonable perspective commands.

The conservative Hayek questions the assumption that individual reason, separated from the concrete processes of social life, possesses the capacity to stand back from the traditions which nurture it and, so, reach a position from which morally to assess those traditions. Individual reason, he argues, is only a tool which guides man's action in a complex environment he is unable fully to understand. Reason is a 'capacity for abstract thought' (*RO* 33) which serves the individual by enabling him to extend the range of

---

[9] *Liberalism and the Limits of Justice* (Cambridge, 1982), 132.
[10] *The Ethics*, Part v, Prop. xxix, in B. Spinoza, *On the Improvement of the Understanding: The Ethics; Correspondence*, trans. R. Elwes (New York, 1955), 262.

phenomena he can master intellectually. Abstraction enables him to reduce complex phenomena to a number of manageable (abstract) rules to guide his decision making. Reason is thus 'merely a discipline, an insight into the possibilities of successful action', and it is a discipline which is necessary 'precisely because our intellect is not capable of grasping reality in all its complexity' (RO 32). Reason's powers of abstraction are, in Hayek's view, extremely limited; thus he argues that man is often served better by custom than by understanding (EP 157). Indeed, man generally learns 'to do the right thing' without comprehending why it is the right thing. Learnt rules supply the lack when the individual seeks guidance and in this sense a 'tradition of rules of conduct, existing apart from any one individual' who learns them (EP 157), governs human life more closely than any individual's rational powers.

This view takes Hayek some distance away from Rawls, for it denies that reason will enable an individual to set out a justification of right action independent of the tradition(s) he shares. The traditions remain primary because reason is able only to theorize about how conflicts within them are to be understood. Reason does not enable man to stand far enough back to comprehend his tradition and to resolve such conflicts. Traditions of rules of conduct thus change, not in response to the strictures of reason, but because of their failures or successes in guiding individuals and their societies' adaptation to changing circumstances (EP 166). Reason is able, at most, to resolve conflicts among particular inconsistent rules; a resolution of more deeply situated conflicts cannot be the work of reason but only of a longer, less fully comprehensible, process of evolution.

The implication of this doctrine in morals is brought out most clearly by Hayek in *The Counter Revolution of Science*, where he attacks the 'rationalist whose reason is not sufficient to teach him those limitations of the powers of conscious reason, and who despises all the institutions and customs which have not been consciously designed' (CRS 163). Such a rationalist, in his view, is wrong to ask for the kind of justification he desires for the acceptance of any general or formal rules of conduct, for this demands that moral justification should take into consideration all the consequences of an action. To this view Hayek responds that general rules cannot be justified by indicating the consequences of their adoption because the very point of adopting rules of behaviour is that, without them, order, if not unattainable, at least cannot be combined with a certain degree of freedom (since the only alternative would be 'direction by a single will') (*CRS* 163). Indeed, without such rules we are less able to estimate the consequences of individual action.

At first sight, this argument appears simply as a rejection of a particular variant of consequentialist moral justification, attacking an argument most consequentialists have modified to meet such objections.[11] Hayek's wider claim, however, is concerned less with consequentialism than the demand that all rules be provided with or have available an explicitly demonstrable *rationale* if they are to command obedience. This, in his view, is an impossible and dangerous demand; impossible because individual reason is not always capable of grasping the value of rules embodied in actions and institutions which arose in response to problems individuals may no longer be aware of; and dangerous because refusing allegiance to institutions for which no such justification exists threatens the persistence of order. Hayek insists that it is essential that reason be less demanding if the conditions of the flourishing of individual reason are to be maintained:

It is essential for the growth of reason that as individuals we should bow to forces and obey principles which we cannot hope fully to understand, yet on which the advance and even the preservation of civilization depend. Historically this has been achieved by the influence of the various religious creeds and by traditions and superstitions which made men submit to those forces by an appeal to his emotions rather than to his reason (*CRS* 162).

In placing such an emphasis on the importance of order and the traditions and institutions which give it continuity, and in stressing that individual reason only has a place in an order of rule-guided behaviour, Hayek reveals the conservative side of his thought. Like

---

[11] See J. Glover, *Causing Death and Saving Lives* (Harmondsworth, 1981), 62–3, who argues that while the problem of correct foresight and calculation may pose 'serious problems for any attempt at a precisely quantified science of utilitarian ethics, . . . it is far from clear that they are fatal to utilitarianism as an approximate guide to conduct. After all, most of us, whether utilitarians or not, take some account of the likely effects of our actions . . .' More serious objections to utilitarianism have come from Bernard Williams. See his recent book, *Ethics and the Limits of Philosophy* (London, 1985). For a powerful defence of consequentialism see S. Scheffler, *The Rejection of Consequentialism: A Philosophical Investigation of the Considerations Underlying Rival Moral Conceptions* (Oxford, 1984), esp. pp. 44–52.

the conservative, he denies that reason can motivate individual conduct: that it can move him to create a particular work or to behave in a certain (moral) way. Indeed, he denies that reason exists as an independent faculty which guides or impels the individual in his construction of his (cultural) environment. As we saw in Chapter 2, Hayek sees the mind, not as 'the capping stone of the hierarchy of complex structures, produced by evolution', but as deeply 'embedded in a traditional impersonal structure of learnt rules' (*EP* 157). The mind must thus be regarded less as the independent originator of human culture than as the product of cultural development: 'mind and culture developed concurrently and not successively' (*EP* 156).

In this respect Hayek's attitude comes very close to that of Oakeshott who, particularly in his essays, 'Rationalism in Politics' and 'Rational Conduct',[12] challenges 'the supposition that mind can be separated from its contents and its activities', that it is 'an independent instrument capable of dealing with experience'.[13] For Oakeshott, no action is 'rational' by itself; what makes it rational is 'its place in a flow of sympathy, a current of moral activity'.[14] But there is no *faculty* called 'Reason', nor one called 'Sympathy'; rather, it is the quality of an action which maintains the coherence of the 'activity' or 'way of living' within which it is located, that makes it 'rational'. The great weakness of the rationalist temper in politics stems from a failure to recognize this character of human conduct. In detaching the operation of reason from the context of the tradition which gives it coherence, the rationalist misunderstands the nature of reason and is led to misconceive its powers. He is led further to believe that society as a whole can be given a rational basis if its operation is founded in, or brought into line with, universal principles—whether principles of human rights or of national self-determination.[15] In Oakeshott's view, however, political activity should be concerned not with the attempt to reconstruct society in accordance with such principles but to attend 'to the general arrangements of a collection of people who, in respect of their common recognition of a manner of attending to its

[12] In his *Rationalism in Politics and Other Essays* (London, 1981), 1–37 and 80–110.
[13] 'Rational Conduct', in *Rationalism in Politics*, p. 86.
[14] Ibid. 109.
[15] 'Rationalism in Politics', p. 6.

arrangements, compose a single community'.[16] Doing this requires both an understanding of the traditions of behaviour of that society which make politics possible, and awareness that political activity consists in the 'exploration' of the 'sympathies' intimated in the customs and institutions of that society.[17]

While Hayek does not picture politics as a 'pursuit of intimations', he is similarly critical of those he dubs 'rationalists', arguing that they do not acknowledge that man's most beneficial institutions—of language, morals, and law—are institutions whose functions and value are not, and perhaps cannot be, fully grasped by the individual mind (*EP* 163). This claim is closely tied up with his thesis that there is a logical limit imposed upon the mind's capacity to understand its own functioning, since it can never present an explanation of its operation which at the same time explains how it is able to present that explanation.[18] The mind cannot step outside itself to view its own operation. Since the mind, as he conceives it, is a system of rules embedded in a social structure also constituted by rules of conduct, it is similarly impossible for the mind to step outside society and view *its* operations from beyond. The difficulty of separating mind from society tells against the possibility of the mind comprehending the operation of the whole. If anything, Hayek argues, we should be seeking not such a comprehensive understanding to enable us to restructure society, but to understand our own practices and the process of 'winnowing' or 'sifting' (*EP* 155) by which they have emerged. For somewhat different reasons, he echoes Oakeshott's call for us to pay greater attention to the search for a historical understanding of our traditions and less to the demand for principles to provide ideological abridgements of them.[19]

Inasmuch as conservatism is a doctrine which not only expresses a preference for what has grown up over a long time (to what has been deliberately contrived by human effort) but also presents philosophical arguments rejecting the claims of individual reason to act as guide in human affairs,[20] there appears to be a case for seeing

---

[16] 'Political Education', in *Rationalism in Politics*, 111–36, at p. 123.
[17] Ibid. 124.
[18] See ch. 2, sect. 2 above.
[19] See Oakeshott, 'Political Education', in *Rationalism in Politics*, p. 128: 'Now, a tradition of behaviour is a tricky thing to get to know. Indeed, it may even appear to be essentially unintelligible.'
[20] See K. Minogue's definition of 'Conservatism', in P. Edwards (ed.), *The Encyclopaedia of Philosophy*, 8 vols. (London, 1967), ii. 195–8.

Hayek as a conservative. Before we can ask how securely his political philosophy is grounded in a conservative outlook, however, we should consider what kind of conservative he might be.

First, he is not, like Oakeshott, a conservative by 'temperament'. For Oakeshott, to be conservative is to prefer 'the familiar to the unknown, to prefer the tried to the untried, fact to mystery, the actual to the possible, the limited to the unbounded, the near to the distant, the sufficient to the superabundant, the convenient to the perfect, present laughter to Utopian bliss'.[21] Change, for him, is to be accommodated rather than welcomed[22] and is regarded as a 'deprivation', a 'threat to identity' which is tolerable only if it comes at slow pace.[23] He prefers that innovation should come at a rate which not only allows adjustment to the consequences of change, but also ensures that 'change is most likely to be limited to what is intended and least likely to be corrupted by undesired and unmanageable consequences'.[24] Hayek, by contrast, regards man as a being who only fulfils his potential or utilizes his intelligence when he strives to adapt himself to change and so, unlike Oakeshott, positively welcomes innovation and 'progress'. While 'progress' may be more easily accepted if it were slower, this does not give us any reason to try to slow the process of innovation so that we may better foresee its direct consequences. 'To confine evolution to what we can foresee would be to stop progress' (*EP* 169) and, for Hayek, despite his emphasis on the value of traditions, progress is of central importance. The character of Oakeshott's conservatism is brought into focus by his observation that, unlike Mill, who abandoned reference to general principle as a reliable guide in politics and put in its place a theory of human progress, he would abandon both 'principle' and the theory of progress as equally deficient referents either for explanation or for practical conduct.[25] Hayek, clearly, does not abandon the appeal to progress either in putting his social explanations or in justifying his political philosophy. (Whether this allows us to regard him as a conservative, particularly since he does not abandon appeal to 'principle' either, is a question we shall turn to presently.)

Secondly, Hayek's conservatism (like Oakeshott's) is not one that

---

[21] 'On Being Conservative', in *Rationalism in Politics*, 168–96, at p. 169.
[22] Ibid. 169–70.
[23] Ibid. 170.
[24] Ibid. 172.
[25] 'Political Education', in *Rationalism in Politics*, p. 136.

displays great attachment to any *particular* practices. He calls not for the state to preserve specific institutions but for the maintenance of the rule of law. Here we may distinguish between two types of conservatism: 'abstract conservatism' and 'substantive conservatism'. (In some respects this labelling parallels Miller's distinction between 'sceptical' and 'full-blooded' conservatism.[26]) Oakeshott would be an example of an abstract conservative while Roger Scruton[27] would come under the description of a substantive conservative. The difference between the two is that they uphold very different things. An abstract conservative like Oakeshott wants primarily to uphold a mode of human interaction which, in his view, is sustained in (not produced by) the political structure he calls 'civil association'. What is important in his vision of the state is that its virtue resides not in the *outcome* of such a mode of association but in the (moral) *character* of this form of community. In the state as 'civil association' individuals are 'indistinguishably and exclusively related in respect of the obligation to subscribe adequately to the non-instrumental conditions which authentic law imposes upon their self-chosen conduct'.[28] While this mode of association involves 'freedom' of a kind, freedom is not a consequence which gives the mode of association its worth. Nor does it have value because it brings 'order'. For Oakeshott, it is not 'order' or 'peace' or 'freedom' which is to be preserved but this mode of association itself.

This viewpoint differs from that of a conservative such as Scruton, mainly because the latter is preoccupied less with the preservation of a particular mode of association which manifests the exercise of human agency than with the preservation of the (existing) civil order which 'reflects . . . the self of man'.[29] In the substantive conservatism of Scruton, it is the actual civil order which must be preserved because it is that order which is the condition in which the individual has been nurtured and can find fulfilment. The conservative's task is to resist the loss of such a condition: 'to resist the loss of ideology'.[30] Seeing that in the modern world man has

[26] D. Miller, *Philosophy and Ideology in Hume's Political Thought* (Oxford, 1981), 204–5.

[27] See his *The Meaning of Conservatism*, 2nd edn. (London, 1984).

[28] Oakeshott, 'The Rule of Law', in *On History and Other Essays* (London, 1984), 119–64, at p. 160.

[29] *The Meaning of Conservatism*, p. 120.

[30] Ibid. 141.

been denuded of the dogmas of received religion and stands in a condition in which 'social continuity' is too fragile to hold him to values which make him a social (human) being, the conservative must defend and sustain the ideology of the order to which the individual is so tenuously attached. The ultimate ideal of the conservative is that of 'legitimate establishment', which commands the allegiance of its subjects through the power of the state. In such an order 'the contrasting conditions of society can achieve their ideological gratification in the condition of subjecthood without recourse to lawless self-determination'.[31]

None of this is to suggest that freedom is held in low regard; rather, it is to say that the order which sustains individuals through their attachments and (uncontracted) obligations to it, is the pre-condition of their autonomy.[32] The maintenance of establishment is vital because without it civil society will remain 'always on the brink of fragmentation'.[33] The conservative, recognizing the magnitude of the threat this poses to man, will not hesitate 'to propose or defend a system which frustrates or diverts even the most innocent of human choices, if he sees those choices in conflict with the order that breeds fulfilment'.[34]

This view contrasts clearly with that of Oakeshott for whom it is that mode of association characterized by relations of choice that requires preservation. While he agrees that the self as a 'substantive personality' is the outcome of an education, a cultivated product whose quality of character is a difficult achievement,[35] he also argues that the autonomy of the self requires that it continually 'disclose[] and enact[] itself in response to contingent situations'.[36] It is only if it may continually engage in acts of choice that the self can exercise its autonomy and remain autonomous: in action it 'both acquires and confirms its autonomy'.[37] Nowhere does Oakeshott suggest that choices are unconditioned and, like Hayek, he claims that autonomy 'does not require indifference to moral or prudential practices or aversion from any but self-made rules'.[38]

---

[31] Ibid. 184.

[32] Ibid. 120.

[33] Ibid. 184.

[34] Ibid. 120.

[35] Oakeshott, *On Human Conduct* (Oxford, 1975), 236.

[36] Ibid. 237.

[37] Ibid.

[38] Ibid. Recall, however, that, for Hayek, moral rules do not invade our freedom only in so far as they are not the arbitrary commands of others, i.e. if they are rules we *would* give to ourselves. See ch. 4 above.

Nor does he claim that conditions which govern the nature of that autonomy ('the conditions which specify the arts of agency'[39]) are unimportant. What he emphasizes, in contrast to Scruton, is that the autonomy of the self and the independence of its conduct requires that the form of human association 'shall be in terms of continuous choices to be associated which reflect the self understanding of the persons concerned'.[40]

If it is right to regard conservatism as 'the politics of imperfection', as an outlook for which the upshot of men's intellectual and moral frailty is that they should not conduct their political affairs in accordance with the abstract projections of individual thinkers, but should let themselves be guided or restrained by customary, established laws and institutions,[41] then both Oakeshott and Scruton are undoubtedly conservatives. Yet they differ inasmuch as Oakeshott's view of the nature of human conduct leads him to confine the activities of the state to the sustaining of general rules which make it possible for people to act as they choose without colliding with one another. And in this respect he is inclined, unlike Scruton, to conserve a tradition of behaviour that no longer exists since, as Quinton observes, 'for more than a century our tradition of politics has embraced far more than the maintenance of rules of conduct to prevent collisions between freely acting agents'.[42] The difference between this abstract conservative stance and the more substantive conservatism of Scruton is illustrated by the latter's acceptance of the welfare state, not as a corruption of traditional behaviour, but as a 'social and political necessity' which, furthermore, cannot be challenged without violating 'what has become a hereditary right' of each citizen.[43] The state, for Scruton, must go beyond the basic functions of preserving a mode of conduct through the rule of law to ensure that poverty and indigence do not breed resentment which might threaten the moral stability of the social order. Its only constraint is that it may not entangle the idea of public welfare in the 'egalitarian crusades' which manifest the rationalist outlook the conservative rejects.[44]

[39] Oakeshott, *On Human Conduct*, p. 237.
[40] Ibid.
[41] See A. Quinton, *The Politics of Imperfection: the Religious and Secular Traditions of Conservative Thought in England from Hooker to Oakeshott* (London, 1978), 13.
[42] Ibid. 96.
[43] Scruton, *The Meaning of Conservatism*, p. 183.
[44] Ibid. 184.

If Hayek is any sort of conservative, he is, like Oakeshott, an abstract one. The kind of order he seeks to preserve is, as we have noted, an 'abstract order'. This emerges most plainly in his discussion of the role of the judge in a liberal order (*RO* 94–122). While the judge is committed to maintaining 'an ongoing order of action', he is not obliged to preserve any status quo in the relations among particular individuals. Unlike Scruton, Hayek does not concede that there may be a place for social hierarchy or 'privilege' in the social order and his account of the role of the judge reinforces this view. (Note, however, that Scruton does *not* contend that privilege and class status are considerations which should affect *judicial* conduct.[45]) The judge's concern is 'only with the abstract relations which must be preserved while the particulars change' (*RO* 120). Hayek's defence of this view mirrors Oakeshott's account of politics as the 'pursuit of intimations' for, just as Oakeshott argues that politics involves the exploration from within of a tradition of conduct, so Hayek contends that the judge, in trying to perform his tasks, 'will always have to move in a given cosmos of rules which he must accept' (*RO* 101).[46] Echoing Oakeshott's thought that rules of conduct should do no more than prevent collisions among free agents, he charges the judge with the task 'of improving a given order of actions by laying down a rule that would prevent the recurrence of such conflicts as have occurred' (*RO* 101).

There is further evidence that the conservatism of Hayek's

---

[45] For Scruton, class distinctions may serve a purpose in reducing the likelihood of social fragmentation. The purpose of 'establishment' is to prevent fragmentation and for this it requires authority. How can it acquire authority, he asks, 'unless men are prepared to recognize—in this or that individual, in this or that office—a vested authority by which they are constrained?' And is it not plausible to suggest, he adds, 'that if this habit of deference arises . . . it is better that it should find the world already provided with *objective signs of authority*, in the form of office, position, and established right? And how, if that is so, can one either prevent or bewail the formation of social classes, in which the unequal distribution of power becomes ratified by an unequal distribution of authority?' See *The Meaning of Conservatism*, p. 180 (my italics). This is a position Hayek attacks when he argues that 'While the conservative inclines to defend particular established hierarchy and wishes authority to protect the status quo of those whom he values, the liberal feels that no respect for established values can justify the resort to privilege or monopoly or any other coercive power of the state in order to shelter such people against the forces of economic change' (*CL* 402–3).

[46] See also *RO* 86: 'The chief concern of a common law judge must be the expectations which the parties in a transaction would have reasonably formed on the basis of the general practices that the ongoing order of actions rests on.'

outlook is closer to Oakeshott's abstract conservatism. In his essay 'Why I Am Not a Conservative', Hayek's criticisms are directed largely at those who defend the idea of privilege and are more concerned with who should govern than with the scope of government (*CL* 403). Only to the extent that conservatives understand the nature of social institutions as spontaneous growths (*CL* 400) and are distrustful of 'reason' (*CL* 406) does he see he has much in common with them. He also follows Oakeshott when he notes that the conservatism he rejects is led by its distrust of reason to assert the 'authority of supernatural sources of knowledge' while he, as a liberal, is led to a position of *scepticism* and tolerance (*CL* 406–7).[47] The abstract conservative is, perhaps, fundamentally a sceptic.

Yet, in spite of the evidence pointing to such an interpretation, can we rightly regard Hayek as a conservative? While the conservative reading of his political theory appears not only defensible as interpretation but also to lend a certain coherence to his thought, this view, I shall now argue, is inadequate both as interpretation and as a way of presenting a consistent foundation for his political philosophy.

Hayek's own reasons, outlined in *The Constitution of Liberty*, for rejecting conservatism are of less significance than might be assumed. It is not his charge that the conservative fears change or progress (*CL* 400), lacks concern about the scope of authority (*CL* 401), is hostile to democracy (*CL* 403), endorses privilege and established hierarchy (*CL* 402–3), or tends to claim the authority of supernatural forces (*CL* 406) that tells against the interpretation of Hayek as a conservative. None of these views goes to the heart of the conservative doctrine. He is not, fundamentally, a conservative because there remains in his theory a rationalistic element which conservatism rejects. The character of the conservative objection to the rationalist nature of his philosophy is captured most neatly in Oakeshott's swift dismissal of Hayek in 'Rationalism in Politics': 'This is, perhaps, the main significance of Hayek's *Road to Serfdom*—not the cogency of his doctrine, but the fact that it is a doctrine. A plan to resist all planning may be better than its opposite, but it belongs to the same style of politics.'[48] Oakeshott,

---

[47] Oakeshott describes himself as a sceptic in 'Political Education', in *Rationalism in Politics*, p. 111.
[48] 'Rationalism in Politics', p. 21.

as a conservative, rejects not only the theory of progress (whether as historical explanation or guide to political activity) but also the idea of using general principles to direct political conduct. Only in a society 'deeply infected with Rationalism' will the 'traditional resources of resistance to the tyranny of Rationalism' be converted into *principles* of resistance—into a self-conscious ideology.[49] In this regard Hayek is unquestionably a rationalist, and this element in his outlook leads him to reject conservatism as simply a 'useful practical maxim', but an inadequate political philosophy because it does not provide 'any guiding principles which can influence long-range developments' (*CL* 411).

In *The Constitution of Liberty* Hayek argued that the 'decisive objection to any conservatism' was that it is unable to offer an alternative to the direction in which society is moving (*CL* 398). Its fate was to be dragged along a path not of its own choosing, and Hayek, as a liberal, considered it important to ask, not only 'how fast or how far we should move, but where we should move' (*CL* 398). Unlike the conservative, he wishes not merely to understand how society functions as a spontaneous order, but also how these spontaneous ordering processes might be utilized. His criticisms of rationalism and rationalists are thus directed less at liberals wishing to 'improve' the functioning of society than those who do not see limits to the extent to which society can be guided by reason.

Now these views expressed in *The Constitution of Liberty* are, in some respects, less important for an understanding of why Hayek is not a conservative, particularly since his ideas have developed in other directions in more recent works. Most importantly, his writings on social evolution argue strongly that human progress *cannot* be guided. In the Epilogue to *Law, Legislation and Liberty* he argues that 'to pretend to know the desirable direction of progress seems to me to be the extreme of hubris' (*EP* 169). Yet this does not make him a conservative, for he clearly retains an emphasis on the importance of progress. His defence of the free market rests on the claim that, through its operation, 'the new which is better has a chance to emerge' (*EP* 169). If we can properly distinguish an 'earlier' from a 'later' Hayek, the later Hayek is clearly less confident about how much we can harness the

---

[49] Ibid. 21–2.

spontaneous ordering forces of society than was the Hayek of *The Road to Serfdom*. There he had written:

The fundamental principle that in the ordering of our affairs we should make as much use as possible of the ordering forces of society, and resort as little as possible to coercion, is capable of an infinite variety of applications. There is, in particular, all the difference in the world between deliberately creating a system within which competition will work as beneficially as possible, and passively accepting institutions as they are. Probably nothing has done so much to harm the liberal cause as the wooden insistence of some liberals on certain rough rules of thumb, above all the principles of *laissez-faire* (RS 13).

The later Hayek, paradoxically, looks both more of an advocate of *laissez-faire* and less of a liberal. While earlier he had written of 'using' the spontaneous forces of society, a recent essay emphasizes the importance of '*relying* on the spontaneous order of society' (*KES* 44, my italics). Even when he suggests that we can try to 'create . . . conditions favourable' to progress, he notes that all we can do then is 'hope for the best' (*EP* 169).

In spite of all this he is not a conservative because of the importance he places on continuing 'progress' and on the deliberate development of principles by which to create conditions which will enhance the prospects of individuals adapting to the changes progress brings. The later Hayek is more sensitive to the limitations of reason and so appears more conservative in the concessions he makes to the importance of tradition in guiding individual conduct. Yet he remains, to the end, interested primarily in how this understanding should guide our attitude to our institutions *with a view to improving* them. The difference between the earlier and the later Hayek, in this respect, is that his earlier writings suggested specific goals could be reached by 'planning for competition' while his later writings suggest the goals he now has in mind are simply individual adaptation to the environment and, ultimately, human survival.

Hayek's rationalistic concern to *improve* social institutions distinguishes him from conservatives such as Oakeshott and Scruton. Unlike Oakeshott, he is not concerned to preserve any particular mode of association as it might be embodied in a tradition of conduct. Nor is he worried by the problems raised by Scruton who is troubled by the dangers of social fragmentation through the (too sudden) disappearance of traditions of behaviour. His concern is, rather, how social institutions might be arranged to ensure human well-being. What is distinctive in this attitude is the view that there are limitations to the extent to which we can 'arrange' institutions to secure particular ends. Any attempt to effect such arrangements must recognize, first, that the nature of society as a spontaneous order reduces the possibility of securing (distributive) outcomes; secondly, that the nature of mind and its relations to society limits the extent to which principles guiding human conduct (including moral principles) can be articulated; and, thirdly, that both these factors counsel against dismissing or seeking to reconstruct traditional modes of behaviour or morality since such traditions embody unarticulated knowledge essential to human survival.

What remains disturbingly unclear in all this, however, is the relationship between the conservative elements in Hayek, which deny the power of reason successfully to reconstruct human institutions and reject the possibility of rationally justifying them, and the more rationalist Hayek who regards traditions in a more instrumental manner. On the one hand, Hayek seems to stand a long way away from the method of Rawls's theory and yet, at the same time, both share a belief that *principles* of human conduct are important and that they ought to be made explicit by political philosophy. This latter concern is most apparent in Hayek's constitutional proposals, which he puts forward not because he thinks his model constitution might be successfully implemented anywhere, but because it would make clear what kinds of general principles he thinks ought to be defended and what kinds of institutions might secure them (*POFP* 107).

At the most abstract philosophical level, what is unclear in Hayek is the relation between freedom and reason. An antinomy between freedom and reason appears in moral philosophy inasmuch as two positions seem incompatible: first, that we are *free* to form opinions about moral questions; and secondly, that answering moral questions is a rational activity. That there exists an antinomy between these two positions is suggested by the consideration that the rationality requirement renders us unfree to form whatever moral opinions we may choose. The reconciliation of these two positions is regarded by many as the task of moral philosophy.[50] Rawls, as we have seen, seeks to effect this reconciliation through

---

[50] See Rawls, *TJ* 516; R. M. Hare, *Freedom and Reason* (Oxford, 1980), 3. But see also C. C. W. Taylor, 'Critical Notice of R. M. Hare, *Freedom and Reason*', *Mind*, 74 (1965), 280–98, esp. pp. 280–1.

the contractarian device of the Original Position which helps to articulate the moral judgements we can form consistently with our nature as free and rational beings. We act freely and rationally when we act according to moral principles which we would have chosen acting as self-interested rational agents in fair or reasonable circumstances. Even if moral principles were inculcated in us through our moral education we remain free, for they are principles which we would choose and whose justification we could set out for ourselves.

Now there is one aspect of Hayek which adopts a very similar solution to the antinomy between freedom and reason. This is the contractarian Hayek who endorses the same Kantian argument that Rawls does: that we are free when we act according to laws which we would give to ourselves. As we have noted, however, the Kantian arguments comprise only a part of Hayek's moral theory; moreover, his conservative hostility to 'reason' seems incompatible with this contractarian approach. We thus see him taking two seemingly contradictory stances.

The first, conservative, anti-rationalist Hayek holds that 'Ethics is not a matter of choice' (*EP* 167) since our morals are not (and cannot be) the product of design but are the result of a natural selection of traditions. This selection 'is not a rational process' but a process which creates reason (*EP* 166). The most we can do, argues this Hayek, is to modify the system of rules 'by seeking to reconcile its internal conflicts or its conflicts with our emotions' (*EP* 167). On such a view alone there is, ultimately, no rational justification we might offer to someone who asks why he ought to act in a particular, moral way. (Thus a conservative like Scruton is led to argue that the impossibility of such an ultimate rational justification requires that, at some point, the abstract, universal 'ought' of liberal theory give way to the 'concrete immediate ought' of family attachments: 'the "ought" of piety which recognizes the unquestionable rightness of local, transitory and historically conditioned social bonds'. Such an 'ought', he argues, recognizes neither equality nor freedom, but only 'the absolute claim of the locally given'.[51]) For this Hayek we are not able to set out for ourselves any rational justification for allegiance to particular moral rules.

[51] Scruton, *The Meaning of Conservatism*, p. 202.

The second, rationalist, Hayek, however, even while maintaining that morality is the product of evolution, does seek to present rational justifications for adhering to what he calls 'traditional morality'. Despite his claim that the mind is unable to distance itself sufficiently from the workings of society to judge its operation, he thinks his theory of spontaneous order has sufficiently explained society's workings to allow him to prescribe certain (traditional) forms of conduct. If this is so, then Hayek can and does present a rational answer, whatever its adequacy, to someone who asks why he ought to act in a particular way. The first Hayek seems to think that no morality is *rationally* justifiable, implying that we are free to do as we please unimpeded by the demands of reason. The second Hayek implies that there are rational considerations which constrain our moral actions and, so, that both freedom and reason can be characterized in a consistent and compatible way.

The question for us is, if Hayek is not a conservative who denies the possibility of rational justification but thinks that the moral views he holds can be justified in such a way as to resolve the antinomy between freedom and reason, what kind of moral theory does underlie his political theory? And can this moral theory also reconcile his conservative anti-rationalism with his rationalist concern to defend principles which would secure the conditions of human progress? We have already rejected the contractarian aspect of Hayek's moral theory as the foundation of his political theory; and our investigation of the anti-rationalist strain in his thought suggests that a rationalistic contractarianism cannot underpin his conservative, anti-rationalist arguments. So we turn now to utilitarianism to see if it might yield a moral theory to lend coherence to the various claims of Hayek's political philosophy.

4. HAYEK AS A UTILITARIAN

As we found in Chapter 2, Hayek rejects both act- and rule-utilitarianism as variants of constructivism which are unable either to account for the existence of rules of conduct or to guide individuals in their practical deliberations about right action. Indeed, he repudiates utilitarianism as a philosophical outlook which is at odds with the epistemological claims at the heart of his political theory. The utilitarian viewpoint, for him, is a profoundly rationalistic one.

Yet we must consider the possibility that his political theory is best characterized as utilitarian because this may provide the only coherent way of reconciling the rationalist and anti-rationalist elements we have identified in his thought. Our question must then be: is there a variant of utilitarianism which will serve to render consistent the Kantian and conservative arguments in Hayek's political philosophy by providing a plausible normative theory to ground the prescriptions he thinks flow from his social theory? This will lead us to consider Gray's claim that Hayek's theory is best understood as a species of indirect utilitarianism.[52]

But first, what precisely is utilitarianism and, more specifically, indirect utilitarianism? Following Sen and Williams, we might define utilitarianism as the coincidence of two different kinds of theory: *welfarism*, which is a theory of the correct way to assess states of affairs claiming that such states have value according to the standards of welfare or preference satisfaction which obtain; and *consequentialism*, which is a theory of correct action claiming that 'actions are to be chosen on the basis of the states of affairs which are their consequences'.[53] Utilitarianism, because it recommends a choice of actions on the basis of consequences, and an assessment of consequences in terms of welfare, is thus best identified as a variant of welfarist consequentialism,[54] and notably one which emphasizes the need to *maximize* welfare. Many utilitarians, however, recognize that the promotion of welfare may be best secured under arrangements in which welfarist considerations are *not* paramount and do *not* guide the choice of actions. The product of this concession is *indirect utilitarianism*: a moral theory which, in conceding that welfare may be more effectively promoted if not directly pursued, sees that the utilitarian criterion may well justify any of a variety of social arrangements—including highly traditionalist systems of morality. Both Sidgwick and J. S. Mill[55] acknowledged this in the nineteenth century, and Hare has defended a variant of indirect utilitarianism in the twentieth.[56]

[52] Gray, *Hayek on Liberty*, pp. 59–61.
[53] A. K. Sen and B. Williams, 'Introduction: Utilitarianism and Beyond', in Sen and Williams (eds.), *Utilitarianism and Beyond*, 1–22, at pp. 3–4.
[54] Ibid. 4.
[55] See J. N. Gray, *Mill on Liberty: A Defence* (London, 1983), ch. 2. See also H. Sidgwick, *The Methods of Ethics*, 7th edn. (Indianapolis, 1981), esp. Part IV, chs. 4 and 5.
[56] See Hare's *Moral Thinking: Its Levels, Method and Point* (Oxford, 1984);

What, then, are the reasons for seeing Hayek as an indirect utilitarian? First, many of his arguments for liberty seem to be utilitarian ones. Our faith in freedom, he notes in *The Constitution of Liberty*, rests on 'the belief that it will, on balance, release more forces for the good than for the bad' (*CL* 31). The liberal social order, whose rules of justice preserve this freedom, is thus defended as the order in which the well-being of the poorest is most likely to rise (*CL* 44). And redistributive intervention is criticized as an ineffective method of reducing inequality and abolishing poverty (*CL* 48). Thus many of Hayek's arguments against socialism seek to show that socialist *aims* are incompatible with socialist *methods*: 'some of the aims of the welfare state can be realized without detriment to individual liberty, though not necessarily by the methods which seem the most obvious' (*CL* 259). Inasmuch as he advocates liberty as a means of increasing (maximizing) welfare he appears to be a utilitarian.

The second reason for seeing Hayek as a utilitarian is that he believes that, while ethical values are not ultimately amenable to scientific investigation, many disputes between socialists and non-socialists can be settled without references to values.[57] For Hayek, the important question is one of how the values shared by most people—at least in the West—may be secured. The implication here is that the dispute he is engaged in is not one about ends but about means to those ends which are, mainly, material prosperity and a measure of personal freedom. Thus he accuses socialists not of immoral intent but of intellectural error—error which stems less from a faulty *moral theory* than from a faulty *political economy*. (Although, of course, this *alone* would not make Hayek a utilitarian.)

Hayek appears to hold a utilitarian political theory, thirdly, because of the importance he places on the instrumental value of rules as constraints which make individual behaviour more predictable. Rules of justice are thus defended, not because they lead to the fulfilment of *legitimate* expectations, but because, by

---

'Ethical Theory and Utilitarianism', in Sen and Williams (eds.), *Utilitarianism and Beyond*, 23–38.

[57] See *RO* 6; see also N. Barry, *Hayek's Social and Economic Philosophy* (London, 1979), 198–202.

conferring legitimacy on particular actions, they make possible a greater *coincidence* of expectations.

Fourthly, he invites classification as a utilitarian because he sees justice as the condition of order. Unlike Kant, he does not think that the moral laws which command justice can be uncovered purely by reason. The purpose of rules of justice for Hayek is to bring order into human affairs and, so, to sustain the conditions necessary for the advance of human endeavour. Thus John Gray, in arguing that, for Hayek, 'a framework of justice is an indispensable condition of the successful achievement of general welfare', is led to compare him with Hume, 'who always saw clearly that the utility of the rules of justice depended on their not being liable to abridgement for the sake of an apparent gain in welfare'.[58] This justification of liberal justice is then given more precise content by a probabilistic and preference-based criterion of utility: a system of rules is useful if it maximizes the chances of any individual chosen at random to achieve his unknown purposes (*S* 173).

Finally, Hayek's utilitarianism seems evident in his proposed measure of the success of a social system: the number of people it is able to sustain. His theory of human evolution as the 'natural selection' of practices which enhance the group's survival prospects leads him to argue that the institutions of justice and property have value because, by making possible the utilization of widely dispersed knowledge, they facilitate increased productivity—which allows populations to increase (*KES* 49).

Yet Hayek is not, in the end, a utilitarian, and any attempt to impose an indirect utilitarian structure upon his political theory must fail. While it cannot be denied that he often invokes utilitarian arguments, this is not sufficient to make his a utilitarian political theory. Before considering the more general arguments against the utilitarian interpretation of Hayek, it is worth looking carefully at the nature of his 'utilitarian' defence of the liberal order and 'traditional morality' as best able to sustain the largest populations.

This argument emerges in the course of Hayek's attempt to defend three 'institutions': private property, 'honesty', and the family. The value of these institutions, in his view, is evident in the fact that those groups which adopted traditions of behaviour embracing the family and private property increased more rapidly

---

[58] Gray, *Hayek on Liberty*, p. 60.

in number than others (*KES* 48). (This very large claim is, incidentally, never substantiated!) While he emphasizes that these institutions facilitate the growth of populations, he does not mean to imply that only the *numbers* of individuals sustained by these institutions are important. If that were his contention then clearly many heavily populated non-liberal orders he rejects (such as the Soviet Union) may well prove to be preferable to the liberal order if they remain stable for long periods of time. (Indeed, all maximizing strategies face the problem of specifying the time period over which success is to be measured.) Moreover, this argument would suggest that an outcome in which larger numbers were sustained at very low standards of living was morally superior to one in which smaller numbers survived at higher standards. Such a view has been thoroughly criticized by Derek Parfit.[59] What Hayek suggests, however, is that the benefits conferred by private property include rising living standards as well as larger populations. As a result of population increase the division of labour is extended, productivity is raised, and the capacity to sustain large numbers is increased (*KES* 49–50).[60]

Hayek further qualifies his claims by arguing that population increase is self-regulating to the extent that growth takes place not in 'highly advanced' market economies (where people no longer use greater wealth to produce larger families) but in economies on the periphery of market society. Thus as more and more regions are absorbed into the market economy, the periphery—and so the rate of population growth—will shrink (*KES* 50). Overpopulation is undesirable, but it is also unlikely.

These qualifications to the most utilitarian of his defences of the market order suggest that it is wrong to say that 'Hayek proposes as a *measure* of utility a calculus of lives—that is, a social system is presumed to generate greater utility if it can support a greater population'.[61] He does not contend either that numbers are all that matter or that greater numbers are valuable because they generate more utility—whether the criterion of utility is hedonistic or preference based. Indeed, he offers no utilitarian criterion by which to evaluate social systems. While the argument that the market

---

[59] D. Parfit, *Reasons and Persons* (Oxford, 1986), ch. 17.
[60] Hayek draws on the work of Julian Simons, *The Ultimate Resource* (Oxford, 1981), to support his case.
[61] Gray, *Hayek on Liberty*, p. 109.

order, in which private property and the family predominate, secures the most rapid increase in mankind does recommend this as an important virtue of market societies, it does *not* suggest that the morally most desirable system is one which maximizes human numbers or human satisfactions. Hayek is not concerned to secure the 'greatest happiness of the greatest number'.

This is important because it indicates that Hayek's arguments are consequentialist but not utilitarian, for they do not point to any welfarist end-state to be achieved. Rather, his argument for the liberal order is that it is a dynamic order governed by mechanisms regulating change. It is an order characterized by 'progress'—by a process of formation and modification of human intellect, a process of adaptation and learning in which desires and values continually change (see ch. 4, sect. 2). Certainly, one of the indicators that society is in a condition of progress is that it is better able to sustain more lives. In the liberal order this is effected by those institutions (such as private property) which enable individuals and groups better to co-ordinate their actions by calculating to secure their expectations. And this 'economic calculus', he argues, is 'a calculus of life: it guides us to do the sorts of things that secure the most rapid increase in mankind' (*KES* 50). But this condition is valued simply for its own sake and not for any further reason or value which is maximized.

In justifying the liberal order as the order of progress, Hayek thus takes a very strongly anti-rationalist stance. And if utilitarianism, in 'promising to resolve all moral issues by relying on one uniform ultimate criterion', appears to be 'the "rational" moral theory *par excellence*',[62] then here is another reason why Hayek cannot be seen as a utilitarian. In his view, progress brings with it changes not only in the form of human achievement but also in human aims and wishes—which are equally subject to that process. Thus it is questionable whether new states of affairs created by progress can properly be regarded as 'better' in any sense. 'Progress in the sense of the cumulative growth of knowledge and power over nature is a term that says little about whether the new state will give us more satisfaction than the old' (*CL* 41). In denying the possibility of comparison among states of affairs, Hayek, in effect, advances two interrelated claims which are incompatible with the utilitarian

[62] Sen and Williams, 'Introduction', *Utilitarianism and Beyond*, p. 16.

outlook. First, he denies the possibility of even a partial or 'incomplete' ordering or ranking of states of affairs. Utilitarian moral theories, even when they concede the difficulty of ranking states of affairs according to any single uniform criterion, insist that, ultimately, what have to be morally evaluated are states of affairs. Secondly, in denying the possibility of comparative evaluation, Hayek rejects the idea that rationality can guide our assessment of different end-states. Reason cannot provide us with the criteria by which to compare states of affairs; it is merely a capacity which is produced or created (and modified) by progress. Thus reason can identify inconsistencies among rules within a situation (or tradition of behaviour) but cannot stand outside the evolutionary process to evaluate the different states of affairs that rational action might lead to.

This objection goes to the heart of the utilitarian doctrine as it is expressed, most notably, in the theory of the impartial spectator. According to this theory, something, say a social system, is right 'when an ideally rational and impartial spectator would approve of it from a general point of view should he possess all the relevant knowledge of the circumstances. A rightly ordered society is one meeting the approval of such an ideal observer.'[63] Hayek's argument denies that such a rational and impartial spectator can possess the knowledge to evaluate a social system. Even if such an observer can be imagined, we would have to know what he would know if we were to choose as he would choose among social systems. This is why Hayek accuses 'constructivist rationalists' of basing their arguments 'on the fiction that all the relevant facts are known to some one mind, and that it is possible to construct from this knowledge of the particulars a desirable social order' (*RO* 14). Utilitarianism is guilty of this. His defence of the liberal order is based not on the claim that its rules will produce end-states we would choose if we knew what alternatives were available, but on the contention that the rules of the liberal order enable us to adapt to a changing environment which is always creating states of affairs which we can never wholly anticipate, let alone choose.

Hayek's argument thus appears to be, like Hume's, a consequentialist argument but not a utilitarian one.[64] But here an important

---

[63] I borrow this characterization from Rawls, *TJ* 184.
[64] John Gray consistently but incorrectly identifies Hume as an indirect

difficulty emerges. How can Hayek be seen as a consequentialist if he denies the possibility of comparing and choosing among states of affairs? This creates a problem for his theory because it would seem that it can be given no clear foundation. If there can be no comparative evaluation of alternative states of affairs, it is difficult to show how a liberal order (which facilitates adaptation to a changing environment) can be regarded as superior or preferable to that condition in which a non-liberal order sustains an impoverished and diminishing population. Unless, the liberal order is justified on the non-consequentialist grounds that the rules of such an order are morally right, with rightness identified through some non-consequentialist moral theory. Yet Hayek's is certainly not a deontological ethic which is ready to posit rights or duties or virtues which are intrinsically obligatory or admirable; so such a non-consequentialist justification of the liberal order is *not* open to him.

These considerations suggest that there is no prospect of indirect utilitarianism rendering consistent and coherent the different arguments invoked in Hayek's political writings. The most important reason why is that utilitarianism, as a rationalistic ethical outlook, cannot reconcile the anti-rationalist elements in his thought with the rationalist—not without changing the character of the anti-rationalist contentions which are central to his thought. The conflict in Hayek's theory is one between a view, on the one hand, that if man is to survive, let alone flourish, he must embrace a system of rules of conduct which enable him to adapt to changing circumstances and so find his way in the world, and a view, on the other hand, that human reason is unable to guide man in the search for such principles, or provide any justification for them, since man is typically led to accept such traditions of behaviour or systems of rules of conduct, not by understanding but by superstitions and myths which have conquered his emotions (*CRS* 162). For Hayek to become a utilitarian of any sort he would have to deny the second view and concede that reason, far from being the mere product of our cultural traditions, is able to evaluate, and justify allegiance to, those traditions and the principles of conduct they enjoin. He would have to become a more Popperian rationalist.

Now here Hayek might object that this is precisely the kind of

utilitarian. See *Hayek on Liberty*, p. 59; *Mill on Liberty*, p. 111. On why Hume is not a utilitarian, see ch. 1 above, and also A. Botwinick, *Ethics, Politics and Epistemology: A Study in the Unity of Hume's Thought* (Lanham, 1980), 119–38.

rationalist he is: an 'evolutionary' or 'critical' rationalist rather than a 'constructivist' or 'naïve' one. In this respect, he would argue, he has clearly recognized that 'one of the tasks of reason is to decide how far it is to extend its control or how far it ought to rely on other forces which it cannot really control' (*RO* 29).

The problem is that he refuses to provide criteria by which reason may decide the proper scope of its control. Indeed, for the anti-rationalist Hayek, if there is one thing that reason *cannot* do it is to identify the scope of its own powers. 'Cultural selection' is not a rational process but one which 'creates reason'; it is not possible for reason to identify the scope of its powers; for those very powers are continually modified by forces beyond its control. Hayek's social theory in fact locates rationality so securely in the social structure of rules and practices that it is hard to see how he could suggest that 'reason' could identify its limits. Mind itself, in this view, is an 'adaptation to the natural and social surroundings in which man lives and ... has developed in constant interaction with the institutions which determine the structure of society' (*RO* 17). It is an order which can exist 'only as part of another independently existing distinct structure or order': it is 'embedded in a traditional impersonal structure of learnt rules, and its capacity to order experience is an acquired replica of cultural patterns which every individual finds given' (*EP* 157). If individual reason is thus embedded in a social structure of rules, if it is, at bottom, capable of little more than classifying and recalling the patterns of experience it encounters, it is hard to see how it might decide how far it is to extend its control or rely on forces it cannot control. Reason, on such a view, does not possess the capacity to initiate such a decision.

Regarding Hayek as a utilitarian of any sort is thus an implausible undertaking because no form of consequentialism is compatible with the dominant anti-rationalist strand of his thought. Furthermore, the incompatibility highlights an important weakness in utilitarianism as a moral theory: that, in emphasizing preference satisfaction as the criterion which should guide ethical reflection and choice, it ignores the process of preference formation and misses the important question of what kinds of preferences are worth having. If preferences are, in part, conditioned by the kind of life led by, and the options available to, the agent, then preference satisfaction cannot be the criterion to guide reflection on the general (ethical) question of what kinds of life are worth living, or on the more specific question (of distributive justice) of what options ought to be available. Considerations such as these, which have led Jon Elster to raise fundamental objections against end-state principles in ethical theory,[65] clearly lie behind Hayek's view that 'progress' is valued not because it brings happiness or satisfaction but because it transforms and extends human intelligence (*CL* 41) and creates greater awareness of the feelings and emotions identified in the expansion of human needs and wants (*S* 314).

Hayek's case for the liberal order thus rests on non-utilitarian arguments in so far as he rejects end-state principles in ethics and insists that liberal institutions do not simply enable individuals to satisfy their preferences but best enable them to discover their wants and needs (or preferences in the broadest sense) as human beings. (If there is any single value implicit in *these* arguments it is perhaps closer to a Millian 'authenticity'[66] than to any form of preference satisfaction.) And here he emphasizes, as we saw in Chapter 3, that discovery is the achievement not of individual reason, but of the *rational* impersonal process of human interaction (*IEO* 15). Individual reason, in so far as it even exists (*IEO* 15), consists simply in the capacity to recognize and classify patterns or regularities in the environment.

Springing from this anti-rationalist perspective, however, is the danger that utilitarianism will not be the only moral theory to be ruled out. It may be the outstandingly rationalist moral theory in positing a single criterion to guide moral judgement, but it is not the only theory which values rationality in moral evaluation. Contractarian theories, for example, are equally concerned to show how moral judgements should be constrained by the demands of rationality. If Hayek's anti-rationalism rules out the 'constructivist rationalism' of utilitarianism, and the equally constructivist approach of contractarian moral theory, it is difficult to see what kind of non-deontological moral theory can be called upon to sustain the normative claims which flow from his social theory. It would seem,

---

[65] Elster, 'Sour Grapes—Utilitarianism and the Genesis of Wants', in Sen and Williams (eds.), *Utilitarianism and Beyond*, 219–38, esp. sect. 3 and at p. 238.

[66] See C. L. Ten's argument that 'Mill's plea for individuality cannot usefully be described as utilitarian', *Mill on Liberty* (Oxford, 1980), p. 8 and ch. 5. But see Gray, *Mill on Liberty*, ch. 4, sect. 2.

then, that Hayek's political philosophy either invokes a number of different, and incompatible, moral theories to defend different claims, or lacks any normative moral theory at all. We should now consider this contention and its implications for his political theory as a whole.

5. HAYEK'S MORAL THEORY

Hayek presents three kinds of argument to defend his liberal social order and the conception of justice he sees at its heart. The first is a contractarian argument which invokes Kantian considerations to deny that patterning principles of social justice can be morally justified. The second is a conservative argument which not only points to the value of established traditions but also repudiates the claim that reason can present complete justifications for the rules governing any social order. The liberal order is preferred as that order which makes the fewest demands upon individual reason, for its principles of justice aim primarily at maintaining the *abstract* order of rules rather than at the rational reconstruction of society according to principles of distributive justice. The third is a utilitarian argument drawing attention to the beneficial conse-quences of a stable regime of liberal justice: progress and material prosperity. While each of these arguments appears in Hayek's work, none, as we have seen, can clearly be held to be fundamental.

Our question must be: can these arguments be structured and reconciled under a single moral theory which would lend coherence to Hayek's politics or must they remain incompatible contentions in a political theory without clear normative foundations? The answer must be that there is no single theory of this kind. The reasons for this are essentially the same as the reasons why no form of utilitarianism or contractarianism or conservatism may be seen to provide the normative underpinnings of his political philosophy. None of these moral viewpoints can reconcile the two conflicting features of Hayek's ethical outlook: the traditionalist outlook which stems from his anti-rationalism and which, finally, casts him in the role of the sceptic in moral philosophy; and the rationalist outlook which leads him to seek to uncover the basic principles which justify, and guide the development of, the liberal order. There remains, therefore, an important and unresolvable conflict in Hayek's thought between the search for a moral justification of the principles of a liberal social order, and a moral epistemology which denies the possibility of such an undertaking.

This leads us, then, to our most fundamental, and most serious, criticism of Hayek's philosophy: that while he has developed in his writings a substantial social theory which purports to explain how particular social institutions enable man to overcome the problems which stem from his limited knowledge, he has not been able to show what kinds of normative conclusions this social theory should guide us towards. Although he has contended that 'Liberalism . . . derives from the discovery of self-generating or spontaneous order in social affairs' (S 162), he has not recognized that such a 'derivation' can only obtain in the context of a moral theory explaining why the nature of social order enjoins the establishment and maintenance of a liberal polity. Although he has presented serious objections to those who envisage the good society as one in which the distribution of benefits and burdens is effected, wholly or in part, by central authority guided by distributive principles, his alternative projections have fallen short in two important respects. First, as we have just noted, he has not shown how these considerations justify a *liberal* social order in which the rule of law prevails to uphold individual entitlements. Secondly, he has not shown how such a social theory enables us to identify the proper scope of individual entitlements—and, in the light of the political outlook he has sought to defend, it means he has not shown why these considerations justify (only) a *classical* liberal social order.

One source of this problem is the theory of spontaneous order and Hayek's exaggeration of its *scope* as an explanatory construct. There is a tendency to call anything grown and unplanned a spontaneous order. Once the idea of spontaneous order is used to explain not only economic and political processes but also the evolution of morals and rationality, the status of the notions of morality and rationality become problematic. This is so particularly because Hayek is led to reject rationality and morality as *philosophical* notions and to regard them as the subjects of *anthropology*. He seeks to explain how the growth of civilization leads individuals to act more 'rationally' but denies that individual reason can assess the civilization which nurtures it. And he attempts to show what part morals play in the preservation of society but does not consider the moral questions which prevail independently of any ethical anthropology: questions about right and wrong, justice and injustice. Ultimately, his philosophy presents an *explanation* of the role or function of rules of justice in the preservation of a social order but not a *justification* of any particular set of rules.

In this regard, Hayek cannot escape the criticism, levelled initially by Kant, against the Humean theory of justice: that, in explaining the nature of justice as an institution in the world of human experience, he has produced only an anthropology of morals rather than a moral philosophy. Now Hume, of course, recognized that his own anti-rationalist account of the nature of moral judgement could only lead to scepticism in so far as it entailed that moral conclusions could not be established by reason. And just as Hayek has argued that many social institutions are often supported by prevailing 'myths' and 'superstitions', so did Hume explicitly acknowledge that conventions and rules (of property, for example) were established and sustained by a mixture of regard for (but not calculation of) their utility and human 'imagination'. While Hume sought to bring to the analysis of politics the temper of a philosopher, he also saw that his philosophical outlook could lead only to the conclusion that there was no possibility of establishing normative claims that could be rationally demonstrated.

Indeed, Hume's politics may be regarded as an attempt to defend this conclusion, for he sought to show that it ruled out both arguments calling for radical change and arguments to demonstrate that the existing order was preferable to all others on rational grounds. This anti-rationalist perspective, while it barred him from establishing any universally valid, substantive normative conclusions in politics, was at least consistently embraced by Hume inasmuch as he sought to establish no such substantive conclusions about the desirable political order. (This is not, of course, to deny that Hume thought it possible to vindicate a moral outlook in terms of human nature and to make comparative judgements about regimes on this basis.) As a political theorist, his project was primarily negative: to deny the rationalist contentions of those whose claims threatened the British Constitution by destabilizing the delicate balance of power between the Crown and the Court and Country parties. His science of politics sought to show no more than that all parties, regardless of philosophical or religious commitment, were guided less by doctrine than by interest. Hume's

Constitution is not a *fully* liberal constitution in so far as his sceptical, anti-rationalist viewpoint disinclined him to construct one.

Although the charge is correct that his account of justice amounts only to a moral anthropology unable to establish any normative conclusions, Hume might happily admit this, for he was not concerned to do any more. He had shown why the artificial virtue of justice emerged in society and that its advantages derived from its strict maintenance, but he made no further positive claims about the nature of the desirable social order.

Yet if Hume's anti-rationalism is consistent with his 'sceptical Whiggism',[67] Hayek's anti-rationalism sits uncomfortably with his self-characterization as 'simply an unrepentant old Whig' (*CL* 409). Unlike Hume, he has tried to defend a 'distinct body of Whig principles', endorsing Acton's contention that ' "the notion of a higher law above municipal codes, with which Whiggism began, is the supreme achievement of Englishmen and their bequest to the nation" ' (and, Hayek ventures to add, 'to the world') (*CL* 409). When Hume defended various liberal viewpoints when he wrote in favour of free trade, a free press (with some reservations), and the political freedoms peculiar to England at the time, he did so without invoking any higher principles. Hayek, however, has consistently sought to establish the principles he thinks underlie the liberal case for such liberties: to present a theory of freedom, defining the justifiable scope of state action in accordance with principles limiting coercion.

The sceptical, anti-rationalist elements in Hayek's theory lead him to a perspective from which he is unable to make any normative prescriptions about the nature of the liberal order. So the prescriptions he makes are given a philosophical grounding in a rationalist moral theory: that of Kant. But this move is inadequate not only because of the flaws in Kant's moral philosophy which, as we saw in Chapter 4, resurface in Hayek's theory of liberty, coercion, and the rule of law: because it generates no substantive, but only formal, demands. It is also inadequate because it keeps at odds, within what purports to be a single philosophy, two fundamentally opposing perspectives: one which asserts the claims of freedom and the other which upholds the claims of reason.

---

[67] A term coined by Duncan Forbes. See his 'Sceptical Whiggism, Commerce, and Liberty', in A. S. Skinner and T. Wilson (eds.), *Essays on Adam Smith* (Oxford 1975), 179–201.

6
Hayek and Modern Liberalism

1. INTRODUCTION

In the subtitle of his trilogy *Law, Legislation and Liberty*, Hayek announced—or reasserted—his intention to provide 'A new statement of the liberal principles of justice and political economy'. This subtitle identifies clearly Hayek's political commitments and philosophical concerns. His political commitment is to a *liberal* ideal, and the philosophical defence of such an ideal, he thinks, requires an elaboration of its guiding *principles*. These principles, which uphold a particular view of human freedom, are, ultimately, principles of *justice*. And because justice is an institution whose purpose is to regulate human freedom in the social world, its principles must be grounded in an understanding of the nature of the social order: in an understanding of *political economy*.

At the deepest level, these concerns reveal an attempt to marry a Kantian view of justice as an institution concerned with the distribution of *freedom*, with a Humean view of justice as an institution preserving *order* among men of limited benevolence, living in a world of scarcity. In this respect, Hayek's undertaking has certain obvious affinities with Rawls's project in political philosophy. And many of the problems which beset Rawls's enterprise have proven equally troublesome for Hayek.

Having examined the main elements of Hayek's defence of a liberal political philosophy, its theoretical roots in the thought of Hume and Kant, and the difficulties it encounters as well as its strengths, our task must now be to assess this defence to ask why it does not succeed, what contribution it makes to our understanding of the questions it addresses and, by implication, why it is worthy of examination. This will afford us a standpoint from which to raise, even if not resolve, two interrelated questions about modern liberalism: first, is it a defensible ideal and, secondly, how might it be defended?

2. HAYEK'S PROJECT AND ITS ASSESSMENT

Hayek does not succeed in his attempt to provide a coherent and plausible defence of the liberal social order primarily because his thought is governed by two incompatible philosophical attitudes. The first embraces a brand of anti-rationalism that he associates with Vico (*CL* 429) and with various representatives of the Scottish Enlightenment (notably Hume) and which, as we have seen, receives its most sustained expression in his critique of 'constructivism'. It is a fundamental thesis of his philosophy that there is a strong connexion between views of reason and particular political standpoints; and the constructivist attitude to reason is, for him, securely tied to an illiberal politics. In Popper's useful terminology, Hayek ties liberalism to an 'epistemological pessimism'.[1] He sees, in the constructivist's optimism about the reason's power to guide man's evaluation of his institutions (*RO* 10) and help him 'achieve a full mastery of the concrete and thus positively master the social process' (*RO* 33), the most dangerous hubris which flourishes in the service of an illiberal ideal. The tendency of this outlook is to enjoin the rational control and direction of society in the pursuit of particular (common) ends—ends which must, in the final analysis, be *imposed* upon those who do not endorse them (*RO* 32). In so far as he sees himself as a critic of constructivism, Hayek's defence of liberalism is grounded in a hostility to rationalism which brings his thought closest to the philosophy of Hume.

As we saw in Chapter 1, Hume's distrust of those who would construct rational justifications for abstract principles defending the Revolution Settlement had its roots in a view of the role of reason in ethics which stemmed from a mitigated scepticism in philosophy and inclined him to a hostility to radicalism in politics. His own defence of what might be regarded as the liberal values of constitutionalism, liberty, the right of rebellion, property, and the rule of law, did not so much seek to uphold or justify particular moral principles as try to show what difficulties would beset any attempt to secure these values upon rational foundations, and what dangers would attend any endeavour to entrench a Constitution, which, happily, favoured liberty, in accordance with philosophical ideals. The anti-constructivist Hayek shares a great deal with

---

[1] K. Popper, *Conjectures and Refutations: The Growth of Scientific Knowledge* (London, 1976), 6.

Hume, for he is hostile to the idea of rational justification of right action. The function of reason is to identify what action we *cannot* take, rather than tell us what action we *should* take. 'Reason is merely a discipline, an insight into the limitations of the possibilities of successful action, which often will tell us what not to do' (*RO* 32). Just as Hume, mainly in his political essays, argued against the extension of public authority and the concentration of political power (in the House of Commons) by pointing to the ills that would ensue given the nature of politics and society, so Hayek, on the basis of his theory of spontaneous order, counsels against social and economic planning as inconsistent with the aims of the planners and inimical to the interests of society. Both thinkers thus defend the upholding of private property by rules of justice, which secure individual entitlements, not by offering any theoretical *foundations* for such rights, but by eliminating alternative distributive criteria. Distribution according to merit or desert or need is rejected as unworkable by their respective social theories.[2] Hayek's advance beyond Hume is to be seen in his more extensive political economy which considers more explicitly the relationship between market processes and the free society.

There are, however, as we have noted, many difficulties confronting Hayek in his guise as anti-constructivist political economist. First, the value of the distinction between the constructivist and the other forms of rationalism is highly questionable. This is not only because he never really makes clear why some thinkers are constructivists and others not. (We observed in ch. 3 that he criticizes social contract theorists such as Hobbes and Rousseau as constructivists, but not his preferred 'liberal' contractarians, Locke and Kant.) The worth of the distinction is an important issue because of the use to which Hayek wishes to put it. His claim is that those who can be identified as constructivist rationalists fail to recognize that society is not the product of conscious design but the unintended product of evolution; and are consequently driven to illiberal conclusions in political philosophy. Yet both parts of this claim are highly suspect, and the falsity of the

---

[2] Indeed, it may be that to argue for one criterion of distributive justice (say, rights) over another (say, need), *requires* the development of a social theory if, as Miller has argued, conceptual argument alone will always be inconclusive. See D. Miller, *Social Justice* (Oxford, 1979). See also C. Perelman, *The Idea of Justice and the Problem of Argument* (London, 1970).

second part does considerable damage to Hayek's critique of constructivism. The plausibility of the first part of his claim is thrown into question by his insistence that such thinkers as Hegel and Marx are constructivists while Vico, Mandeville, Hume, Ferguson, and Smith are not. There can surely be no doubt that Hegel and Marx did *not* think of society as the product of conscious design. Indeed, it is a crucial feature of their social philosophies that society is understood as the product of the historical evolution of human institutions. In this respect, some have argued that Vico is a precursor of Hegel and Marx,[3] while others have located the sources of Hegel's view of civil society as a system of interdependence in the work of Locke, Hume, Smith and, especially, Ferguson.[4] Some better explanation is therefore needed as to why Hegel and Marx are constructivists while Smith and Ferguson are not.

The more serious problem, however, is in the suggestion that there is a necessary connexion between an appreciation of the nature of mind and society as the unintended products of evolution, as spontaneous orders, and a sympathy with the liberal ideal of an 'Open Society', for this is precisely the connexion Hayek does *not* establish. Several observations suggest that there may be no such connexion.

First, a number of 'constructivists' have been far from hostile to liberalism. It was the 'constructivist rationalist' Bentham who, as Arthur Diamond points out, chastised the 'critical rationalist' Smith for failing to realize how far the invisible hand could reach, and argued against Smith's advocacy of government imposed interest rate ceilings.[5] Indeed, the English utilitarians, whom Hayek criticizes as false individualists who paved the way for socialism, generally insisted that the state's functions be limited because of human ignorance (the state cannot know what will make the individual happiest), stressed the importance of general rules, had a considerable confidence in the market economy, and a strong

---

[3] This point is made by A. M. Diamond, 'F. A. Hayek and Constructivism in Ethics', *Journal of Libertarian Studies*, 4 (1980), 353–66, at p. 357.

[4] See S. Avineri, *Hegel's Theory of the Modern State* (Cambridge, 1980), 141n.; Z. A. Pelczynski, 'The Hegelian Conception of the State', in Pelczynski (ed.), *Hegel's Political Philosophy: Problems and Perspectives* (Cambridge, 1971), 1–29, at p. 10 and n. 26.

[5] Diamond, 'Hayek and Constructivism', p. 357.

hostility to monopolies.[6] Among non-utilitarians, Rawls, a self-confessed contractarian constructivist, has offered an account of justice which is *liberal enough* to be greeted favourably by Hayek.[7]

Secondly, many have explicitly accepted that society is a spontaneous order, the product of evolution and not of human design, while insisting that its future development can, indeed should, be guided to ensure that the form this development takes is benign. This attitude has been rejected by Hayek when it has come from Hegel or from Keynes,[8] but has nonetheless been defended by J. M. Buchanan, a thinker with great sympathy with Hayek's liberalism. Buchanan, who has averred that the only principle in economics worth stressing is the principle of the spontaneous order of the market,[9] criticizes Hayek for being 'so distrustful of man's explicit attempts at reforming institutions that he accepts uncritically the evolutionary alternative'.[10] Similarly, Karl Popper has emphasized 'that *only a minority of social institutions are consciously designed while the vast majority have just "grown", as the undesigned results of human action*',[11] only to advocate a form of 'piecemeal social engineering' which recognizes this fact. Clearly, an acceptance of the notion of spontaneous order as an explanatory construct does not in any way commit one to any particular view about whether, and how far, it is legitimate to try to direct the course of social or institutional development.

Thirdly, it is quite unclear where a number of Hayek's liberal thinkers would be placed in the 'constructivist rationalist versus

---

[6] These points are made by J. W. N. Watkins, 'Philosophy', in A. Seldon (ed.), *Agenda for a Free Society: Essays on Hayek's* The Constitution of Liberty (London, 1961), 31–50, at p. 47.

[7] In the 'consolidated preface' to the one-volume edition of *Law, Legislation and Liberty* (first published 1982), p. xvii, Hayek says that Rawls and he agree on 'the essential point', and that the differences between them are 'more verbal than substantial'.

[8] See J. M. Keynes's *The End of Laissez-Faire*, where he quotes Burke to defend the view that the problem (' "one of the finest problems in legislation" ') was to determine ' "what the State ought to take upon itself to direct by the public wisdom, and what it ought to leave, with as little interference as possible, to individual action." ' From E. K. Bramstead and K. J. Melhuish (eds.), *Western Liberalism: A History in Documents from Locke to Croce* (London, 1978), 706.

[9] J. M. Buchanan, *Freedom in Constitutional Contract: Perspectives of a Political Economist* (London, 1977), 25.

[10] J. M. Buchanan, *The Limits of Liberty: Between Anarchy and Leviathan* (Chicago, 1975), 194 n. 1, and also 183 n. 3. See also R. A. Arnold, 'Hayek and Institutional Evolution', *Journal of Libertarian Studies*, 4 (1980), 341–52.

[11] K. Popper, *The Poverty of Historicism* (London, 1976), 67.

critical rationalist' distinction. Hayek never makes plain where Humboldt, Kant, Locke, J. S. Mill, and Herbert Spencer stand. Locke and Mill, as contractarian and utilitarian respectively, look clearly to be constructivists, and Kant, with his faith in reason's power to identify the moral law, is surely the constructivist rationalist *par excellence* if we accept Hayek's claim that: 'The illusion that leads constructivist rationalists regularly to an enthronement of the will consists in the belief that reason can transcend the realm of the abstract and by itself is able to determine the desirability of particular actions' (*RO* 32). If any thinker has thought it possible that reason alone should guide moral conduct, and can be accused of elevating the will to the rank of source of law (both moral and legal), it is Kant.[12] Yet Hayek has no hesitation in branding Kant a liberal, and goes so far as to say that, on the issues that are his concern in *Law, Legislation and Liberty*, 'thought seems to have made little advance since David Hume and Immanuel Kant' (*RO* 6).

If Kant does possess those liberal credentials Hayek suggests (and Rawls implies) he has, then it would seem that there is no necessary, or even strong, connexion between the constructivist's rationalism and illiberal politics. Indeed, while particular positions in epistemology and social theory may be *compatible* or *consistent* with particular political outlooks, Hayek has offered insufficient argument to show that certain epistemological doctrines *entail* particular political philosophical conclusions, or that political doctrines are only defensible if grounded in certain epistemological assumptions. He is not justified in claiming that: 'If the constructivist rationalism can be shown to be based on factually false assumptions, a whole family of schools of scientific as well as political thought will also be proved erroneous' (*RO* 5–6).

The absence of any strong connexion between constructivist rationalism and an illiberal politics is perhaps not so surprising, however, given the other side of Hayek's philosophy which is, as I have argued, much more clearly Kantian and inconsistent with the Humean strain in his thought. Like Hume, Hayek has argued, on the basis of his anti-constructivist viewpoint, that reason can only guide us by indicating what courses of action are *not* open to us but cannot supply us with justifications for right action. Reason's

---

[12] For Kant, as we saw in ch. 1, *Wille* lays down the principles of right and wrong and cannot itself err.

limited powers also means that we cannot construct our ideal social institutions or guide their evolution in preferred directions. Yet, on the other hand, Hayek, quite unlike Hume, is not content to allow evolution to take its course, or even to disavow any adherence to the principles which must underlie the laws of the good society.

At the most superficial level, this is apparent in his rejection of conservatism as a doctrine fated to be always 'dragged along a path not of its own choosing' (CL 398). Indeed, he thinks that the 'decisive objection to any conservatism' is that, 'by its very nature it cannot offer an alternative to the direction in which we are moving' (CL 398). At a deeper level, however, it is evident in the Kantian character of his defence of liberty and the rule of law, and, more particularly, of his insistence that justice obtains only under a system of rules in which the freedom of each is compatible with the freedom of all. For Hayek (like Rawls) thinks that this requirement generates the conclusion that, in a just society, individuals must be accorded entitlements which delineate protected domains within which their decisions are sovereign or, in other words, individuals must be accorded a determinate measure of *liberty*. Moreover, he believes that this conclusion offers us a standard by which to judge, and to redirect, our society.

This *constructivist* turn in Hayek's thought is most clearly evident in the following passage from the conclusion of *Law, Legislation and Liberty*:

What I have been trying to sketch in these volumes . . . has been a *guide* out of the process of degeneration of the existing form of government, and to *construct* an intellectual emergency equipment which will be available when we have no *choice* but to *replace* the tottering structure by some better edifice than resort in despair to some sort of dictatorial regime. Government is necessarily the product of *intellectual design*. If we can *give it a shape* in which it provides a beneficial framework for the free growth of society without giving to any one power to control this growth in the particular, we may well hope to see the growth of civilization continue (POFP 152).

As the italicized words illustrate, Hayek has not wavered from his intention to provide a *guide* to how to handle our (degenerating) system of government, to *construct* the principles we need when we come to try to *replace* our existing (spontaneously evolved) institutions. For all his criticisms of constructivist rationalism, his philosophical concern is not simply *description* but also *evaluation* and *prescription*. And Hayek has not been slow to prescribe: his 'moral constitution', while not proposed as a 'scheme for present application' (*POFP* 107), is a rational construction embodying abstract principles by which to assess and guide the development of (*a*) constitutions in places which lack any 'strong constitutional tradition', and (*b*) supra-national institutions regulating relations among national governments (*POFP* 108–9). And its basic principles make clear that it is fundamentally a 'constitution of liberty': the 'fundamental rights' it articulates 'are intended to protect . . . individual liberty in the sense of the absence of arbitrary coercion' (*POFP* 111).

Now here it might be objected that *none* of this is inconsistent with the Humean strand of Hayek's thought, for he is still arguing against the attempt to *direct* or *control* society's development through some central agency. All he is doing is offering a guide to how we might act, *given the existence of spontaneous ordering processes*. Thus, in the paragraph following the passage quoted above, Hayek writes: 'We ought to have learnt enough to avoid destroying our civilization by smothering the spontaneous ordering process of the interaction of the individuals by placing its direction in the hands of authority. But to avoid this we must shed the illusion that we can deliberately "create the future of mankind" . . .' (*POFP* 152). His counsel is that we are ill-advised to act in defiance of such processes but not that these processes cannot be harnessed at all. We should not 'plan *against* competition' but we can 'plan *for* competition', as *The Road to Serfdom* argued.

Indeed, it might be said that many of Hayek's practical proposals for the 'denationalization of money',[13] the removal of trade unions' legal immunities,[14] and dramatic action to combat inflation,[15] betray, not the constructivism of a rationalist but a call for an end to 'intervention' of any sort in the social process. Yet two observations tell against this interpretation. First, as we saw in Chapter 3, Hayek is not a simple advocate of *laissez-faire* but maintains that the important problems for liberals concern the rules

[13] See Hayek, *Choice in Currency: A Way to Stop Inflation* (London, 1976); *The Denationalization of Money: The Argument Refined*, 2nd edn. (London, 1978).

[14] Hayek, *1980s Unemployment and the Unions: The Distortion of Relative Prices by Monopoly in the Labour Market* (London, 1984).

[15] Hayek, *Full Employment at Any Price?* (London, 1978).

or laws which define property and freedom of contract. Secondly, he repudiates the conservative's pragmatism and is unwilling to allow that public policy remain an unsystematic treatment of each problem 'on its own merits'. These concerns make it clear that Hayek is not willing to concede that we might continue to develop laws and build institutions without being guided by principles which can be rationally justified and which, ultimately, have liberty as their primary value.

If there is a reason why Hayek turns out to be a constructivist of sorts it may be that it is difficult for liberals in general, and classical liberals in particular, not to be. This is because they see that, while spontaneous orders are best understood as orders in which activities are co-ordinated to a high degree, producing collective benefits which were no part of anyone's intention, it is also true that co-ordination is imperfect. Spontaneous orders can generate 'prisoners' dilemmas': situations in which rational maximizing action produces undesirable collective outcomes. In market orders this may be reflected in the generation of 'negative externalities' or 'public bads' which cannot be eliminated by market processes because the structure of rules specifying rights or entitlements makes the cost of the necessary economic transactions prohibitive, or simply does not specify the rights necessary to make such transactions possible. Similar difficulties arise with the problem of supplying public goods.

While classical liberals shy away from the idea of intervening in the market—because the danger is that any agency with the power to intervene has the opportunity to direct society according to some parochial conception of society's collective ends—the problem is that, without some kind of constructivist intervention, the stability, and very survival, of the spontaneous order may be threatened. Some classical liberals may be prepared to put up with certain 'ineliminable' negative externalities, or an undersupply of public goods. And to some extent, their case is a strong one: the costs of intervention often outweigh any anticipated benefits. When the structure of rules and entitlements threaten, however, to make undesirable outcomes a pervasive feature of social life, and to generate what amounts to a spontaneous *dis*order, the case for constructivist intervention becomes stronger.

The classical liberal thinker who has most consistently advanced the view that there is a need for rational reconstruction at the constitutional level is James Buchanan.[16] In Buchanan's view, without constitutional reform, modern social democracies are likely to degenerate into 'anarchistic jungles' in which rules serve, not to facilitate 'free relations among free men', but to intensify conflict over scarce resources. What is needed is reform, generated by constitutional agreement, to create the rights that will allow such conflicts to be negotiated by individual participants in society.

The alleged failure of existing social arrangements in many of these situations cannot legitimately be attributed to markets or to government, if we think of these as alternative processes of postconstitutional contracting. The social dilemma reflected in apparent results . . . stems from incomplete constitutional agreement, from first-stage failure to define and to limit individual rights. Resolution of this dilemma lies not in any explicit redistribution of rights among persons, not in some reshuffling of claims, but in the *creation* of newly defined rights in areas where none now exist, at least none that can offer a basis for predictability and exchange.[17]

As we noted earlier, Buchanan is thus critical of Hayek's inclination to leave too much to the operation of evolutionary processes in looking for solutions to social dilemmas.

Yet the suspicion of rationalist schemes for reconstruction that leads to this difficulty in Hayek's thought also generates similar problems for Buchanan, who has consistently criticized the idea of trying to demonstrate the superiority of any one set of subjectively determined social values. Constitutional reconstruction must come as the result of agreement among the contending interests in the status quo: anything other than this would amount to imposing the values of one particular outlook upon all others. Yet the unwillingness to engage in the task of normative ethical construction leaves Buchanan in a similar bind to that in which Hayek finds himself. He is unable to prescribe any course of action without appeal to the ethical constructions which must govern any account of constitutional contract, but are prohibited by his own social philosophy.[18]

---

[16] His most important works include: *The Limits of Liberty*; *Freedom in Constitutional Contract*; J. Buchanan and G. Tullock, *The Calculus of Consent* (Ann Arbor, 1962); J. Buchanan and G. Brennan, *The Reason of Rules: Constitutional Political Economy* (Cambridge, 1985).

[17] Buchanan, *The Limits of Liberty*, p. 179.

[18] See the critique of Buchanan by Norman Barry, 'Unanimity, Agreement, and Liberalism: A Critique of James Buchanan's Social Philosophy', *Political Theory*, 12 (1984), 579–96.

None the less, Buchanan has at least acknowledged the need for some form of social construction, informed by an appreciation of the limitations of direct governmental intervention and centralized direction. The anti-rationalist elements in Hayek's thought do not permit this concession, despite the fact that he has consistently put forward proposals for social reform.

This tension in Hayek's thought, between the rationalist advocacy of liberal reform and the anti-rationalist critique of all social reconstruction, has inclined one commentator to describe his political theory as 'Utopian non-engineering'.[19] While the word 'Utopian' might exaggerate a little the rationalist character of his thought, this term captures well the unstable nature of the Hayekian system of ideas. For, in the end, a Humean scepticism about the powers of reason is incompatible with a Kantian insistence on the priority of rationally justifiable principles. Hayek has tried to cast himself in the image of that most improbable of creatures: the principled sceptic.

3. HAYEK'S CONTRIBUTION TO MODERN LIBERAL THEORY

If these difficulties do indeed burden Hayek's work, what is it, one might ask, that justifies such detailed scrutiny of his political philosophy? Hayek's writings bear examination by those interested in the problem of defending liberalism, and in the wider issues of political theory it raises, not because they have generated any novel solutions to the traditional problems of political philosophy: the problems of justice and political obligation. Nor because he has developed, as has Rawls, a sustained *philosophical* argument attempting to reconcile two apparently incompatible philosophical viewpoints: as we have seen, the philosophical assumptions of Hume and Kant appear in Hayek's thought as inconsistent presuppositions which he makes insufficient attempt to reconcile, and which render his system of ideas fundamentally unstable. Hayek's political thought is worthy of attention because he has offered a distinctive conception of a liberal social order, one which presents an important challenge, not only to liberalism's critics, but also to many of its self-proclaimed defenders.

[19] R. Vernon, 'The "Great Society" and the "Open Society": Liberalism in Hayek and Popper', *Canadian Journal of Political Science*, 9 (1976), 261–76, at p. 269. For a discussion of the Austrian character of this problem in Hayek's liberalism see M. Francis, 'The Austrian Mind in Exile: Kelsen, Schumpeter and Hayek', in M. Francis (ed.), *The Viennese Enlightenment* (London, 1985), 63–87.

To see clearly the character of Hayek's challenge, however, it is necessary to understand the state of play in contemporary theorizing about liberalism.

Modern political theory has been dominated by the work of John Rawls. In his own much discussed contribution to political philosophy, Robert Nozick remarked that, henceforth, political theorists interested in the problem of justice would have to work within Rawls's theory or explain why not.[20] For the most part, political philosophers have accepted Nozick's assessment. Even leaving aside the great volume of critical writing dealing directly with Rawls, most work defending, refining, or criticizing the liberal conception of justice has found it difficult not to respond to his theory. This literature reveals two major concerns among political philosophers. The first is with the substantive question of the nature of the just society, which leads these writers to ask what is the proper role of the state, or what rights individuals have, or how the benefits and burdens of social life should be distributed. The second is with the procedural or methodological question of how an account of the just society may be justified. The two concerns are not always easily distinguished, however, since methodological strictures are often adopted because they lead to certain substantive conclusions—or, at least, rule out others.

The debates over both substantive and procedural questions have focused primarily on the idea of 'neutrality' as fundamental to any liberal conception of the good polity. Generally, those who see themselves as liberals argue that neutrality is of crucial importance. Two kinds of claims are made. The first is that the liberal state must exemplify neutrality inasmuch as its laws must not prefer any particular conception of the good life as superior to others: the various conceptions of the good to be found in a pluralist society must be accorded equal respect. As one writer puts it, 'Liberalism dictates official neutrality among the projects to which individuals might come to commit themselves.'[21] The second claim is that the principles governing a liberal polity must be principles chosen under 'neutral' conditions: they must be principles whose selection is not determined by any particular conception of the good life, even though the principles themselves will rule out some ways of

---

[20] In *Anarchy, State, and Utopia* (Oxford, 1980), 183.
[21] L. Lomasky, *Persons, Rights, and the Moral Community* (Oxford, 1987), 167.

life (indeed, they would be pointless if they did not). Rawls's own theory is most readily interpreted in this way.

Not all liberals have found the idea of neutrality attractive or philosophically persuasive. Some, like William Galston, have argued that a coherent defence of liberalism requires a stronger commitment to a particular, liberal, conception of the good life.[22] For the most part, however, the attack on the idea of neutrality has come from critics of liberalism who see the idea of state neutrality as both unattainable and undesirable, and the idea of procedural neutrality as philosophically incoherent.[23] The so-called communitarian critics of liberalism, who include such figures as Alasdair MacIntyre, Michael Walzer, Benjamin Barber, Michael Sandel, and Charles Taylor, among others, have pressed the view that any plausible conception of a political order cannot aspire merely to neutrality among competing conceptions of the good life.[24] A society, they insist, is more than an association of individuals bound together by contractual ties: it is a community which coheres because people share common practices and beliefs. At some deep level, they suggest, people must share an understanding of the character of the good life if they are to be able to associate in human communities. Politics is not simply about protecting or enforcing individual rights but about securing the common good.[25] And they emphasize that 'we cannot justify political arrangements

---

[22] See Galston, 'Defending Liberalism', *American Political Science Review*, 76 (1982), 621–9; *Justice and the Human Good* (Chicago, 1980).

[23] See particularly M. Sandel, *Liberalism and the Limits of Justice* (Cambridge, 1982); 'Liberalism and the Claims of Community: The Case of Affirmative Action', in M. Cohen (ed.), *Ronald Dworkin and Contemporary Jurisprudence* (London, 1984), 227–37. See also 'A Reply by Ronald Dworkin', in the same volume 247–301, esp. pp. 291–4. See also R. A. Rodewald, 'Does Liberalism Rest on a Mistake?', *Canadian Journal of Philosophy*, 15 (1985), 231–51.

[24] A. MacIntyre, *After Virtue: A Study in Moral Theory* (London, 1981); 'Moral Arguments and Social Contexts', *Journal of Philosophy*, 80 (1983), 589–92; M. Walzer, *Spheres of Justice: A Defence of Pluralism and Equality* (Oxford, 1983); 'Philosophy and Democracy', *Political Theory*, 9 (1981), 379–99; 'Liberalism and the Art of Separation', *Political Theory*, 12 (1984), 315–30; '*Spheres of Justice*: An Exchange', *New York Review of Books*, 21 July 1983, 43–4; B. Barber, *Strong Democracy: Participatory Politics for a New Age* (Berkeley, 1984); C. Taylor, 'Atomism', *Philosophical Papers*, 2 vols. (Cambridge, 1985), ii. 187–210; 'The Nature and Scope of Distributive Justice', *Philosophical Papers*, ii. 289–317; 'The Diversity of Goods', in A. K. Sen and B. Williams (eds.), *Utilitarianism and Beyond* (Cambridge, 1984), 129–44.

[25] For a particularly clear statement of this viewpoint see M. Sandel, 'Morality and the Liberal Ideal', *New Republic*, 7 May 1984, 15–17.

without reference to common purposes and ends, and that we cannot conceive our personhood without reference to our role as citizens, and as participants in a common life'.[26]

The communitarian challenge has had a substantial impact on contemporary theorizing about liberalism. It has not only presented a critical standpoint from which to assess the liberal ideal, but has also persuaded some that, if liberalism is defensible, it can only be so for existing liberal societies which should endorse the practices and values of their own traditions. Liberalism is to be embraced, not because the idea of a polity which is neutral and allows different conceptions of the good life to flourish is commendable or capable of independent justification, but because a polity respecting the traditional liberal rights is a part of 'our' heritage or history. This view has been defended most ably by Richard Rorty, who has sought, in his most recent political writings, to 'convince our [liberal] society that loyalty to itself is morality enough, and that such loyalty no longer needs an ahistorical backup'.[27] The communitarian critique of liberalism has, however, also invited a liberal response,[28] particularly from those who were the most prominent targets of communitarian criticism, such as Ronald Dworkin[29] and John Rawls.[30]

Interesting though they are, these discussions return to some familiar themes in liberalism's history. Those who emphasize the importance of neutrality exhibit a concern that is central to liberalism: a concern that the political order not be transformed

[26] M. Sandel, 'Introduction', in M. Sandel (ed.), *Liberalism and Its Critics* (Oxford, 1984), 5.

[27] Rorty, 'Postmodernist Bourgeois Liberalism', *Journal of Philosophy*, 80 (1983), 583–9, at p. 585. See also his 'Solidarity or Objectivity', in J. Rajchman and C. West (eds.), *Post-analytic Philosophy* (New York, 1985), 3–19; *Consequences of Pragmatism* (Brighton, 1982), chs. 1, 11, and 12; and, for a general statement of his philosophical pragmatism, *Philosophy and the Mirror of Nature* (Oxford, 1983).

[28] See e.g. A. Gutmann, 'Communitarian Critics of Liberalism', *Philosophy and Public Affairs*, 14 (1985), 308–22; R. B. Thigpen and L. A. Downing, 'Liberalism and the Communitarian Critique', *American Journal of Political Science*, 21 (1987), 637–55.

[29] See Dworkin's earlier essays, 'Liberalism', in S. Hampshire (ed.), *Public and Private Morality* (Cambridge, 1978), 113–43; 'Neutrality, Equality, and Liberalism', in D. Maclean and C. Mills (eds.), *Liberalism Reconsidered* (Totowa, 1983), 1–11. A part of his response to communitarianism is to be found in his *A Matter of Principle* (Cambridge, Mass., 1986), esp. Part 3; and *Law's Empire* (London, 1986), esp. chs. 6 and 7.

[30] See in particular Rawls's essay 'Justice as Fairness: Political not Metaphysical', *Philosophy and Public Affairs*, 14 (1985), 223–51.

into an 'enterprise association',[31] organized and directed to pursue particular ends. The early liberal writers conceived of the polity as the context within which the divisions and conflicts which were ineliminable features of society were kept in check, so that the members of that civil association might pursue their particular goals in peace. The institutions of political order were there, we might say, to *neutralize* the conflicts of interest which surfaced as people pursued those various goals. As we noted in Chapter 1, this conception of the political order was rejected by liberalism's earliest critics who wished to replace the idea of a pluralistic, secular society with a communitarian ideal of a more highly unified social order in which the interests of the individual and the political community were in closer harmony. The liberal individualist viewpoint, it was held, conceived of man as an isolated, asocial creature, concerned only with his own selfish projects, and, from this mistaken picture of human nature, proceeded to construct an account of the polity which forgot his nature as a social being. It was in this spirit that Rousseau offered his criticisms of Hobbes's view of man in the state of nature, Hegel and Herder their criticisms of Kant's ideal of autonomy,[32] and Marx his critique of pre-communist society. Liberalism's modern critics, while pointing to more recent targets, have, for the most part, simply repeated these complaints—prompting one writer to remark 'how distressingly recurrent and hackneyed is a certain pattern of antiliberal thought'.[33]

Yet this is not entirely fair. While the criticisms modern communitarians level against their liberal opponents are familiar ones, it is also true to say that some charges have gone unanswered. Contemporary liberal theorists have generally failed to address the objection that their models of the good polity, resting as they do on inadequate accounts of human nature and social processes, are unable to explain how human beings can form any kind of social order at all. Theorists such as Rawls and Bruce Ackerman offer accounts of the principles of social justice in a liberal state without pausing to explain whether such principles would prove workable

[31] The phrase is Michael Oakeshott's. See his *On Human Conduct* (Oxford, 1975), 114–18.
[32] On this see C. Larmore, *Patterns of Moral Complexity* (Cambridge, 1987), esp. ch. 5.
[33] Ibid. 93.

in any social order, given the nature of man and the nature of society. It is here that Hayek's contribution is most important, for his political theory, despite its shortcomings, supplies an answer to liberalism's oldest adversaries, as well as presenting a challenge to its modern defenders.

Hayek's first contribution to modern liberal theory has been to show clearly the plausibility of the idea of a social order as a means-connected system without a common hierarchy of ultimate ends.[34] More than this, he has brought out the difficulties which emerge with any attempt to organize or direct society in the pursuit of particular collective goals. In his theory of spontaneous order he tries to show that stable social formations can emerge as the result of individuals pursuing their separate goals in ignorance of the aims of their fellows and of the social patterns that are thus created. In some respects, Hayek's contribution here is not particularly novel: what he offers is an account of the invisible-hand processes which Mandeville, Hume, and Smith had identified as crucial to the understanding of social order as the undesigned product of human interaction. What is distinctive in Hayek's theory is his account of social institutions and rules of conduct as bearers of *knowledge*. Society may profitably be viewed as a network of practices and traditions of behaviour which convey information to guide individual conduct. These institutions serve not only to facilitate the matching of means with pre-determined ends, but also stimulate the discovery of human ends. If this is to be achieved, however, it is crucial that society is not brought under the governance of a single conception of the ends of life which is held to subsume all the various purposes human beings pursue, for this can only stifle the transmission and the growth of knowledge.

A part of Hayek's achievement here has been to show that what Hegel called 'civil society' is indeed a cohesive order in which individuals come to know one another, and to know their own purposes or ends, and which has the resources to deal with most of the disorders that arise in civil life. What is worth stressing, however, is that his conception of civil society is one of a network of communities, traditions, and conventions which bind individuals in ties of custom and habit, rather than one of an economic system in which individual association is governed only by needs and the rules of contract. 'Each of us', he suggests, 'is . . . a member of

[34] I borrow this phraseology from Larmore, ibid. 107.

many different overlapping and interlacing societies to which he may belong more or less strongly or lastingly. Society is a network of voluntary relationships between individuals and organized groups, and strictly speaking there is hardly ever merely one society to which any person exclusively belongs' (*POFP* 140). Society is not simply an aggregation of Robinson Crusoes, utility-maximizers who co-operate only for personal gain, but an association of communities: 'spontaneous formations which are founded on contacts closer and more intimate than those that can exist in the large unit' (*IEO* 28). A liberal social order, for Hayek, is one which is governed by principles which allow such groups to form, and to coexist; although without the conventions and traditions which flourish in such a society, and which not only make human behaviour predictable (*IEO* 24) but also make men moral (*IEO* 24 n.), liberal principles could never be adopted.

The implication Hayek draws from his account of the extended society as an association of traditions and practices is that there is little prospect of governing it by invoking shared conceptions of desert or moral worth of the kind found in particular communities. Once the 'circle of other people in relation to whom one had to obey moral rules' was extended, there had to be a reduction of the 'content' of the moral code (*MSJ* 147). The political order could be either one which confined itself to the task of maintaining a stable system of rules to preserve a peaceful coexistence, or one which exercised the authoritarian powers needed to impose a particular moral conception upon all. The latter alternative, for Hayek, is not only undesirable in itself but self-defeating inasmuch as the most probable effect of such an endeavour would be to destroy the spontaneous ordering processes which make civil life possible.

In defending such a view Hayek, in effect, pleads guilty to one charge levelled by modern communitarians like Sandel against liberalism. The root of liberalism's difficulties, Sandel maintains, lies in its distancing of the self from its ends. It fails to see that the self is not an independent construct but, in some important sense, a political construct. 'By putting the self beyond the reach of politics, it makes human agency an article of faith rather than an object of continuing attention and concern, a premise of politics rather than its precarious achievement.'[35] The concern of politics, in Hayek's conception, is not the character of the individual, or his develop-

[35] Sandel, *Liberalism and the Limits of Justice*, p. 183.

ment as a moral agent. That is the concern of the traditions and conventions which civilize him; a liberal politics is possible only when this has been achieved, and the sole purpose of liberal politics is the preservation of the conditions in which such practices may prevail. In this regard, Hayek's political theory calls attention to the value of liberalism's oldest, and currently most neglected, concern: peace.[36]

Hayek's contribution to the defence of liberalism against its communitarian detractors has been to offer a rationale for a liberal political order which rests, not upon contestable claims about individual rights, nor on any idealized conception of the person, but on a social theory which purports to show why the preservation of civil life requires a political order which facilitates peaceful coexistence, rather than one which aims at a more complete cultural unity. And his most important claim is that the order which preserves such a peace not only allows societies to coexist, but also enables them to form. The state, for Hayek, although an indispensable structure, is 'very far from being identical with society', and its concern can only be that of providing the conditions 'within which self-generating orders can form' (POFP 140). To bring the state to attempt more than this will ensure not the creation of a greater harmony of human interests, but a greater divisiveness as different groups seek pre-eminence.

Whether or not Hayek's social theory is, in the end, thought persuasive (and, as we have noted earlier, there are many respects in which it has been found wanting), it presents an argument worthy of consideration by liberalism's critics. For it takes on the task of defending a political theory *in their terms*—by presenting a social theory explaining why only a polity governed by liberal concerns is a practicable ideal.

It is also a theory worthy of more careful study by those who see themselves as liberalism's defenders. Although Hayek shares with them a conviction that the good polity cannot be one which is organized in the service of particular collective goals, and that the idea of 'neutrality' is of central importance to a liberal order, what he offers is a *conception* of neutrality which is distinctive, and highly critical of other so-called liberal views.

While modern liberals are agreed that the state must be neutral in

[36] 'The possibility of men living together in peace and to their mutual advantage without having to agree on common concrete aims, and bound only by abstract rules of conduct, was perhaps the greatest discovery mankind ever made' (MSJ 136).

its treatment of citizens, they differ over how neutrality is to be understood. Many recent contributions to the defence of liberalism may be seen as attempts to restate the doctrine of neutrality, and to draw out its implications for the rights of individuals and the role of the state. Nozick, for example, argues that neutrality permits no more than a minimal state, whose only concern is the preservation of order, while Dworkin suggests that many other state activities, ranging from implementing 'affirmative action' programmes to subsidizing the arts, are quite consistent with neutrality.[37] Clearly, neutrality may be understood in more ways than one.

At least three versions of political neutrality may usefully be distinguished.[38] In the first, neutrality requires that no political action be taken if its purpose is to promote or enable individuals to pursue an ideal of the good. In the second, neutrality forbids any political course which affects the likelihood that a person will pursue one conception of the good rather than another. And in the third, neutrality demands that the state ensure that all citizens are equally able to pursue and promote any ideal of the good they choose. Libertarian theories like Nozick's adopt the first, narrow, view of neutrality, while egalitarian theories like Dworkin's or Rawls's adopt the third, more comprehensive, view. It is enough to note, without entering into a detailed consideration of the ways in which these conceptions of neutrality manifest themselves in the literature of liberal theory, that the important conflict is between the first view that neutrality is attained only if the state refrains from involvement in people's pursuit of the good, and the latter two views that neutrality may require such involvement to ensure that the odds are not stacked against certain persons or ideals.

Hayek's liberalism is most readily associated with the first view of neutrality, although certain qualifications must be made to distinguish him from Nozick. His conception of neutrality does not impose the absolute prohibitions on state action that Nozick's does, since he is prepared to see the state involved in a number of activities—such as minimal welfare provision—which Nozick's theory forbids.[39] This indicates a certain looseness on Hayek's part

[37] See Dworkin, *A Matter of Principle* (Cambridge, Mass., 1986).
[38] In this analysis I draw freely from Joseph Raz's especially helpful discussion of the idea of neutral political concern in his *The Morality of Freedom* (Oxford, 1985), 110–33.
[39] Although Nozick clearly has some reservations about these matters since he concedes that state involvement may be required to avert 'catastrophic moral horror'. See *Anarchy, State, and Utopia*, p. 29 n.

since, as I argued earlier, he offers no justification for giving the state such tasks. Yet it also points to the difference between the ways Hayek and Nozick reach their conclusions about what neutrality involves. Nozick begins by stipulating that individuals have rights and from this deduces the conclusion that only the minimal state is justifiable. He rejects the comprehensive conception of neutrality because it is ruled out by his view of individual rights. Hayek, however, begins at the other end by rejecting the comprehensive conception of neutrality, and so offers a narrow view of neutrality as the only feasible alternative. His conclusions thus issue not from any controversial moral doctrines but from his social theory.

In developing this argument Hayek makes two contributions to modern discussions of liberalism that make his theory worth further consideration (although again it must be borne in mind that his achievement remains compromised by the difficulties drawn out by this study). The first is his use of social theory to challenge the prevailing comprehensive conceptions of neutrality. The neutrality that theorists like Dworkin seek, which requires the redistribution of resources in society to equalize opportunities, Hayek purports to show is unattainable given the nature of social order.

There are several reasons why this is so. First, the nature of society as a spontaneous order in which people react to changes in their circumstances suggests it may be impossible to preserve distributive patterns without resorting to strategies which invade the liberties which theorists like Rawls wish to accord unconditional priority. This is made more probable by the fact that government would have to be granted the powers needed to achieve its distributive goals.

Secondly, once the state ceases to be merely the defender of order and becomes the forum in which distributive questions are settled, politics becomes the means through which various groups try to secure 'justice' or the 'common good' conceived in terms of their particular interests. This is unfortunate for the ideal of neutrality because it increases the possibility of particular interests coming to rule in the name of the common interest, and imposing their own views of the good upon all. 'All groups whose members pursue the same or parallel aims will develop common views about what is right for members of those groups. Such views, however, will be right only for all those who pursue the same aims, but may be wholly incompatible with any principles by which such a group can be integrated into the overall order of society' (*MSJ* 137).

Thirdly, even if the state is not captured by any one set of interests, for as long as it remains the means through which groups pursue their goals, it is more likely to become a divisive instrument than one for the reconciliation of conflicts of interest (*MSJ* 137). In so far as it restricts itself to the task of preserving the abstract framework within which civil society can prevail, the state plays a vital role. Once it descends into civil society, however, and becomes embroiled in the substantive issues therein, it becomes the source of disorder.[40]

Now, whether or not Hayek's account of the nature of the state and civil society is wholly acceptable, it presents an important case. For it puts the charge that comprehensive conceptions of neutrality can have practical relevance only if one accepts a mistaken view of the state—and, indeed, a mistaken social theory more generally. The challenge for those who reject Hayek's understanding of the liberal ideal of neutrality is to present an account of social and political processes which would support their alternative conceptions.

Hayek's second contribution to modern liberalism in developing his defence of a narrow conception of neutrality lies in his revival of the idea of the liberal polity as a *modus vivendi* rather than an expression of a comprehensive philosophical doctrine. The problem with some conceptions of liberalism is that they appeal to values or doctrines which are not simply controversial but unduly restrict what the polity may recognize as an allowable conception of the good life. Mill, for example, makes particular appeal to the ideal of individuality in offering a liberal view of liberty as defensible because it enables that individuality to flourish. Yet the immediate implication of this is that ways of life which do not value individuality cannot be accorded the same respect or protection since they uphold values which are at odds with the fundamental values of the liberal state. Similarly, the Kantian conception of the liberal order, which emphasizes the importance of autonomy as a substantive ideal, is forced to concede that ways of pursuing the good life which do not value autonomy cannot so easily be

---

[40] In this regard see Charles Murray's study of the impact of welfare programmes on poverty levels in his *Losing Ground: American Social Policy 1950–1980* (New York, 1985).

tolerated by a state which is founded on that ideal. If there is a rationale for such tolerance it cannot be that it is required by the value of autonomy.

Much of the criticism levelled against the liberal idea has tried to show that the neutrality it professes is in fact bogus. 'The liberal state . . . is no more neutral than the conception of the good on which it rests.'[41] Many of these criticisms miss the mark because they hold that neutrality demands that no activities are excluded or prohibited by regulative procedures. Such procedures are not only unavailable in principle but would also be pointless. And there is no need to interpret the neutrality requirement in this way. Nor is it necessary, however, to appeal to substantive conceptions of the good life, or even to substantive claims about the minimal requirements for the pursuit of any conception of the good. Once such claims are advanced, however, as they have been by Kant, Mill, and modern writers who follow them, liberalism opens itself up to the charge that the neutrality it professes has been compromised.

Hayek's liberal theory, if we can prescind from the difficulties which trouble it, points to the possibility of finding political principles which do not rest on controversial claims about human ends or the good life by seeking a *modus vivendi*. 'The fundamental liberal insight', as Charles Larmore has recently argued, 'is the inescapable controversiality of ideals of the good life and thus the need to find political principles that abstract from them.'[42] Hayek's contribution has been to suggest how this is possible, for in offering an account of society as an order which is the product of individuals associating and yet also foments man's moral and intellectual development, he indicates that the least demanding solution to the problem of social order may be to find those political principles which allow such societies to form and to coexist.

Now, this is a view that many liberals who are unsympathetic to Hayek's libertarianism may find congenial. Amy Gutmann, for example, who has argued for a more egalitarian liberalism,[43] writes in response to the communitarians:

The major aim of liberal justice is to find principles appropriate for a society in which people disagree fundamentally over many questions,

---

[41] I. Shapiro, *The Evolution of Rights in Liberal Theory* (Cambridge, 1986), 285.
[42] *Patterns of Moral Complexity*, pp. 129–30. See also ch. 5 more generally.
[43] In *Liberal Equality* (Cambridge, 1980).

including such metaphysical questions as the nature of personal identity. Liberal justice therefore does not provide us with a comprehensive morality; it regulates our social institutions, not our entire lives. It makes claims on us 'not because it expresses our deepest self-understandings,' but because it represents the fairest possible *modus vivendi* for a pluralistic society.[44]

Yet agreement between Hayek and the dominant strand of liberal theory may not be quite so easily secured. For a great deal turns on what is understood by a *modus vivendi*, and thought necessary to secure it. For Gutmann and Larmore, a liberal *modus vivendi* may well involve the growth of the mechanisms of participatory democracy, and need not compromise egalitarian ideals. A Hayekian conception of the liberal order as a *modus vivendi*, however, would not be of this nature. The conclusion he draws from his social theory is that a liberal order must be ruled by a limited government whose primary task is to maintain the framework within which individuals and groups may pursue their respective aims, regardless of the shape the resulting society assumes.

Rawls, however, in his most recent essay,[45] explicitly rejects the idea of a *modus vivendi*. For him, what is needed is a political conception of justice which will command the allegiance of a diversity of moral viewpoints in a pluralist society. Only such a public philosophy which was able to sustain an 'overlapping consensus' of views would ensure social unity in 'long run equilibrium'. A *modus vivendi* would amount to little more than a temporary truce, in which time the more powerful interests would be able to marshall their forces, later to impose their own attitudes upon all. This contrasts with Hayek who sees social stability as possible only under political institutions which removed social justice from the agenda of politics.

This lack of agreement does not, however, reduce the interest of Hayek's contribution to liberal theory. Indeed, it suggests one way liberals may approach the problem of dealing with differences that divide them: by returning to issues in social theory. His work

[44] A. Gutmann, 'Communitarian Critics of Liberalism', p. 313. Gutmann quotes from Larmore's review of Sandel's *Liberalism and the Limits of Justice*. Larmore's defence of the idea of a *modus vivendi* is developed more fully in *Patterns of Moral Complexity*, ch. 5.

[45] John Rawls, 'The Idea of an Overlapping Consensus', *Oxford Journal of Legal Studies*, 7 (1987), 1–25.

deserves examination because he draws attention to the need to consider the nature of society and the way in which this constrains our choice of political principles. For, if Hayek is right, many kinds of principles may be ruled out as unworkable. In other words, the *circumstances* of justice need much more careful investigation than they have been given.

Hayek's endeavours, while they have not succeeded in establishing a coherent liberal philosophy, do push contemporary liberal theory in a promising direction. For they show, first, that the defence of the liberal order need not assume that man is an isolated, asocial, utility maximizer: the defence of liberalism can, and should, be grounded in a more plausible account of man and society. And they suggest, secondly, that, while it will prove difficult to establish philosophical foundations for liberal rights, or a liberal theory of liberty, an understanding of the nature of social processes may offer a surer guide by telling us what kinds of rights and liberties *cannot* be adopted if the liberal ideal is to survive.

BIBLIOGRAPHY

ACKERMANN, B., *Social Justice and the Liberal State* (New Haven, 1980).

ALCHIAN, A. A., 'Uncertainty, Evolution and Economic Theory', *Journal of Political Economy*, 58 (1950), 211–21.

ARBLASTER, A., *The Rise and Decline of Western Liberalism* (Oxford, 1985).

ARDAL, P. S., *Passion and Value in Hume's Treatise* (Edinburgh, 1966).

ARNOLD, R. A., 'Hayek and Institutional Evolution', *Journal of Libertarian Studies*, 4 (1980), 341–52.

AUNE, B., *Kant's Theory of Morals* (Princeton, 1979).

AVINERI, S., *Hegel's Theory of the Modern State* (Cambridge, 1980).

BARBER, B., 'Justifying Justice: Problems of Psychology, Politics and Measurement in Rawls', in N. Daniels (ed.), *Reading Rawls: Critical Studies of* A Theory of Justice (Oxford, 1978), 292–318.

—— *Strong Democracy: Participatory Politics for a New Age* (Berkeley, 1984).

BARRY, B., *The Liberal Theory of Justice: A Critical Examination of the Principal Doctrines in* A Theory of Justice *by John Rawls* (Oxford, 1973).

BARRY, N., 'Hayek on Liberty', in J. Gray and Z. Pelczynski (eds.), *Conceptions of Liberty in Political Philosophy* (London, 1984), 263–88.

—— *Hayek's Social and Economic Philosophy* (London, 1979).

—— 'The Tradition of Spontaneous Order', *Literature of Liberty*, 5 (1982), 7–58.

—— 'Unanimity, Agreement, and Liberalism: A Critique of James Buchanan's Social Philosophy', *Political Theory*, 12 (1984), 579–96.

BERLIN, I., 'Two Concepts of Liberty', in his *Four Essays on Liberty* (Oxford, 1976), 118–72.

—— *Vico and Herder: Two Studies in the History of Ideas* (London, 1976).

BOSANQUET, N., *After the New Right* (London, 1983).

BOSWELL, J., *Life of Johnson*, ed. R. W. Chapman (Oxford, 1983).

BOTWINICK, A., *Ethics, Politics and Epistemology: A Study in the Unity of Hume's Thought* (Lanham, 1980).

BRAMSTEAD, E. K., and Melhuish, K. J. (eds.), *Western Liberalism: A History in Documents from Locke to Croce* (London, 1978).

BRITTAN, S., *The Economic Consequences of Democracy* (London, 1977).

—— *Participation Without Politics: An Analysis of the Nature and Role of Markets*, 2nd edn. (London, 1979).

—— *The Role and Limits of Government: Essays in Political Economy* (London, 1983).

BUCHANAN, A. E., *Ethics, Efficiency, and the Market* (Oxford, 1985).

—— *Marx and Justice: the Radical Critique of Liberalism* (London, 1983).

BUCHANAN, J. M., *Freedom in Constitutional Contract: Perspectives of a Political Economist* (London, 1977).

—— *The Limits of Liberty: Between Anarchy and Leviathan* (Chicago, 1975).

BUCHANAN, J., and BRENNAN, G., *The Reason of Rules: Constitutional Political Economy* (Cambridge, 1985).

BUCHANAN, J., and TULLOCK, G., *The Calculus of Consent* (Ann Arbor, 1962).

BURTON, J., *Picking Losers . . .? The Political Economy of Industrial Policy* (London, 1983).

BUTLER, E., *Hayek: His Contribution to the Social and Economic Thought of Our Time* (London, 1983).

CAMPBELL, D. T., 'Evolutionary Epistemology', in P. A. Schilpp (ed.), *The Philosophy of Karl Popper*, 2 vols. (La Salle, 1974), i. 413–63.

CAPALDI, N., 'Introduction: The Problem of Hume', in D. F. Norton, N. Capaldi, and W. L. Robison (eds.), *McGill Hume Studies* (San Diego, 1979), 3–22.

COPLESTON, F., *A History of Philosophy*, Vol. 6: *Modern Philosophy*, Part II: *Kant* (New York, 1964).

CRAGG, A. W., 'Hayek, Justice and the Market', *Canadian Journal of Political Science*, 13 (1983), 563–74.

CROWLEY, B. L., *The Self, the Individual, and the Community: Liberalism in the Political Thought of F. A. Hayek and Sidney and Beatrice Webb* (Oxford, 1987).

DASGUPTA, P., 'Utilitarianism, Information and Rights', in A. K. Sen and B. Williams (eds.), *Utilitarianism and Beyond* (Cambridge, 1983), 199–218.

DESCARTES, *The Philosophical Works of Descartes*, trans. E. Haldane and G. Ross, 2 vols. (New York, 1955).

DIAMOND, A. M., 'F. A. Hayek and Constructivism in Ethics', *Journal of Libertarian Studies*, 4 (1980), 353–66.

DIETZE, G., 'Hayek on the Rule of Law', in F. Machlup (ed.), *Essays on Hayek* (London, 1977), 107–46.

DUNN, J., *Western Political Theory in the Face of the Future* (Cambridge, 1979).

DURKHEIM, E., *The Division of Labour in Society*, trans. W. D. Halls (London, 1984).

DWORKIN, R. M., *Law's Empire* (London, 1986).

—— 'Liberalism', in S. Hampshire (ed.), *Public and Private Morality* (Cambridge, 1978), 113–43.

—— *A Matter of Principle* (Cambridge, Mass., 1986).

—— 'Neutrality, Equality, and Liberalism', in D. MacLean and C. Mills (eds.), *Liberalism Reconsidered* (Totowa, 1983), 1–11.

—— 'A Reply by Ronald Dworkin', in M. Cohen (ed.), *Ronald Dworkin and Contemporary Jurisprudence* (London, 1984), 247–301.

—— 'Rights as Trumps', in J. Waldron (ed.), *Theories of Rights* (Oxford, 1985), 153–67.

—— *Taking Rights Seriously* (London, 1978).

—— 'We Do Not Have a Right to Liberty', in R. L. Cunningham (ed.), *Liberty and the Rule of Law* (London, 1979), 169–84.

EDGAR, D., 'The Free or the Good', in R. Levitas (ed.), *The Ideology of the New Right* (Oxford, 1986), 55–79.

ELSTER, J., *Making Sense of Marx* (Cambridge, 1985).

—— 'Sour Grapes—Utilitarianism and the Genesis of Wants', in A. K. Sen and B. Williams (eds.), *Utilitarianism and Beyond* (Cambridge, 1983), 219–38.

FEINBERG, J., *Doing and Deserving* (Princeton, 1976).

FINNIS, J., *Fundamentals of Ethics* (Oxford, 1983).

—— *Natural Law and Natural Rights* (Oxford, 1980).

FLEW, A., 'Social Science: Making Visible the Invisible Hands', *Quadrant*, Nov. 1981, 24–9.

FORBES, D., 'Hume and the Scottish Enlightenment', in S. C. Brown (ed.), *Philosophers of the Enlightenment* (Brighton, 1979), 94–109.

—— *Hume's Philosophical Politics* (Cambridge, 1978).

—— 'Sceptical Whiggism, Commerce, and Liberty', in A. S. Skinner and T. Wilson (eds.), *Essays on Adam Smith* (Oxford, 1975), 179–201.

FRANCIS, M., 'The Austrian Mind in Exile: Kelsen, Schumpeter and Hayek', in M. Francis (ed.), *The Viennese Enlightenment* (London, 1985), 63–87.

FREEMAN, M., *Edmund Burke and the Critique of Political Radicalism* (Oxford, 1980).

FRIEDMAN, M., *Capitalism and Freedom* (Chicago, 1962).

FRIEDMAN, M., and FRIEDMAN, R., *Free to Choose: A Personal Statement* (London, 1980).

—— *The Tyranny of the Status Quo* (Harmondsworth, 1985).

GALBRAITH, J. K., *The Affluent Society* (Harmondsworth, 1962).

GALEOTTI, A., 'Individualism, Social Rules, Tradition: The Case of Friedrich A. Hayek', *Political Theory*, 15 (1987), 163–81.

GALSTON, W., 'Defending Liberalism', *American Political Science Review*, 76 (1982), 621–9.

—— *Justice and the Human Good* (Chicago, 1980).

GLOVER, J., *Causing Death and Saving Lives* (Harmondsworth, 1981).

GRAY, J. N., 'Classical Liberalism, Positional Goods, and the Politicization of Poverty', in A. Ellis and K. Kumar (eds.), *Dilemmas of Liberal Democracies: Studies in Fred Hirsch's* Social Limits to Growth (London, 1983), 174–84.

—— 'F. A. Hayek on Liberty and Tradition', *Journal of Libertarian Studies*, 4 (1980), 119–37.

—— 'Hayek and the Rebirth of Classical Liberalism', *Literature of Liberty*, 5 (1982), 19–66.

—— 'Hayek as a Conservative', *Salisbury Review* (Summer 1983).

—— *Hayek on Liberty*, 2nd edn. (Oxford, 1986).

—— 'Hayek on Liberty, Rights, and Justice', *Ethics*, 92 (1981), 73–84.

—— *Liberalism* (Milton Keynes, 1986).

—— 'Marxian Freedom, Individual Liberty, and the End of Alienation', in E. Paul, F. Miller, J. Paul, and J. Ahrens (eds.), *Marxism and Liberalism* (Oxford, 1986), 160–87.

—— *Mill on Liberty: A Defence* (London, 1983).

GUTMANN, A., 'Communitarian Critics of Liberalism', *Philosophy and Public Affairs*, 14 (1985), 308–22.

—— *Liberal Equality* (Cambridge, 1980).

HAAKONSSEN, K., *The Science of a Legislator: The Natural Jurisprudence of David Hume and Adam Smith* (Cambridge, 1981).

HAMOWY, R., 'Hayek's Concept of Freedom: A Critique', *New Individualist Review*, 1 (1961), 28–31.

—— *The Scottish Enlightenment and the Theory of Spontaneous Order* (Carbondale, 1987).

HAMPSHIRE, S., *Spinoza* (London, n.d.).

HARE, R. M., 'Ethical Theory and Utilitarianism', in A. K. Sen and B. Williams (eds.), *Utilitarianism and Beyond* (Cambridge, 1984), 23–38.

—— *Freedom and Reason* (Oxford, 1980).

—— *Moral Thinking: Its Levels, Method and Point* (Oxford, 1984).

HARRISON, J., *Hume's Moral Epistemology* (Oxford, 1976).

—— *Hume's Theory of Justice* (Oxford, 1981).

HAYEK, F. A., *Choice in Currency: A Way to Stop Inflation* (London, 1976).

—— *The Constitution of Liberty* (London, 1979).

—— *The Counter-Revolution of Science: Studies in the Abuse of Reason* (Indianapolis, 1979).

—— *The Denationalization of Money: The Argument Refined*, 2nd edn. (London, 1978).

—— 'Freedom and Coercion: A Reply to Hamowy', *New Individualist Review* 1 (1961), 28–32.

—— *Full Employment at Any Price?* (London, 1978).

—— *Individualism and Economic Order* (Chicago, 1980).

—— *Knowledge, Evolution and Society* (London, 1983).

—— *Law, Legislation and Liberty: A New Statement of the Liberal Principles of Justice and Political Economy*, 3 vols. (London, 1982).

Vol. 1: *Rules and Order*.

Vol. 2: *The Mirage of Social Justice*.

Vol. 3: *The Political Order of a Free People*.

—— *New Studies in Philosophy, Politics, Economics and the History of Ideas* (Chicago, 1978).

—— *1980s Unemployment and the Unions: The Distortion of Relative Prices by Monopoly in the Labour Market* (London, 1984).

—— *Prices and Production* (London, 1932).

—— *The Road to Serfdom* (London, 1979).

—— *The Sensory Order: An Inquiry into the Foundations of Theoretical Psychology* (London, 1952).

—— *Studies in Philosophy, Politics and Economics* (London, 1978).

—— 'The Trend of Economic Thinking', *Economica*, 13 (1933), 121–37.

HEGEL, G. W. F., *Philosophy of Right*, trans. T. M. Knox (Oxford, 1978).

HERZOG, D., *Without Foundations: Justification in Political Theory* (Ithaca, 1985).

HIRSCH, F., *Social Limits to Growth* (London, 1978).

HUME, DAVID, *Dialogues Concerning Natural Religion*, ed. H. D. Aiken (New York, 1975).

—— *Enquiries Concerning Human Understanding and Concerning the Principles of Morals*, introduction by L. A. Selby-Bigge, 3rd edn. revised by P. H. Nidditch (Oxford, 1975).

—— *Essays Moral, Political and Literary* (London, 1910).

—— *The History of England from the Invasion of Julius Caesar to the Accession of George III*, 8 vols. (London, 1810), vol. i.

—— *A Treatise of Human Nature: Being an Attempt to Introduce the Experimental Method of Reasoning into Moral Subjects*, ed. L. A. Selby-Bigge, revised by P. H. Nidditch (Oxford, 1978).

JACKSON, M. W., *Matters of Justice* (London, 1986).

—— 'On Her Majesty's Service', *Bulletin of the Australian Society of Legal Philosophy*, 43 (1987), 298–301.

JAGGAR, A., *Feminist Politics and Human Nature* (Brighton, 1983).

KANT, I., *The Critique of Judgement*, trans. J. C. Meredith (Oxford, 1982), Part II: *The Critique of Teleological Judgement*.

—— *The Critique of Practical Reason*, trans. L. W. Beck (Indianapolis, 1978).

—— *The Critique of Pure Reason*, trans. N. Kemp Smith (London, 1970).

—— *The Groundwork of the Metaphysics of Morals*, rendered as *The Moral Law*, ed. H. J. Paton (London, 1972).

—— *The Metaphysical Elements of Justice*, trans. J. Ladd (Indianapolis, 1978).

KANT, U., *Prolegomena to any Future Metaphysics That Will Be Able to Present Itself as a Science*, ed. and trans. by P. G. Lucas (Manchester, 1978).

KIRZNER, I. M., *Competition and Entrepreneurship* (Chicago, 1978).

—— 'The Primacy of Entrepreneurial Discovery', in *The Entrepreneur in Society* (Sydney, 1983), 59–80.

KRISTOL, I., 'The Shaking of the Foundations', in his *On the Democratic Idea in America* (New York, 1973), 22–30.

—— ' "When Virtue Loses All Her Loveliness"—Some Reflections on Capitalism and the "Free Society" ', in his *On the Democratic Idea in America* (New York, 1973), 90–106.

LADD, J., 'Review of Riley, *Kant's Political Philosophy*', *Political Theory*, 12 (1984), 124–7.

LARMORE, C., *Patterns of Moral Complexity* (Cambridge, 1987).

LAVOIE, D., 'A Critique of the Standard Account of the Socialist Calculation Debate', *Journal of Libertarian Studies*, 5 (1981), 41–87.

—— 'Introduction' to 'An Economic Critique of Socialism', *Journal of Libertarian Studies*, 5 (1981), 1–6.

—— *Rivalry and Central Planning: The Socialist Calculation Debate Reconsidered* (Cambridge, 1985).

LEONI, B., *Freedom and the Law* (Los Angeles, 1972).

LEPAGE, H., *Tomorrow Capitalism: The Economics of Economic Freedom* (La Salle, 1982).

LEVIN, M., 'Negative Liberty', *Social Philosophy and Policy*, 2 (1984), 84–100.

LIVINGSTON, D., *Hume's Philosophy of Common Life* (Chicago, 1984).

—— 'Time and Value in Hume's Social and Political Philosophy', in D. F. Norton, N. Capaldi, and W. L. Robison (eds.), *McGill Hume Studies* (San Diego, 1979), 181–201.

LOCKE, D., 'The Trivializability of Universalizability', *Philosophical Review*, 77 (1968), 25–44.

LOMASKY, L., *Persons, Rights, and the Moral Community* (Oxford, 1987).

MACCORMICK, N., *Legal Right and Social Democracy* (Oxford, 1982).

MACINTYRE, A., *After Virtue: A Study in Moral Theory* (London, 1981).

—— *Against the Self-Images of the Age: Essays on Ideology and Philosophy* (London, 1971).

—— 'Moral Arguments and Social Contexts', *Journal of Philosophy*, 80 (1983), 589–92.

MACK, E., 'Hayek on Justice and the Market: A Reply to MacLeod', *Canadian Journal of Political Science*, 13 (1983), 563–74.

MACKIE, J. L., *Ethics: Inventing Right and Wrong* (Harmondsworth, 1979).

MACKIE, J., *Hume's Moral Theory* (London, 1980).

MACLEOD, A. M., 'Hayek on Justice and the Market: A Rejoinder to Cragg and Mack', *Canadian Journal of Political Science*, 13 (1983), 575–7.

—— 'Justice and the Market', *Canadian Journal of Political Science*, 13 (1983), 551–62.

MACPHERSON, C. B., *The Political Theory of Possessive Individualism* (Oxford, 1962).

MENGER, C., *Problems of Economics and Sociology*, ed. with an introduction by L. Schneider, trans. F. J. Nock (Urbana, 1963).

MERTON, R. K., 'The Unanticipated Consequences of Purposive Social Action', *American Sociological Review*, 1 (1936), 894–904.

MILL, J. S., *John Stuart Mill on Politics and Society*, ed. G. Williams (Glasgow, 1976).

—— *Utilitarianism, Liberty, and Representative Government* (London, 1962).

MILLER, D., 'Justice and Property', *Ratio*, 22 (1980), 1–15.

—— *Philosophy and Ideology in Hume's Political Thought* (Oxford, 1981).

—— *Social Justice* (Oxford, 1979).

MILLS, C. WRIGHT, *The Marxists* (Harmondsworth, 1962).

MINOGUE, K., 'Conservatism', in P. Edwards (ed.), *The Encyclopaedia of Philosophy*, 8 vols. (London, 1967), ii. 195–8.

MISES, L. VON, 'Economic Calculation in the Socialist Commonwealth', in F. A. Hayek (ed.), *Collectivist Economic Planning: Critical Studies in the Possibilities of Socialism* (London, 1935), 87–130.

—— *Human Action: A Treatise on Economics*, 3rd rev. edn. (Chicago, 1966).

—— *Socialism: An Economic and Sociological Analysis*, trans. J. Kahane (Indianapolis, 1981).

MOORE, J., 'Hume's Theory of Justice and Property', *Political Studies*, 24 (1976), 103–19.

MOSSNER, E. C., *The Life of David Hume* (Oxford, 1980).

MURPHY, J. G., *Kant: The Philosophy of Right* (London, 1970).

MURRAY, C., *Losing Ground: American Social Policy 1950–1980* (New York, 1985).

NIELSEN, K., *Radical Egalitarianism* (Totowa, 1984).

NISHIYAMA, C., and LEUBE, K. (eds.), *The Essence of Hayek* (Stanford, 1984).

NOZICK, R., *Anarchy, State and Utopia* (Oxford, 1980).

—— 'On the Randian Argument', in J. Paul and E. Paul (eds.), *Reading Nozick* (Oxford, 1982), 206–31.

—— *Philosophical Explanations* (Oxford, 1984).

OAKESHOTT, M., *On History and Other Essays* (London, 1984).
—— *On Human Conduct* (Oxford, 1975).
—— *Rationalism in Politics and Other Essays* (London, 1981).
O'DRISCOLL, G. P., *Economics as a Coordination Problem: The Contributions of Friedrich A. Hayek* (Kansas City, 1977).
OLSON, M., *The Logic of Collective Action: Public Goods and the Theory of Groups* (New York, 1970).
—— *The Rise and Decline of Nations: Economic Growth, Stagflation and Social Rigidities* (New Haven, 1982).
OPPENHEIM, F., *Political Concepts: A Reconstruction* (Oxford, 1981).
PARFIT, D., *Reasons and Persons* (Oxford, 1986).
PARKINSON, G., 'Spinoza on the Freedom of Man and the Freedom of the Citizen', in Z. A. Pelczynski and J. N. Gray (eds.), *Conceptions of Liberty in Political Philosophy* (London, 1984), 39–56.
PATEMAN, C., *The Problem of Political Obligation: A Critique of Liberal Theory* (Berkeley, 1985).
PELCZYNSKI, Z. A., 'The Hegelian Conception of the State', in Pelczynski (ed.), *Hegel's Political Philosophy: Problems and Perspectives* (Cambridge, 1971), 1–29.
PERELMAN, C., *The Idea of Justice and the Problem of Argument* (London, 1970).
PETTIT, P., 'The Freedom of the City: A Republican Ideal', in P. Pettit and A. Hamlin (eds.), *The Good Polity* (Oxford, forthcoming).
—— 'A Theory of Justice?', *Theory and Decision*, 4 (1974), 311–24.
PETTIT, P., and BRENNAN, G., 'Restrictive Consequentialism', *Australasian Journal of Philosophy*, 64 (1986), 438–55.
PLANT, R., *Equality, Markets and the State*, Fabian Tract 494 (London, 1984).
—— *Hegel: An Introduction*, 2nd edn. (Oxford, 1983).
—— 'Hegel and Political Economy I', *New Left Review*, 103 (1977), 79–92.
—— 'Hegel on Identity and Legitimation', in Z. A. Pelczynski (ed.), *The State and Civil Society: Studies in Hegel's Political Philosophy* (Cambridge, 1984), 227–43.
—— 'Hirsch, Hayek, and Habermas: Dilemmas of Distribution', in A. Ellis and K. Kumar (eds.), *Dilemmas of Liberal Democracies: Studies in Fred Hirsch's* Social Limits to Growth (London, 1983), 45–64.
PLANT, R., LESSER, H., and TAYLOR-GOOBY, P., *Political Philosophy and Social Welfare: Essays on the Normative Basis of Welfare Provision* (London, 1980).
POLANYI, M., *The Logic of Liberty: Reflections and Rejoinders* (Chicago, 1980).
—— *The Tacit Dimension* (London, 1967).

POLANYI, M., and PROSCH, H., *Meaning* (Chicago, 1975).

POPPER, K., 'Campbell on the Evolutionary Theory of Knowledge', in P. A. Schilpp (ed.), *The Philosophy of Karl Popper*, 2 vols. (La Salle, 1974), ii. 1059–64.

—— *Conjectures and Refutations: The Growth of Scientific Knowledge* (London, 1976).

—— *Objective Knowledge: An Evolutionary Approach* (Oxford, 1981).

—— *The Poverty of Historicism* (London, 1976).

QUINTON, A., *The Politics of Imperfection: The Religious and Secular Traditions of Conservative Thought in England from Hooker to Oakeshott* (London, 1978).

RAND, A., *Atlas Shrugged* (New York, 1957).

—— *Capitalism: The Unknown Ideal* (New York, 1967).

—— *The Fountainhead* (New York, 1943).

RAWLS, J., 'The Basic Liberties and their Priority', in S. M. MacMurrin (ed.), *The Tanner Lectures on Human Values* (Cambridge, 1982), iii. 1–89.

—— 'The Basic Structure as Subject', *American Philosophical Quarterly*, 14 (1977), 159–65.

—— 'The Idea of an Overlapping Consensus', *Oxford Journal of Legal Studies*, 7 (1987), 1–25.

—— 'Justice as Fairness: Political not Metaphysical', *Philosophy and Public Affairs*, 14 (1985), 223–51.

—— 'Kantian Constructivism in Moral Theory', *Journal of Philosophy*, 88 (1980), 515–72.

—— *A Theory of Justice* (Oxford, 1976).

—— 'A Well-Ordered Society', in P. Laslett and J. Fishkin (eds.), *Philosophy, Politics and Society*, 5th series (Oxford, 1979), 6–20.

RAZ, J., *The Morality of Freedom* (Oxford, 1985).

—— 'The Rule of Law and Its Virtue', in his *The Authority of Law: Essays on Law and Morality* (Oxford, 1983), 210–32.

REISS, H. (ed.), *Kant's Political Writings*, trans. H. B. Nisbet (Cambridge, 1970).

RILEY, P., *Kant's Political Philosophy* (Totawa, 1983).

ROBERTS, P. C., *Alienation in the Soviet Economy: Toward a General Theory of Marxian Alienation, Organizational Principles, and the Soviet Economy* (Albuquerque, 1971).

ROBERTSON, J., 'The Scottish Enlightenment at the Limits of the Civic Tradition', in I. Hont and M. Ignatieff (eds.), *Wealth and Virtues: The Shaping of Political Economy in the Scottish Enlightenment* (Cambridge, 1983), 137–78.

RODEWALD, R. A., 'Does Liberalism Rest on a Mistake?', *Canadian Journal of Philosophy*, 15 (1985), 231–51.

RORTY, R., *Consequences of Pragmatism* (Brighton, 1982).

RORTY, R., *Philosophy and the Mirror of Nature* (Oxford, 1983).

—— 'Postmodernist Bourgeois Liberalism', *Journal of Philosophy*, 80 (1983), 583–9.

—— 'Solidarity or Objectivity', in J. Rajchman and C. West (eds.), *Post-analytic Philosophy* (New York, 1985), 3–19.

ROTHBARD, M., *The Ethics of Liberty* (Atlantic Highlands, N.J. 1982).

—— *Man, Economy and State* (Princeton, 1962).

RUGGIERO, G., *The History of European Liberalism*, trans. R. G. Collingwood (London, 1927).

RYAN, A., *J. S. Mill* (London, 1974).

—— *The Philosophy of John Stuart Mill* (London, 1970).

RYLE, G., *The Concept of Mind* (Harmondsworth, 1976).

SANDEL, M., 'Liberalism and the Claims of Community: The Case of Affirmative Action', in M. Cohen (ed.), *Ronald Dworkin and Contemporary Jurisprudence* (London, 1984), 227–37.

—— *Liberalism and the Limits of Justice* (Cambridge, 1982).

—— 'Morality and the Liberal Ideal', *New Republic*, 7 May 1984, 15–17.

—— 'The Procedural Republic and Unencumbered Self', *Political Theory*, 12 (1984), 81–96.

—— (ed.), *Liberalism and Its Critics* (Oxford, 1984).

SCANLON, T. M., 'Contractualism and Utilitarianism', in A. K. Sen and B. Williams (eds.), *Utilitarianism and Beyond* (Cambridge, 1984), 103–28.

SCHEFFLER, S., *The Rejection of Consequentialism: A Philosophical Investigation of the Considerations Underlying Rival Moral Conceptions* (Oxford, 1984).

SCRUTON, R., *Kant* (Oxford, 1982).

—— *The Meaning of Conservatism*, 2nd edn. (London, 1984).

SEIDMAN, S., *Liberalism and the Origins of European Social Theory* (Oxford, 1983).

SEN, A. K., 'Behaviour and the Concept of Preference', *Economica*, 40 (1973), 241–59.

—— 'The Impossibility of a Paretian Liberal', in his *Choice, Welfare and Measurement* (Oxford, 1983), 285–90.

—— 'Liberty, Unanimity and Rights', in his *Choice, Welfare and Measurement* (Oxford, 1983), 291–326.

—— 'Rational Fools: A Critique of the Behavioural Foundations of Economic Theory', in F. Hahn and M. Hollis (eds.), *Philosophy and Economic Theory* (Oxford, 1979), 87–109.

SEN, A. K., and WILLIAMS, B., 'Introduction: Utilitarianism and Beyond', in A. K. Sen and B. Williams (eds.), *Utilitarianism and Beyond* (Cambridge, 1984), 1–22.

SHAPIRO, I., *The Evolution of Rights in Liberal Theory* (Cambridge, 1986).

SHEARMUR, J., 'The Austrian Connection: Hayek's Liberalism and the Thought of Carl Menger', in B. Smith and W. Grassl (eds.), *Austrian Economics: Philosophical and Historical Background* (London, 1986), 210–24.

—— 'Hayek and the Wisdom of the Age', in A. Seldon (ed.), *Hayek's 'Serfdom' Revisited* (London, 1984), 67–85.

SHELL, S. M., *The Rights of Reason: A Study of Kant's Philosophy and Politics* (Toronto, 1980).

SIDGWICK, H., *The Methods of Ethics*, 7th edn. (Indianapolis, 1981).

SIMONS, J., *The Ultimate Resource* (Oxford, 1981).

SMART, J. J. C., 'An Outline of a System of Utilitarian Ethics', in J. J. C. Smart and B. Williams, *Utilitarianism: For and Against* (Cambridge, 1980).

SOWELL, T., *Knowledge and Decisions* (New York, 1980).

SPINOZA, B., *On the Improvement of the Understanding: The Ethics; Correspondence*, trans. R. Elwes (New York, 1955).

STEELE, D. R., 'Posing the Problem: The Impossibility of Economic Calculation under Socialism', *Journal of Libertarian Studies*, 5 (1981), 7–22.

STEINER, H., 'Can a Social Contract be Signed by an Invisible Hand?', in P. Birnbaum, J. Lively, and G. Parry (eds.), *Democracy, Consensus and Social Contract* (London, 1978), 295–316.

—— 'The Concept of Justice', *Ratio*, 16 (1974), 206–25.

—— 'Critical Notice of Nozick, *Anarchy, State and Utopia*', *Mind*, 86 (1977), 120–9.

—— 'Individual Liberty', *Proceedings of the Aristotelian Society*, 75 (1974–5), 33–50.

STOVE, D., *Popper and After: Four Modern Irrationalists* (Oxford, 1984).

TAYLOR, C., 'Atomism', in his *Philosophical Papers*, 2 vols. (Cambridge, 1985), ii. 187–210.

—— 'The Diversity of Goods', in A. K. Sen and B. Williams (eds.), *Utilitarianism and Beyond* (Cambridge, 1984), 129–44.

—— 'Kant's Theory of Freedom', in Z. Pelczynski and J. N. Gray (eds.), *Conceptions of Liberty in Political Philosophy* (London, 1984), 100–22.

—— 'The Nature and Scope of Distributive Justice', in his *Philosophical Papers* (Cambridge, 1985), ii. 289–317.

TAYLOR, C. C. W., 'Critical Notice of R. M. Hare, *Freedom and Reason*', *Mind*, 74 (1965), 280–98.

TEN, C. L., *Mill on Liberty* (Oxford, 1980).

THIGPEN, R. B., and DOWNING, L. A., 'Liberalism and the Communitarian Critique', *American Journal of Political Science*, 21 (1987), 637–55.

ULLMAN-MARGALIT, E., *The Emergence of Norms* (Oxford, 1977).

VERNON, R., 'The "Great Society" and the "Open Society": Liberalism in Hayek and Popper', *Canadian Journal of Political Science*, 9 (1976), 261–76.

WALDRON, J., 'Theoretical Foundations of Liberalism', *Philosophical Quarterly*, 37 (1987), 127–50.

—— (ed), *Theories of Rights* (Oxford, 1985).

WALKER, R. C. S., *Kant: The Arguments of the Philosophers* (London, 1978).

WALZER, M., 'Liberalism and the Art of Separation', *Political Theory*, 12 (1984), 315–30.

—— 'Philosophy and Democracy', *Political Theory*, 9 (1981), 379–99.

—— *Spheres of Justice: A Defence of Pluralism and Equality* (Oxford, 1983).

—— '*Spheres of Justice*: An Exchange', *New York Review of Books*, 21 July 1983, 43–4.

WARD, K., *The Development of Kant's View of Ethics* (Oxford, 1972).

WATKINS, J. W. N., 'Philosophy', in A. Seldon (ed.), *Agenda for a Free Society: Essays on Hayek's* The Constitution of Liberty (London, 1961), 31–50.

WILLIAMS, B., *Ethics and the Limits of Philosophy* (London, 1985).

WILLIAMS, H., *Kant's Political Philosophy* (Oxford, 1983).

WOLFF, R. P., *The Autonomy of Reason: A Commentary on Kant's* Groundwork of the Metaphysics of Morals (New York, 1973).

—— *The Poverty of Liberalism* (Boston, 1968).

—— *Understanding Rawls: A Reconstruction and Critique of* A Theory of Justice (Princeton, 1977).

ZLABINGER, A., and LEUBE, K. (eds.), *The Political Economy of Freedom: Essays in Honour of F. A. Hayek* (Munich, 1984).

INDEX